THE SCIENCE OF FAMILY LAW

Tools For Successful Practice

AUSTRALIA
Law Book Co.
Sydney

CANADA and USA
Carswell
Toronto

HONG KONG
Sweet & Maxwell Asia

NEW ZEALAND
Brookers
Wellington

SINGAPORE and MALAYSIA
Sweet & Maxwell Asia
Singapore and Kuala Lumpur

THE SCIENCE OF FAMILY LAW

Tools For Successful Practice

By

Anne Hall Dick

*Mediator and Specialist in Family Law Accredited
by the Law Society of Scotland*

and

Tom Ballantine

*Mediator and Specialist in Family Law Accredited
by the Law Society of Scotland*

EDINBURGH
W. GREEN/Sweet & Maxwell
2001

Published in 2001 by W. Green & Son Ltd
21 Alva Street
Edinburgh EH2 4PS

*Printed in Great Britain by Athenaeum Press,
Gateshead, Tyne & Wear*

No natural forests were destroyed to make this product;
Only farmed timber was used and replanted

A CIP catalogue record for this book is available from the British
Library

ISBN 0 414 013 700

© Anne Hall Dick & Tom Ballantine 2001

FOREWORD

Family law is one of the most demanding and one of the most personally rewarding aspects of legal practice. Clients arrive angry, distressed and bewildered. The treatment they receive in a solicitors' office can make the difference between descent into hopelessness and impoverishment on the one hand and financial security with a positive approach to the future on the other. This is a book about putting clients onto the right side of that divide in a professional and cost-effective manner.

The Science of Family Law is a companion volume to *The Art of Family Law*, by the same authors. *The Art of Family Law* explores the attitudes and interpersonal skills necessary to a family lawyer. *The Science of Family Law* develops the theme. It proposes a systematic approach to practice which is designed to leave the solicitor free to respond creatively to clients. Sound administrative structures are placed alongside an explanation of law and procedure. There is a fresh approach to drafting with a focus on clarity and accessibility. In the modern world not only should parties be able to comprehend the documents in a case, but lawyers from outside Scotland should also be able to understand pleadings, without requiring a lexicon of obscure terms. The essential elements of family law litigation and practice are here in a contemporary and helpful form.

This is a book by practitioners for practitioners. The authors have a wealth of experience in family law. They write as those driven by the urgency of real clients with pressing needs. Some problems are simple to address, others are more complex. This book provides a helpful starting point in a wide range of cases. It is unique in its combination of approach, administrative advice, procedural guidance and black letter law. It is a book destined to make a difference to the practice of family law.

Janys Scott
Advocate

ACKNOWLEDGEMENT

This Practice Manual from the coal face of family law owes much to the labours of those who specifically commented on and contributed to the text. Particular thanks are due to Janys Scott and Margaret Scanlan for their generosity in giving their time, wisdom and experience. Thank you also to Liz McFarlane, Iain Talman, John Pollock, Ewan Malcolm, Sheila Barker, Alison Cleland, Telfer Blacklock, George Thomas, and George Jamieson.

Thank you too to Wendy Sheehan who, as well as commenting on the text, contributed the chapter on human rights.

This book owes much to those who have written related topics before us. In particular, we acknowledge our debt to Sheriff I.D. MacPhail's *Sheriff Court Practice*.

The Law Society of Scotland and the Scottish Legal Aid Board provided much valued assistance.

A project of this sort required understanding from our business partners at Mowat Dean and Anne Hall Dick & Co. Thank you to Hugh Mackay, Peter Dean, Wendy Sheehan and Liz McFarlane. Thank you to Lynne Corrigan, Louise Steel, Debbie Gray and Angela Purcell for their indispensable secretarial skills.

Finally, to Neil McKinlay, Carole McMurray and all at Greens, thank you for your invaluable professional help.

The strengths of this book are drawn from the specific input already mentioned and from the general understanding gained from our interaction with family law colleagues in the Family Law Association and CALM. Any weaknesses are entirely our own work!

May the book provide help and encouragement to all family lawyers.

CONTENTS

CHAPTER 4

THE NUTS AND BOLTS OF FINANCIAL PROVISION
INCLUDING PENSION SHARING

CHAPTER 5

WRITTEN AGREEMENTS

CHAPTER 6

PLEADINGS

CHAPTER 7

DRAFTING THE INITIAL WRIT—BASIC CASES

CHAPTER 8

THE INITIAL WRIT—COMPLEX SITUATIONS

CHAPTER 11

KEY STEPS TO THE OPTIONS HEARING

CHAPTER 12

DEBATES AND APPEALS

CHAPTER 13

THE PROOF

CHAPTER 14

LEGAL AID

CHAPTER 15

ENFORCEMENT

CHAPTER 16

THE HUMAN RIGHTS ACT 1998—IMPLICATIONS FOR
FAMILY LAWYERS

CHAPTER 1

INTRODUCTION—A SYSTEMATIC APPROACH

An overview

To be a family lawyer demands full use of both head and heart! Family lawyers need to combine wide legal knowledge with highly developed interpersonal skills. A significant proportion of the work may be done on Legal Aid. The narrow profit margin will call for efficient streamlining but the need for unhurried face-to-face advice giving at relevant times must be accommodated. The mechanics of navigating a family law case from start to finish can be daunting. Keeping up-to-date with the black letter law can seem a full-time task even without dealing with any clients. Having the procedural paperwork streamlined and efficient systems in place is an essential foundation to build on. It will allow sufficient time to be available for clients and enable the inevitable urgent steps required from time to time to be taken without overloading the system.

Family lawyers represent a gateway to valuable information. Since information is becoming more and more readily available at the click of a mouse it is correspondingly important for us to add value in some significant way. Family law clients are individuals going through change. Fifty years ago if a couple separated it was seen as their failure. Twenty-five years ago there was a tendency to portray separation as a route to personal growth. Now we recognise the breakdown of a relationship as a time of enormous emotional and practical change. The attitude of the people involved will determine how far the constructive potential is realised and the destructive element minimised. The needs of any children involved must be considered with the utmost care. Destructively selfish, violent or bullying behaviour must be contained. As family lawyers, we not only provide information but also have to help people deal with choices and consequences arising from that information.

Clients will expect you to have total command of the fast breeding legislation and case law and the ability to produce appropriate and accurate documentation with ease. You will tend to be judged by how helpful and prompt a service you have provided. The good news is that if you do the groundwork and have efficient systems in place to allow you to combine your people skills and legal knowledge you will find the work endlessly fascinating and rewarding.

We would like to help you either set up a workable framework or check your existing set up, hopefully finding both reassurance and some additional assistance. This book sets out to deal with the nuts and bolts of family law practice. Just don't forget that although a well managed family law practice should allow you to keep your practising certificate and a reasonable relationship with your bank manager and feel on top of your work the people skills make a particular impact on clients. Both elements are essential.

Tools of trade

Chapter 2 outlines the key legislation and sources of case law. Build in the time to keep up-to-date with the law. It can be useful to keep a digest of significant cases as they are reported. Things are never still in family law. Try to avoid stockpiling one year's supply of Scots Law Times to read at one sitting! We also suggest other useful material and equipment for you to assemble and use.

Processing information and the nuts and bolts of financial provision

Our job as family lawyers is a combination of advising, negotiation and litigation. Negotiation tends to be the largest element. The raw material for any of those steps is, in addition to knowing your way round the law, knowing your way round the people involved. At any stage you need to be able to ask the right questions and find a way of managing the information you receive in response. Chapter 3 sets out a suggested framework for assembling and managing information. Chapter 4 takes a look at how to use the information productively and appropriately. It includes a consideration of pension sharing with styles for separation agreements and writs.

Written agreements

For most clients who want to take things further after an initial meeting the next stage will be to explore the possibility of resolving whatever issues are outstanding by way of negotiation or mediation. Either way in most cases the outcome would be set out in a written contract. Chapter 5 provides examples of agreements which could be used to set out whatever formula emerges. Negotiation is a fascinating process which has to be recognised as a significant skill in its own right.

Pleadings and court procedure

If your client is at the receiving end of a writ, needs protection from a violent partner, has to prevent the removal of a child from their care or destruction of property or if the negotiation process hits the buffers your systems will have to cope with the demands of litigation. A divorce action may follow a concluded separation agreement. Chapters 6, 7 and 8 describes the procedure involved, gives guidance about written pleadings and provides examples of writs for some common remedies.

Interim hearings and interim steps

Interim hearings are a very significant feature of family law litigation. Overall, very few cases reach the stage of proof but decisions made and steps taken in the early stages of litigation can have a huge impact on the eventual outcome whether by settlement or judicial decision. Chapter 9 looks at interim hearings and various steps which might need to be taken in the course of litigation.

Child welfare hearings and decisions about children

Disputes over arrangements for children are particularly demanding to deal with. Child welfare hearings are playing a very significant role in family litigation. The variety of ways in which they are conducted in different courts and by different Sheriffs has proved a striking and rather unsettling feature. The involvement of children has introduced a new element which has potential benefits but also opens the possibility of creating additional stress and anxiety for young people. Chapter 10 looks at decisions about children in more detail.

Steps to the family options hearings

Family Options hearings have made less impact than child welfare hearings. It was hoped, when they were introduced, that Family Options hearings would allow a more interactive role for the Sheriffs and create an opportunity for some significant input at a relatively early stage. In fact they have become in most courts limited to a procedural formality. The steps leading up the Options Hearings and the Hearings themselves are important stages in defended litigation and are covered in Chapter 11.

Debate and appeals

Debates in family law cases continue to be uncommon but because the legislation and case law has become increasingly complex there is more likelihood of legal points arising. It's important to be ready to deal with a debate and some basic guidance is given about that in Chapter 12. As the law in relation to children and financial provision has become more complex so has the use of appeal procedure become more common. This is also considered in Chapter 12.

Proof

Cases which do go to proof can involve very extensive and complex factual and financial information. As many family lawyers deal mainly with advising clients and negotiating we tend to develop problem-solving skills. To be effective in litigation these skills need to be supplemented and expanded. Although in almost all cases a well negotiated settlement is preferable to an unpredictable outcome in litigation it is important for your client that the possibility of litigation is one you can contemplate with equanimity! If the prospect of a proof is clearly daunting for you your ability to negotiate effectively is likely to be reduced. Guidance is given in Chapter 13 about the conduct of a proof.

Legal aid

Most family lawyers do feel a sense of responsibility to allow clients access to the legal system regardless of their means and carry out work under the legal aid system. Because of the low hourly rate it is quite a challenge to maintain the appropriate standard of work without either losing contact entirely with your own family or struggling to make ends meet. An efficiently run practice is the starting point and we end this chapter with an outline of practices and procedures which have proved useful for us. Some further suggestions are made in Chapter 14.

Enforcement

We must never forget that for the client the registered Agreement or court order is only the starting point. The words must be made to deliver their promise. In probably the majority of cases formal enforcement is not necessary but when it is required appropriate action is crucial. Some aspects of enforcement are covered in Chapter 15.

Human Rights

All areas of law have been affected by the Human Rights Act 1998, effectively incorporating the European Convention on Human Rights into United Kingdom domestic law. Chapter 16 outlines the impact on family law of this significant development.

Office Systems

All this work has to be tackled within the context of an office system. Standardisation of the routine stages is the way to allow you to devote your individual skills to your clients rather than spend time fire fighting. You avoid the search for misfiled papers, the panic over courts dates or the frustration of elusive information.

You and your office staff must work as a team over this. The amount of control you have over office systems will depend on many factors including your own place in the scheme of things. The following suggestions could be tried as macro or micro systems.

Office practice manual

It's very helpful to compile an office practice manual with instructions for carrying out routine tasks. This is necessary for some objective quality control schemes and is likely to be necessary if civil legal aid develops in the same way as criminal legal aid. Quite apart from those factors it is just very useful to work with your staff and draw up instructions covering matters such as—

- procedure for dealing with incoming and outgoing mail (whether by e-mail, fax or snail mail)
- the office filing system
- opening and closing files
- guidance with dealing with clients at reception and on the phone
- dealing with legal aid forms
- secretarial aspects of court procedure
- general secretarial knowledge such as a system of references and layouts
- diary system
- the operation and procedures for your computer system
- a list of contacts such as stationary suppliers and tradesmen
- use of styles
- a database of experts
- interaction with the cash system

The exercise of drawing up these instructions is likely to illustrate how much more complex office life is than you realise! It will highlight gaps in knowledge all round and if done in a constructive way will help you all work together better. One object is to allow appropriate and supervised delegation of tasks which can be carried out by staff other than solicitors. Another is to ensure consistency and streamlining. A fruitful by-product is discovering how much knowledge and experience is to be found in any legal office and using that resource for the general benefit. You and your colleagues should enjoy the exchange of information and feel satisfaction in producing a reference manual. This can be compiled in a generously sized ring binder and updated when appropriate.

Incoming and outgoing mail

Traditionally, lawyers have been accused of using obscure jargon. Family lawyers should be aware more than most of how helpful clients find it when we do use plain English. However, whether the words are Latin or plain (or baroque) English the practice of law still involves processing them in vast quantities. They flood like a tide in and out of the office and can threaten to swamp the system. Once the supervised mail opening session has been completed, it should be helpful for your secretary to be given sufficient training to be involved in a preliminary sifting of incoming correspondence. The secretaries could sort the letters and messages into appropriate piles for each responsible solicitor then, if suitably experienced, into subdivisions of matters you are likely to want to deal with, tasks they may have the experience to deal with (such as service of writs) and correspondence which seems likely to simply need filing. A folder with appropriate subdivisions could be used. This could then be passed to you to check then passed back to activate the appropriate next step.

Remember that if you are in a position to sign outgoing mail for colleagues, you are liable to share responsibility for any of its deficiencies! Try to avoid pressure by setting time aside in the diary for dealing with outgoing mail and resist dealing with telephone calls simultaneously. Check that there is a consistent system about dealing with enclosures and if possible, double check yourself. The staff dealing with outgoing correspondence should also have a specific time set aside for doing that task which is a particularly responsible one.

Filing system

Although the combination of scanning, word processing and e-mail may lead at last to the paperless office, for the moment, an efficient filing system is at the heart of a smooth running office. Although it may be usual for anyone working on a file to deal with sorting out their own filing, at that stage, it can be enormously helpful for one member of staff to be responsible for the welfare of the filing system in general, and any unallocated paperwork in particular. To avoid the frustration of files which have gone walkabout you could have a system of cards (perhaps in different colours) naming staff members so that the appropriate card can be placed in the filing cabinet to indicate the whereabouts of the file when removed.

Opening, closing and destroying files

The procedure for opening files in many offices will stimulate activity in the accounts system. The main thing is to ensure that any new matter is recorded throughout the office system as soon as possible and that each new matter is opened in a prompt and consistent way. Before any file is closed there should be a checklist to ensure that the work has been completed, any relevant documents returned to the client and that there is no outstanding fee or mysterious credit or debit balance!

It can be helpful to set up a label for files which sets out the basic information about the client at the outset and provides room for subsequent details you might wish to have at a glance. An example is given at the end. The space for additional information can be used for adding the case number if matters end up in litigation or to flag up the existence of a power of arrest.

Since storage for the future is a problem best tackled in the present it is important to set up a system which will make it clear when files may be destroyed. The guidance from the Law Society is that files dealing with divorce and "consistorial" matters should be kept for five years after final completion, for example after orders relating to custody, access, residence or contact or financial provision have ceased to have effect. Taking into account the potential for deferred payments, "earmarking" and pension sharing, the period of storage could be quite significant.

Dealing with clients at reception and on the phone

Family law clients are likely to be particularly fragile. That will make them prone to anger or distress. Either way, it imposes a weighty responsibility on members of staff who are in the front line. It makes it particularly important to have clear guidelines including the sort of issues which could be tackled by reception staff and sensible measures for their safety. Ensure that clients are told to bring evidence of identity (and income if legal aid is a possibility) to their first meeting. It's very important the member of staff who deals with this is helped to find ways of explaining to the client diplomatically. If the client understands it's partly because of rules all solicitors have to follow and partly to check the possibility of legal aid he or she is less likely to feel put off. If your firm doesn't undertake legal aid work evidence of income won't be necessary but the position about legal aid should be explained.

Dealing with legal aid forms

It's useful to prepare instructions about legal aid procedure setting out the steps which can be carried out by the secretarial staff with guidance about what is involved. One particularly helpful responsibility a secretary can take is to be aware of the need to submit form SU2 if an urgent step is carried out and remind you if you have forgotten to instruct one!

It is also important to have a diary forward system to check that legal aid papers have been returned and submitted within the time limit once an SU2 has been lodged or steps under an SU4 authorised.

Secretarial aspects of court procedure

Experienced legal secretaries should be able to serve writs and motions without detailed instructions. If your secretary has not yet reached this stage it would be a good investment of your time to provide appropriate training and supervision. Clearly, you will take responsibility for the work carried out.

General knowledge

Every office will have its own system of references and layouts. Court procedure imposes different requirements for different courts and some universal practices. Keeping a record of your own and various courts' demands as and when you come across them can create an extremely valuable reference point for both experienced and new members of staff. This can be done by incorporating appropriate instructions in the office practice manual and the relevant styles stored as templates in your computer.

Diary system

In any family law practice there is a need to have a record of appointments made and relevant court dates. It will usually also be necessary to have a system of recording files to be checked for progress or specific events such as the return of legal aid papers. Unless you have an electronic diary system you may wish to have an appointments diary which is maintained by the receptionist or secretary and a separate court diary. The responsibility for maintaining a court diary is substantial. You may keep one for your own cases or share one with colleagues. Either way, it is essential that there is an utterly clear system for making and checking entries including provision for a substitute to take responsibility if you are ill or when you manage to escape on holiday! If you do have an electronic diary it is wise to also maintain a separate paper court diary. Computer crashes are enough of a nightmare without being compounded by the spectre of a missed court appearance. Printing out one copy of the next day's diary can avoid chaos if there is a glitch. A networked diary system with internal e-mail is feasible for even small offices. The benefits are significant. The need for emergency plans if they fail simply underline how helpful they are in operation.

The operation and procedure of your computer system

Most offices will now be using computer systems to a greater or lesser degree. Even if it is only for word processing the benefit of a computer is substantial. Many systems integrate accounts, client database and word processing. A well thought out "house-keeping" system is needed to get the most out of any use of computers. Two distinct components are client work and office styles. It is very important to keep these distinct. The work for each client is best kept in a separate directory for each client. The most straightforward system is to have a "folder" for each letter of the alphabet and within that folder a "file" for each client, allocating each client a distinct but simple computer reference using a combination of the first few letters of their surname and numbers allocated in sequence. Make absolutely sure your computer backup system is reliable and is being activated preferably on a daily basis. Also use a reliable virus checker. You will test your own wellbeing if you fail to keep your computer system in good shape.

Styles

We hope you might find the styles we are suggesting of help to either start or add to your collection of styles. If you are able to set up a central store of styles as templates in your computer system this will ensure that any changes are immediately implemented for all members of staff. It is useful to have a systematic approach to instructions given within styles to make sure that there is sufficient clarity about what parts to leave in or take out. Remember to add to your styles a general version of any new documents you have to prepare from scratch. Also bear in mind the need to be on the alert for changes which may have to be made to existing styles. And most importantly, never be so trusting of your styles that you overlook checking the finished article for a client. Styles are aids to the production of appropriate documents, not replacements for solicitors' brains!

It is possible to use office styles as an element of an office practice manual. An index of styles can be compiled incorporating the standard style letters and documents for each aspect of the work in the appropriate order with some explanation and instructions for use. The styles themselves can contain guidance and instructions for their use and indicate what other office styles should also be activated. The combination of these steps should facilitate an orderly progress through information giving and gathering, negotiating or litigating and avoid the need to dictate standard letters from scratch. It will not, of course, deal with the subtleties of negotiation or the intricacies of litigation but the more the basic steps are standardised the more time you will have to devote to making progress!

Contacts and experts

Try to avoid the frustration of being unable to lay hands on details of contacts and experts. Set up and maintain a database of contacts and experts using your computer system or indeed a trusty ring binder.

Interaction with the cash system

Encourage an understanding of how the accounts system works amongst other members of staff. An accurate flow of information from the secretarial side of the office to the accounts department and back is crucial. The more the reason for accurate and detailed information is made clear the more likely accuracy will be achieved.

Conclusion

The suggestions about a systematic approach are intended to help you put in place routines and have standard documents available which will free you to respond creatively to your clients. There is no set way for you (just as there will rarely be one right way for your clients). The trick is to use the information available to make the basics clearer and allow you to evolve your own style.

CHAPTER 2

TOOLS OF THE TRADE

One of the experiences all lawyers have in common is of memorising hundreds of legal cases for exams. Memorized in the few weeks before the exam, the cases are almost invariably forgotten within the few days after. Beyond improving a person's memory it is difficult to see what educational value this has. In the practical world of family law, thank goodness, the need is not for a voluminous memory but rather some knowledge, access to relevant materials and a well organised approach to research.

It is difficult to overstate the importance of an ability to organise your own mind and materials to let you perform at your best. Coupled to a knowledge of the essentials of family law and a realistic assessment of the limits of our knowledge it allows us to make the most of our other qualities as legal advisers.

Main legislation

To give a foundation from which to use text books we need to have available the main legislation. The following are central—
    Domicile and Matrimonial Proceedings Act 1973
    Divorce (Scotland) Act 1976
    Adoption (Scotland) Act 1978
    Matrimonial Homes (Family Protection) (Scotland) Act 1981
    Family Law (Scotland) Act 1985
    Family Law Act 1986
    Children (Scotland) Act 1995
    United Nations Convention on the Rights of the Child
    Human Rights Act 1998
    Ordinary Cause Rules
Scottish Family Law Legislation, edited by Professor K. Norrie, is the best place to find most of the relevant legislation gathered in one place. It is in looseleaf format and is regularly updated. The annotations provide a useful gloss on the primary legislation. At the risk of sounding like self-publicists, it should be noted that the W. Green version of the Family Law (Scotland) Act 1985 (annotated by Anne Hall Dick) provides an excellent

starting point for case law relating to that piece of primary legislation.

Foundation texts

These materials are there to make sure that your own understanding of the basics of family law is correct. This is the type of knowledge that you should remember but may need to refresh your memory on. The statutory basis for divorce, grounds on which an exclusion order can be granted, the initial principles governing the division of matrimonial property on divorce. Because we deal with these concepts day in day out we sometimes forget the subtleties behind them. The availability of the relevant written material gives us the opportunity to double check our understanding and develop and refine what we know.

Family Law in Scotland by Professor J. Thomson. Professor Thomson is one of the most entertaining and clear writers about family law. Because it is not limited to talking about children and married relationships, this book is a good introductory overview to the law governing all family relationships including adoption and the role of local authorities in relation to children.

Family Law by Lilian Edwards and Anne Griffiths. Published in 1997, this is another useful introduction to family law. The book is laid out to take the reader through the status, rights and responsibilities of a person in the family law context. The book starts from the foetus and moves through to end with adult relationships.

The underlying theme is that "as the permanence of marriage has declined, increasingly the focus of modern law is on the indissoluble parent-child link rather than on the suspiciously transient bond of matrimony".

This thesis supports a greater emphasis on the legal position of unmarried people in the book.

Divorce in the Sheriff Court by S. A. Bennett. Now in its sixth edition, this provides some good initial guidance on procedures peculiar to divorce and ancillary matters such as protective measures, children, property and money with some basic styles included.

Sheriff Court Practice by I. D. Macphail. This is now in its second edition. It may strike you as odd to include a text that is not wholly concerned with family law in a listing of basic texts, but no family lawyer can function in the family law field without a knowledge of procedural law and the mechanisms of the Sheriff Court. This book has saved many lawyers from sleepless nights and anxiety with its comprehensive, authoritative and practical guidance. Although we have included it under basic texts its range is such that it encompasses most of the deeper procedural issues you will face. In writing this book we have to acknowledge our debt to it. It is indispensable and should be on your shelf.

Butterworth's Scottish Family Law Service. Another useful looseleaf volume covering all relevant main areas of family law. It has the benefit of being kept up-to-date by virtue of its format. It is particularly useful on enforcement procedures.

Going deeper

While on many occasions a short simple explanation will suffice, on others, more is required.

The Law of Husband and Wife in Scotland by E. Clive. Professor Clive manages to compress a huge amount of information into one volume. Now in its fourth edition, like Macphail, this text is indispensable to the serious family law practitioner. It covers in an authoritative way the stages from formation through to termination of marriage.

Child and Family Law by Elaine Sutherland. Another detailed look at the family designed with a wider audience in mind than just lawyers. The status and rights of children in the family are given a particular emphasis.

Child law

The Law Relating to Parent and Child in Scotland by J. B. Wilkinson and K. McK. Norrie. Now in its second edition this is another indispensable text that tells you most of what you need to know about the law with regard to children and their carers. If it doesn't have it, it will give you a pretty good idea where to find it.

Parental Responsibilities and Rights by George Jamieson. A useful text although hampered by the fact it was published before much of the relevant case law on its subject matter was available. Good as an introduction to international child abduction law.

Children's Rights in Scotland by Alison Cleland and Elaine Sutherland. A book that brings together the views of several respected family legal thinkers in its different chapters. It has the benefit of a definite focus on the rights of the child and the interaction of those rights with the United Nations Convention on the Rights of the Child.

Child and Family Law: Cases and Materials by Richard Mays. This brings together some of the main cases and materials in the field of Scots child and family law, up to April 2000.

Specialist areas

Adoption

Adoption of Children in Scotland by P. G. B. McNeil, Q.C. Now in its third edition, this text is essential for anyone intending to work in this area as the only authoritative text dedicated exclusively to adoption. The text starts by discussing what adoption is and works its way through to the end of the relevant Court procedures involved in adoption.

Children's Hearings

Children's Hearings and the Sheriff Court by B. Kearney. Now in its second edition, it is clearly set out and guides the reader from the initial children's hearing through applications to the Sheriff for findings in relation to the hearing and appeals to the Sheriff Court and Court of Session

Children's Hearings in Scotland by K. McK. Norrie. An up-to-date practical guide to the process. This goes from initial investigation through the hearing process to the determination of any supervision requirement.

Interdict

The Law of Interdict by S. Robinson. All the main texts on family law include useful sections on interdict. This is a helpful backup text that is useful precisely because it looks at the law of interdict in itself providing a context for the narrower applications of the law in family cases.

Pleadings/court craft

Advocacy Skills by Michael Hyam. A good short and clear guide to preparation for and the conduct of different stages of examination in Court.

Advocacy by Andy Boon. Directed at the English lawyer, the text is helpful in running through the components required for skilful advocacy.

Evidence

The Law of Evidence in Scotland by Walker and Walker, now in its second edition, is the key work in this vital area. Chapter 28 is devoted entirely to evidence in family actions.

Publications

Scots Law Times is a weekly publication giving significant decisions in the civil and criminal courts with Court news and articles on legal topics of interest. This provides a useful mechanism for keeping up to date with developments in family law. Its broad remit means that most of the cases fall outwith the family law field. However that same breadth allows you to keep in sight developments in other areas of law that are of significance to the family law practitioner for instance over civil court procedure, evidence and contract.

Scottish Civil Law Reports. Dedicated entirely to civil law, this has similar benefits and weaknesses to the *Scots Law Times*. As the cases covered are often different from the S.L.T. it is another valuable up-to-date source of information about developments in the law.

Greens Weekly Digest is a weekly publication giving brief resumes of cases over the full spectrum of civil and criminal law. Helpful in flagging up decisions of which a full copy of the relevant judgment might be worth obtaining.

Publications specific to family lawyers

Greens Family Law Reports. Because of its concentration on the family law field alone this is a particularly valuable publication. The layout includes a helpful Digest before the reports themselves which is particularly useful for updating research beyond the most recent textbooks.

Greens Family Law Bulletin. Pretty well essential reading for the serious family lawyer. It includes family law news, invaluable articles on practical issues as well as updates on new cases and legislation. For a succinct means of keeping your finger on the pulse this is hard to beat.

The Internet

The internet can be a useful source of information. This is not the place for a detailed introduction to its use. The only points we would make are what you would expect as a matter of common sense—

- It is best used as a follow up to, rather than in place of, traditional sources of information
- Use it in the most targeted way you can. Search engines can give you large numbers of tangential or irrelevant hits
- Have an address book of useful addresses to avoid duplication of effort

Your own digest

It is extremely helpful to create your own digest of research materials. The key to this is good librarian skills and the determination not to let quality be swamped by quantity! There is a temptation to keep a copy of every family law decision that passes before your eyes in a large forbidding box file or more likely box files. The files are never visited or if visited are so voluminous that the information needed is never found.

What is required is an accessible, properly demarcated series of research files broken down between particular subjects. The more material you need to keep on say, finances the more you may choose to create new demarcations—"section 9 principles", "pensions", "businesses" and so on.

An alternative to keeping copies is to maintain a very brief summary of relevant cases on computer. This is more work but helps you truly "digest" the case for information and makes it more likely you will find the material again!

As always the balance to be achieved is between accessibility and completeness.

The Family Law Association

We should both, as long-standing members of the Association, confess an interest in recommending this. The Association has become the lead organisation in providing a resource to outside individuals and agencies on the views of family lawyers in Scotland. Membership of the organisation commits lawyers to a conciliatory approach to resolving family disputes. Members are kept in touch with developments in the family law field by the *Bulletin* published by the Association. Just as important, the Association through its membership network, seminars and social events, provides an invaluable source of information and support to and between family law practitioners. Finally, the Association gives all family law practitioners a voice in addressing issues that affect them and their clients. If you are serious about family law, you should be a member.

CHAPTER 3

INFORMATION GATHERING AND GIVING

Introduction

Information is the raw material for decision-making. No matter what form of dispute resolution is used, the quality of the information introduced into the process will be a significant factor in the quality of the outcome. Clear and objective information can often narrow the area of dispute so much as to suggest an acceptable way forward. It can provide reassurance: it can flag up potential problems. Dealing with information is a circular process. Details have to be obtained and their consequences explained. That will normally lead to further exploration with further information gathering and giving.

Since family lawyers are helping people both solve problems and also adjust to change, fact-finding will inevitably be tinged by an emotional overlay. The eddies of emotion affecting the client will have an impact on the solicitor and a consequent effect on the more practical elements. A key element in navigating the turbulent waters is to have a solid administrative structure which can absorb a substantial part of the stresses.

This applies as much to information giving as gathering. Standard forms and letters to be used for clients can ensure that points are covered which might otherwise be overlooked. They can also serve as a record that the information has been given. Examples of standard paperwork are given.

File layout

Files can become looming, threatening presences! Make your files friends, not enemies! If you develop a set way of dealing with the paperwork it will allow you easier access to necessary information and avoid fruitless searching and time wasting.

Interview sheets

At the first interview you should aim to collect sufficient information about the client, relevant adults and children and their personal and financial circumstances to allow you to assess potential eligibility for legal aid and broadly how your client stands in law if financial provision is relevant. If you use interview sheets to ensure that you cover the necessary points it will leave you all the more able to deal with how the client is reacting and coping. They can be updated as things change.

Progress sheets

Although each interview with the client will be vivid at the time the inevitable pressure of work will make it impossible to keep a mental note of progress. Reading over correspondence and notes before each interview would be very time-consuming. Keeping a separate, very brief record of major developments can allow you to bring back to mind the important features.

Record sheets

If you use a standard way of recording any work you carry out for the client it will make the file much easier to follow, ensure that the time spent is accounted for and remind you on each occasion to be clear what has to happen next. The back of the record sheets can be used to make notes from an interview or points arising when reading through incoming correspondence or documents.

Standard letters

Since you will be explaining complicated legal issues to people who are under stress it is important to let them have a summary of your discussion in writing. It's helpful to have standard paragraphs which can be used to confirm the broad legal points although these will need expanding and amending to suit particular circumstances.

Questionnaire about matrimonial property

Enlist the client's help as early as possible in assembling the necessary detailed information. When you reach the stage of collecting more detailed financial information clients can be encouraged to provide the necessary details and paperwork by being given a questionnaire to complete. This can be the starting point for a schedule setting out the information. Some of this exchange of information could be done using the internet if you have appropriate safeguards.

Schedule of matrimonial property

Assembling information about the matrimonial assets and liabilities in a tabular form makes the overall picture easier to grasp. Using a spreadsheet facility can prevent unnecessary time communing with a calculator. The schedule can be incorporated into a Separation Agreement or used in the context of a court action.

Letter of engagement

It is not only necessary but also good practice to provide the client with clear information about the basis of fee charging and what to do if they are unhappy with the work you are doing. Guidance about other points of contact within the firm and other general information helps promote a good solicitor client relationship.

Relevant organisations and publications

Since you are a potential gateway to all sorts of helpful information it's useful to maintain a list of relevant organisations and publications to provide for clients.

You can find some suggestions at the end.

File Layout

Despite (or because of?) the onward march of technology the promise of the paperless office remains unfulfilled. With an increasing use of scanners and networked computer systems within offices and the flicker of computer screens and rattle of printers a normal feature in courts things might change quite quickly. Most correspondence and pleadings are likely to be exchanged electronically in the foreseeable future. It's certainly wise to establish a good "housekeeping" system for your computer system with a clear hierarchy for client directories and a system of maintaining and updating styles as templates. However, more trees still seem likely to be sacrificed for the legal profession! It's useful to have a systematic approach to dealing with the mass of written material which mounts up.

Paperwork in relation to clients tends to fall into four categories—

1. A chronological record of meetings and correspondence.
2. Questionnaires, schedules, drafts, precognitions and copy documents.
3. Original documents (birth and marriage certificates, valuations and such like).
4. Cash room information (record of outlays, receipts, fee notes and such like).

It can be helpful to keep the categories separate. Original documents can be put in an envelope attached to the file with a tag and the other three categories kept separate within the file. The record of meetings and correspondence with the basic client information as the starting point can be kept on the right-hand side of the file. If the tag with questionnaires and schedules or precognitions with copy documents becomes rather overloaded a ring binder can be used instead.

The main thing is to have a system which everybody understands and follows and which is flexible enough to accommodate various categories of work. Information should be easy to find and the record of work clearly set out if a detailed fee note is required.

Interview Sheets

Client data

It will be clear from information given when the appointment was made or at the very beginning of the first interview if you are dealing with issues arising from the separation of a married or unmarried couple, difficulties faced by a young person, the legal position of an adult in relation to a young person who is not their child or some less definable category. In any event, you will need details of their financial circumstances and a history of the events leading to your involvement. It can be helpful to have a set of interview sheets dealing with couples, adoption, young people as clients and third parties (such as grandparents).

The interview sheets for couples are necessarily the most complex and an explanation of them should clarify any points arising from the interview sheets for young people which can be found in the Appendix.

Married and unmarried couple interview sheets

First page—personal and family information

A1a	***MARRIED / UNMARRIED COUPLE***
Date of first interview:	date of amendments:
Info. sheets given.	**(Check with client)** **Tick when received.**

<u>FULL NAME OF CLIENT:</u>	ADDRESS FOR DATABASE & CORRESPONDENCE (IF DIFFERENT FROM CURRENT ADDRESS):
Identification given:	
Current Address:	

TO BE DISCLOSED: YES/NO
Is that the Family Home - YES/NO
Rented / Owned   Client / Partner / Joint
Telephone number: Home   Work
E-mail Address   **Mobile**
Age   D.O.B.
Occupation:
Place of Work:
If unemployed, previous Employers:
<u>FULL name of relevant partner:</u>
Current address:
Is that the Family Home - YES/NO   Rented / Owned   Client / Partner / Joint
Age   D.O.B.
Occupation:
Place of Work:
Date and Place of Marriage:
OR date relationship started
Date of Separation
Names and D.0.B.'S of Client's Children: (1)
(2)
(3)

(4)	
Any not from this relationship ?	Any other relevant children?
Children with client/partner:	Contact:
Schools Attended:	
Child Minder:	
M&B Certificates: Produced / to be ordered?:	Where registered?
Habitual residence in Scotland?	
Previous decree of divorce/parental orders:	
Date and Court	

Notes

Keep track of the inevitable changes of surname, address, occupation and every other aspect of your clients' lives by using a different colour of ink to mark changes. Note the date of the change at the same time. Always check if it is acceptable to contact the client at their home address and make it very clear on the file if that is not the case. If the address has to be kept under wraps have some way of marking that out very vividly. A fluorescent red sticker on the front of the file can do the trick! In those relatively rare but extremely worrying cases where secret addresses may be vulnerable and under serious and sinister investigation it is vital for anyone who might deal with any aspect of the case whether incoming correspondence, telephone calls or visitors to the office to be aware of the situation.

Full names should always include the client's original surname and any subsequent and intervening surnames. This can be quite a lengthy exercise! It does avoid frustrating delays at a later stage particularly in relation to divorce actions if all that information is clear from the outset.

Always ask for the spelling of even the most innocuous name! What may seem a very simple name on inquiry could turn out to have a spelling similar to a nightmare hand of Scrabble! Creatively phonetic Gaelic is another of the potential pitfalls!

Remember you need to ask for sufficient evidence of identity. Clients do have to be alerted to this when making a first appointment.

Dates of marriage and birth can often be elusive but it is worth trying to pin them down. If they are clearly speculative rather than definitive make a note to that effect. If you might have to order any of the certificates it is worth having information about the place of registration at the outset.

The "relevant partner" for this sheet is the individual causing the client current problems. Relevant information about any new partners comes later.

Details of Income & Expenditure

DETAILS OF INCOME & EXPENDITURE

INCOME DETAILS	CLIENT	RELEVANT PARTNER
Income Support		
Which Office?		
Working Family Tax Credit		
Disabled Person's Tax Credit		
Child Benefit		
Pay from Employment		
Is O/T usual		
Job Seekers Allowance		
Contribution Based	YES/NO	YES/NO
Incapacity Benefit		
Other Benefit (Specify)		
Investments/other		
Aliment received		

EXPENDITURE	CLIENT	RELEVANT PARTNER
Housing costs		
Rent/loan repayments		
Endowment policies		
Building contents		
Gas/electricity		
Telephone		
Car costs		
Food		
Council tax		
Other		
Aliment Paid		
CONTRIBUTION?	AMOUNT	DATE TO BE PAID
Benefit book/pay slip examined?	Place of birth:	
N.I. number;	Mother's original surname:	
Is client living with new partner?	YES/NO If yes, name:	
If YES, do they have an income **and/or** capital?	YES/NO	
If YES, give details of income and capital:		

Notes

In most cases it is useful to ascertain at the first interview the income details of both your client and the relevant partner and any current partner. The expenditure information may not be covered at that point but may be completed at a later interview. If from income it looks as if your client may qualify for legal aid then check the capital details on the next sheet. If appropriate, go back and complete the information at the foot of this sheet in connection with legal aid.

Remember to ask specifically for the client's last take home pay. It is quite common for a client to give their basic rather than actual income. You should ask to see their pay slip or benefit book if they might be eligible for Advice & Assistance. Clients should be advised when they make their appointment to bring that paperwork if they want to explore eligibility for Legal Aid. The receptionist has a challenging task to cover all the necessary points without overwhelming the client. An abundance of people skills is called for at that stage.

Sometimes asking for the place of birth or mother's original surname provokes an explanation that the client is adopted. He or she will usually know the information but often feel it is relevant to mention about the adoption. That may be done in a very matter of fact way which may need no further comment other than recognising the information. On the other hand, it may be clear that the adoption is a sensitive area for the client and care should be taken in how the information is acknowledged.

Capital Details

CAPITAL DETAILS
Relevant date values unless marked otherwise as current (c)– show estimates as (e)

MATRIMONIAL/SHARED HOME	CLIENT	PARTNER	JOINT
Value of house			
Amount of loan			
Name and Address of lenders			
Reference number			

Net value of house			
Endowment loan			
YES/NO			
Policy details			
OTHER ASSETS			
Time share/holiday			
Home/other property			
Household contents			
OtherInsurance policies			
Bank accounts			
Savings			
Investments			
Pensions			
Business Interests			
Vehicles			
Other			
Any inheritance or			
gifts or previous assets			
Other resources			
LIABILITIES			
Bank loans			
Car loans			
Credit cards			
Other			

Notes

For unmarried couples, this may be of more limited relevance. It is intended to provide only a broad outline of what is around. More detailed accurate information can be gathered at the next stage. These details will allow some idea of possible options and an indication of what further information is necessary.

For married couples, it is always important to check if the matrimonial home is also matrimonial property. That may well usually be the case but not always. If not, that may have very major implications and is not a point you would wish to emerge somewhere down the line! It may be appropriate to mention the difference between occupancy rights and property rights briefly at this stage without being drawn into a full dissertation about matrimonial property.

Much of the information will be "guesstimates". Reassure the client that a rough idea is helpful and keep notes where figures are very approximate. Remember to make it clear that you understand a client may well not know the full picture and emphasise that you are only looking for a general indication of the assets and liabilities that are or may need to be taken into account.

If the matrimonial assets are clearly extensive all that you would need at this stage are global figures. You should explain to the client that you will be looking for detailed information for the next stage and will provide paperwork to help there. It is quite likely that such a client will have or can provide copies of beautifully worked spread sheets. Be grateful! Check you know what they mean!

It is important to make a habit of asking if either your client or his or her partner put money from an inheritance, gift or resources from before the marriage or an inheritance or gift from a third party acquired during the marriage into any of the matrimonial assets. It is also useful to know if there are other resources around even if not matrimonial property.

Since the ownership of or liability for assets and liabilities is relevant in considering the mechanics of any settlement it is useful to have this information from the outset. There is the risk that a client will start with the assumption that ownership or liability has huge significance in terms of ultimate division. Avoid reinforcing that impression. Explain where appropriate at this stage the difference between the law of contract and family law. The trick is to do that simply and quickly to avoid going in to lecture mode!

Once you have these details you can obtain relevant information about the breakdown of the relationship on a separate sheet to give you more material about possible options then have a preliminary discussion with the client about the way forward. At the end of the interview you can note the outcome and specifically what tasks you and the client are to undertake. It is a particularly useful exercise to go through this step while the client is still there. It allows you to summarise the ground you have covered and check that you and the client do have the same impression of what has to happen next. This can be done on the record sheet which should also be used to note any work undertaken for the client. The progress sheet can be used to ensure some preliminary matters have been dealt with.

Progress Sheet

PROGRESS SHEET		
Summarising Letter to be sent? YES/NO		
Couple Counselling discussed	To be Attempted	YES/NO/PERHAPS
Mediation:	To be Attempted If so–CALM/FMS	YES/NO/PERHAPS
OBJECTIVES AND PRIORITIES		
SUMMARY		

Notes

Check with the client if he or she would like a letter summarising what you discussed at the first meeting. It is likely to be helpful as you will have covered a lot of ground with the client who may well be anxious and not best placed to absorb complex legal information! Be aware that the Legal Aid Board may challenge the need for such a letter You should always gently explore the possibility of couple counselling either as a couple or as an individual. It is important to do that in a careful way to avoid the client feeling you have judged his or her account of the difficulties in the relationship and found it trivial. Equally, it can avoid a client feeling they have stepped on the conveyor belt to permanent separation. Clients should also be aware of the option of mediation. Both these options are unlikely to be appropriate if there has been a history of physical or mental abuse in the relationship.

In the box above "summary" it is useful to note your client's main objectives and anxieties and any significant features that might otherwise be overlooked as time goes on such as source of funds. This should be done in whatever shorthand will alert you to important aspects and need not be an elegant precis!

Similarly, the summary is intended to mark only the most significant steps along the way and should not be more than a few words noted after there have been developments which should not be overlooked. It should simplify rather than complicate your life!

Separation Agreement Framework

SEPARATION AGREEMENT FRAMEWORK

List Proposals	Amendments
CHILDREN Based With	
Contact With	

DIVISION OF ASSETS	CLIENT	PARTNER
Matrimonial Home		
Time share/Holiday home		
Household contents (see overleaf if very detailed)		
Insurance Polices		
Savings		
Investments		
Pensions		
Business Interests		
Vehicles		
Other		
Capital Sum		

APPORTIONMENT OF LIABILITIES	CLIENT	PARTNER
Bank Loans		
Other Loans		

FINANCIAL SUPPORT:		
PA:	AMOUNT:	DURATION:
ALIMENT		

Notes

Once proposals start emerging it can be useful to record and check them against the separation agreement framework. This can allow you to see the whole picture and make sure it still makes sense!

Summarising Letters

The following are paragraphs which could be used to confirm the broad legal position to clients. It allows clients to have information for reference. It allows you the reassuring knowledge that not only was the information given, but can be seen to have been given! Obviously, any specific quirks peculiar to the client must also be outlined.

Parental rights and responsibilities

Since the terms "custody" and "access" remain all too vivid for some clients it is useful to start off reinforcing the current legal framework.

Married couples

"The Children (Scotland) Act 1995 emphasises the responsibilities parents have rather than their rights. It discourages parents from asking for Court Orders unless they are absolutely necessary. It encourages parents to remain as involved as possible with their children after separation and in fact says that a parent not living with a child has a duty to keep in touch with that child. Instead of using the words "custody" and "access" the Court orders that can be requested are for a residence order to have a child living with a parent or a contact order where the object is to have the child spend some time with the parent asking for the order. Even if residence or contact orders are made, both parents should still be involved in major decision making. There is also the provision to ask the Court for orders for specific matters.

When parents separate they have 3 choices:

Negotiation:

1. The parents can agree between them the best arrangements for their children. The agreement can be informal but may also be put in writing (a separation agreement).

Mediation:

2. If parents want to co-operate but need some help to decide what arrangements would be best for the children they can go to a Family Mediation Service or a Solicitor/Mediator where they will be helped to do this.

Litigation:

3. If parents cannot agree between themselves what is best for the children they can ask the court to decide.

As you will realise going to court is stressful for everyone. It is better for the children if the parents can agree things between themselves rather than have to go to court.

However, if there is a danger that the other parent might snatch the children it is very important to ask the Court for an order, particularly if there is a danger that the children might be taken out of the country.

The Law does not consider that either the mother or the father automatically has a better claim. The decision is based on what is in the best interests of the child. That will depend on who is best able to provide for the practical and emotional needs of the child.

The views of any child involved are also very important. A child of twelve or over is assumed to be old enough to say what their views are. With younger children it depends on their maturity. Parents are normally supposed to take into account the views of the other parent and children (where appropriate) in any major decision making."

Unmarried couples

"If a child's parents are not married then only the mother has any automatic right over the child even if the father is shown on the birth certificate. An unmarried father can only get his name put on the original birth certificate if he is present when the birth is registered.Only the mother has automatic legal rights over the child unless this is changed by the court.If the father wants either contact with or care of the child this could be done by agreement with the mother. Sometimes mediation can be a useful way of tackling this.If there is no agreement he must ask the court in which case he would have to prove what he seeks is in the best interests of the child. The Children (Scotland) Act 1995 did not change the basic rule that unmarried fathers have no automatic legal rights. The Act emphasises the responsibilities parents have rather than their rights. It discourages parents from asking for Court orders unless they are absolutely necessary. Instead of using the words "custody" and "access" the Court orders that can be requested are for a residence order to have a child living with a parent or a contact order where the object is to have the child spend some time with the parent asking for the order. There is also the provision to ask the Court for orders for specific matters. The Act allows an unmarried father to gain parental rights and responsibilities by a formal agreement signed by both parents. The wording of this agreement has to follow a special form and must be registered."

Grounds for divorce

Many clients have a very firm idea that divorce is granted because of the "irretrievable breakdown" of a marriage but assume a subjective assessment to that effect should be enough.

Underlining the need for proof and specific grounds is usually necessary and helpful. Flag up any likely changes.

"All divorces are granted because of the irretrievable breakdown of a marriage but there are only certain ways that can be proved, known as the grounds for divorce. If the couple are not yet separated or have been separated for less than two years the only two grounds for divorce are by proving the other person has committed adultery or behaved unreasonably. If one person left without any justification and against the other one's wishes then after two years apart the other partner could ask for a divorce based on the grounds of desertion. If after two years apart both want a divorce then the irretrievable breakdown can be proved by the fact of non cohabitation for two years or more together with the consent of the other person.

If the fault based grounds of adultery, unreasonable behaviour or desertion don't apply and only one person wants a divorce then they would have to wait for five years and use the ground of non-cohabitation for five years or more to prove the irretrievable breakdown. Where there are no children under 16 and no financial issues to be sorted out by the Court then a simple and cheaper divorce is available by submitting a form to the court. It can be applied for after two years if both want to be divorced or five years if only one person want to be divorced."

Proposed changes

"It seems quite likely that within the foreseeable future the rules will be changed to say that a father who is shown on the birth certificate will have automatic rights and responsibilities in the same way as a married father. This is simply a proposal and might not be made law but there should be reports about it in the Press from time to time."

The family home—married couples

The family home

"Normally both husband and wife have occupancy rights in the family home (known as the matrimonial home). It usually does not matter which of the couple is owner or tenant. Both have the right to remain in the house.

If it is necessary for the physical or mental welfare of one of a couple or the children caused by the behaviour of one of the parties then the court can be asked to exclude the person causing the risk from the family home. A power of arrest can be attached to an order like that which makes the order more immediately effective.

While a couple are married it is not automatic that one of them can insist that the house is sold. In a divorce action one of the couple can ask the court for continued occupancy rights or transfer of title or tenancy as part of the overall financial settlement."

Spousal support

It may be necessary to consider spousal support as either a short-term or longer term measure.

Spousal support

"When a married couple separate and one is working and the other is not or is on a lower income the one who is worse of may ask their partner for financial support called aliment, usually paid weekly or monthly. The amount depends mainly on the needs and resources of both households.

The one who has left the family home can be asked to pay towards specific outgoings to do with the house, eg, mortgage repayments. Quite often rather than do this the amount of aliment requested is calculated to help the one remaining in the family home to pay these outgoings."

Child support

Since working family tax credit does not trigger the involvement of the Child Support Agency (unlike the position with family credit) there may be more "private ordering" of child support. In view of Commissioner's Case No. C.S.C.S./5/97, 1999 Fam. L.R.

37, the Child Support Agency are not dealing with child support if that matter has been covered in a written agreement registered in the Books of Council and Session unless income support or other qualifying benefit is in payment. The question of child support accordingly remains an issue which could be sorted out between the parties if they wished in many cases. The position will be changed yet again with the imminent overhaul of the Agency.

Clients are understandably anxious to have some guidance about the appropriate level for child support. The proposal to have a level of child support fixed as a percentage of the net income of the parent not living with the children can give some assistance. It is important to point out that the proposed 15 per cent for one child, 20 per cent for two children and 25 per cent for three or more should only be taken as a rough guide. There will be departures from that percentage if the non resident parent has children in his or her household or is on a low income and an element of discretion for other significant factors. It should be more satisfactory to focus on the real needs and resources of both households. Unfortunately, this usually discloses a chronic shortage of resources and over abundance of needs!

The obligation to support older children who are in full-time education can sometimes be overlooked. It is an increasingly significant factor for many couples and should be taken into account from the outset. Parents who have hitherto been justifiably proud of the academic record of their offspring may be suddenly daunted at the financial implications of any leaning in that child towards medicine or architecture!

Child support

"If there are children then both parents have an obligation to contribute towards the childrens' support. The parent who does not have the children living with them most of the time should provide financial support for the children. For parents with care of the children who receive Income Support the Child Support Agency will automatically tell the absent parent how much maintenance they have to pay for the children. Other parents with care who do not receive that benefit can either enter into a voluntary contract about aliment or can apply to the Child Support Agency for an assessment of how much maintenance the other parent should pay if they do not have an existing Court order or agreement. The obligation to maintain children continues after divorce."

Financial support for young people

"Where there are children aged sixteen and over who are likely to go on to further education it is useful to bear in mind that both parents have financial obligations to young people in appropriate full time education or training up to and including the age of twenty four. Between the age of sixteen and eighteen financial support for a child can be paid from one parent to the other or from the parent to child direct. Where the support is for a young person of eighteen and over the support is paid to them."

Debt

Joint debt can be a real trap for the unwary. Many people have failed to take on board the implications of a joint bank account or joint loan. They may take what they feel is the fair interpretation that whoever benefited from the money should repay the debt. It is important to spell out the legal position.

Joint bank accounts and debt

"At the time of separation there are many practical matters to sort out including safeguarding the position about any joint bank accounts. Remember that you could be responsible for the whole amount due on any joint account. It is important to sort out any joint debt."

Financial provision on divorce

This could obviously extend to several volumes of information let alone a paragraph or so! Since you are likely to have focused on the detail of the client's particular circumstances it can be helpful to give a very broad overview to ensure that some of the more general points are not lost. Equally, it is crucial to summarise any significant specific points which have arisen.

Financial provision on divorce

"On divorce the general idea is that all the property acquired by either husband or wife during the marriage is considered matrimonial property and the value of it should be shared fairly at the end of the marriage up to the date of separation. This can involve one party transferring property to the other or a balancing payment of capital being made, so that each ends up with a fair share. "Fairly" usually means equally, although there are cases where the division is not simply one half each. Any debt incurred during the same period has to be taken into account. Matrimonial property includes savings from during the time of the marriage, any business interests built up during the marriage and the value of pension and life insurance interests A house or contents bought in contemplation of a marriage are included in matrimonial property. Otherwise it is only assets acquired after the marriage and before the separation that are included. In some circumstances "fair sharing" might mean that the wife has the family home transferred to her (and takes over responsibility for the secured loan) instead of receiving any money from the husband's pension interests although it is now possible for pension interests to be shared if that would be more appropriate. Every case is different. Gifts from third parties and inherited money are not included in matrimonial property. If either of you put such gifts or inherited money or resources you had before the marriage into matrimonial property that may also affect the division. Other special circumstances can be taken into account.

In addition to sharing matrimonial property there can be a request for money either as a lump sum (capital) or as periodical payments (known as periodical allowance) to one party (usually the wife) from the other (usually the husband). This happens where one person needs extra financial support, for example, to allow her or him a period of not more than three years to adjust to living independently of the other's financial support or because the divorce will otherwise cause grave financial hardship."

Legal aid

Remember that you have a duty to advise a client as to how they stand about the possibility of legal aid. Even if you are in a firm which does not do legal aid work you must let the client know if they could qualify and explain that they would have to go elsewhere if they wished to pursue that option. If legal aid is involved various things should be underlined for the clients at different stages. The following is simply a starting point!

Legal fees

"You qualify under the Advice and Assistance Scheme. That means the only payment you have to make is the amount of any contribution you have been told about unless you receive any money or property as a result of the work we do for you. If (except in some restricted circumstances) you did receive any money as a result of advice or court action covered by the Legal Aid Rules then your fees are likely to have to come out of whatever you do receive. There are some exceptions to that for financial settlement on separation or divorce but the general rule is that fees do have to come out of any money or property recovered."

Court proceedings

"If matters have to be resolved in a court action then you could apply for a different kind of Legal Aid. If you are on Income Support you should be able to have your legal costs paid by the Legal Aid Board and only have to pay yourself if you recovered money as a result of the action taken. If you are on a low income help with legal costs may still be possible although you may be asked to pay a contribution towards your fees. If the advice is about difficulties with your partner then your partner's income is not included in the calculation. If you are living with a new partner then the new partner's income has to be considered along with yours."

Mediation if advice and assistance applies

"If you are considering using mediation about financial issues by a Solicitor Mediator and since you qualify under the Advice and Assistance Scheme it is important to let me know before you have a meeting with the mediator because your share of the mediation cost can be covered but only if I specifically ask the Legal Aid Board for their authority. The costs involved are subject to the clawback mentioned above."

Questionnaire about matrimonial property

There can be found at the end a questionnaire about matrimonial property. A copy of this can be sent to a client after the first meeting, or at a later stage to give a clearer picture of the precise nature of the matrimonial property. It can be used to establish the whereabouts of relevant paperwork such as policy documents. The questionnaire can form the basis of a draft schedule of matrimonial property. Legal expenses are an issue for most people. Encouraging clients to provide full information as early and as comprehensively as possible can reduce expense for the client and frustration for you.

It can be quite a challenge to complete the picture of matrimonial property particularly if they include business interests. You should seek advice from an expert familiar with the legislation. It is important to keep up to date with the case law. Consideration of the different approaches to business valuations was given in *McConnell v. McConnell,* 1997 Fam. L.R.97. A list of information likely to be required for a business valuation is given at the end of the book. The basis of the valuation of the pension interests has become rather more straightforward, although the options and issues arising from it are increasingly complex. The cash equivalent transfer value (CETV) is used (even if the pension is in payment). If it is felt there could be features that might warrant a request for a departure from equal sharing, then advice should be sought from an Actuary. This might arise if the member was in poor health (which would not be taken into account in the calculation for the CETV) or where the accrual of benefit was uneven, or if there is a possibility of temporary underfunding in the scheme at the time of valuation. Because the regulations now make it clear that the CETV is the starting point, it is likely that very strong arguments would be required to justify a departure from equal sharing and expert advice would certainly be required. This is reinforced by *Stewart v. Stewart,* 2001 Fam. L.R. 72. If pension interests are a significant part of the matrimonial assets, financial and actuarial advice is likely to be necessary.

Statement of income and expenditure

It is usually helpful at an early stage for a client to work out his or her budget. This may be relevant in considering whether your client could take over the matrimonial home or in relation to the question of support. Some clients already have the figures etched in their minds: others may have no idea where to begin. For the first category, the exercise of completing a statement of income and expenditure will be mainly of help to you and in negotiations. For the second category, the exercise will be the start of a process of learning how to cope with new challenges and help and support should be given. Sometimes a projected budget will be more relevant and the form amended to suit.

Schedule of matrimonial property

If your client has completed the questionnaire about the matrimonial property it should be fairly straightforward to assemble the information as a schedule. It can be helpful to start the draft schedule as soon as you have an outline of assets and liabilities. The schedule can then be updated as further information is assembled. The schedule with supporting vouching could be kept on a treasury tag, in a clear plastic envelope or in a ring binder for ease of reference. A spread sheet facility could be used to make it easier to keep all the totals up-to-date accurately. If any of the information on the schedule is provisional or estimated make that clear.

Letters of engagement

When writing to the client setting out the terms on which you are working for him or her it is important to strike the right balance between providing the information clearly without sounding coldly commercial. It may be helpful to provide a separate contact within the office to discuss the question of fees. The solicitor dealing with the client will wish to focus on being helpful and problem-solving. A first interview in particular can create a climate that would make a detailed discussion of the basis of fee charging difficult. On the other hand, there is no doubt that clients want and need to know what they will be charged and what methods of payments might be open. It may be easier for clients to discuss these aspects with another member of staff.

It is also very important to make it clear who else within the firm might be able to deal with queries if you are not available. Clients can feel very frustrated if you are not at the other end of telephone but reassured if another member of staff is able to help. It may well be worth outlining any regular "away fixtures" you have such as court commitments and any time of the day which you set aside for telephone calls to increase the chance of interface with a client should that be necessary.

Relevant organisations and publications

Solicitors are likely to be one of the first point of contact for someone who is experiencing problems at home but is not sure what do next. For that reason it is particularly important to make sure that the client is aware of other sources of help and information. It is a good idea to compile a list of organisations and publications which might be of interest and help. You will find a list at the end with the details of national organisations. It would be helpful for your clients if you obtained and added local information.

CHAPTER 4

THE NUTS AND BOLTS OF FINANCIAL PROVISION INCLUDING PENSION SHARING

Introduction

Once all the information has been assembled the next stage is to look at the range of workable options. Often the matter uppermost for clients will be sorting things out for their children. Making decisions about children is dealt with in a later chapter. Arrangements for children and financial and property issues are often linked in practice. It is important to recognise this and ensure plans are child friendly so far as possible while trying to avoid children being used as levers to promote an adult agenda. A very full range of skills is needed throughout to help family law clients deal with both the emotional and practical factors.

Financial provision as regulated by the Family Law (Scotland) Act 1985 is complex. It is essential to be familiar with the range of orders possible in terms of s. 8 of the Act, the principles set out in s. 9 and the provisions of ss. 10–14 to assess what is a fair settlement to aim for by way of negotiation or litigation.

It is usually helpful to start from a complete schedule of financial information. If you have a figure for the net matrimonial property and details of income and expenditure some shape for the possibilities usually begins to emerge.

In compiling the schedule remember to check for and exclude property belonging to the parties before the marriage (other than property acquired before the marriage to use as a family home or furniture for it) or property acquired by succession or by way of gift from a third party even after the marriage. Equally, remember those exclusions will still be considered as resources which might be a factor in testing the reasonableness of any division (s.8(1)(b)).

Consider if circumstances have to be taken into account to justify some departure from the starting point that fair division will be equal division (ss.9(1)(a) and 10(1)). Watch out for the possibility of a discount where a non-matrimonial source of funds has been used to acquire matrimonial property. Bear in mind that the strength of this argument will be significantly lessened if the matrimonial property has been acquired in joint names and will be very difficult to establish if the joint acquisition is the matrimonial home. (*Cunningham v. Cunningham,* 2001 Fam. L.R. 12.)

Keep up to date with cases dealing with the s. 9 principles. Remember that the most common departure from equal sharing has been because it was necessary to allow a family home to be kept or provided for the benefit of children. Watch out for claims based on financial advantage/disadvantage where there is non-matrimonial property especially business interests. Check that any career disadvantage suffered to the benefit of the other partner has been adequately balanced by the overall financial provision. Recognise that the impact of *Wallis v. Wallis,* 1993 S.L.T. 1348 allowing the transferee of joint property to receive the "windfall" of its increase in value can be mitigated by backdated interest or offsetting of outlays paid by the transferor, although only in certain circumstances. Mitigation is less likely to be appropriate if the transferor owed a duty of support to the transferee.

Always explain to clients that the legal framework is available for guidance in negotiations and would be the benchmark in litigation. It remains open for parties to take into account their own scale of values. The key element is for decisions to be made from the basis of clients understanding their legal rights. An important part of providing advice as a family lawyer is to help clients check they are making decisions which are measured plans for the future rather than a desperate attempt to escape the past.

Offsetting or splitting?

It is wise to explain to clients that in working out a fair division the idea is to leave each person with a fair share of the net assets overall rather than necessarily dividing up each asset and liability. It can be helpful to say that each person should be left with a list of assets and liabilities that comes to about half the value of the net matrimonial property (or some other proportion depending on the other factors discussed above).

Prior to the introduction of pension sharing it was probably most usual to deal with financial division by way of offsetting—one party would keep the house and the other retain pension interests with some "fine tuning" using policies and/or investments. Then, and now, it is, of course, possible to deal with any required 'balancing' payment by deferred payment or instalments (usually with interest running).

Pension sharing

Since pension sharing became an option in divorces started after December 1, 2000 in terms of s. 8(1)(baa) and s. 8A offsetting is less automatically the most obvious way forward in many cases. There may, as a result, be more pressure on considering the feasibility of selling a matrimonial home in negotiations. The need to consider the benefit of continuity and stability for children remains an important factor to take into account.

Independent financial advice

The option of pension sharing introduces elements which clearly involve financial advice and clients will need to be advised to take seek appropriate guidance. This will fall into two stages. Firstly, the decision of whether to offset or pension share is likely to be affected by a comparison between potential income from either a pension share or investment of other assets. Secondly, the pension share available to the non-member may either be by internal or external credit. If there is an option of taking the pension share out the scheme by way of external credit, again, financial advice is required to inform the decision about how to proceed.

Advantages of pension sharing

If the pension is the main or only asset, it is the only way of achieving fair sharing.

If your client's partner is the pension holder ("the member") and has been financially irresponsible in the past leading to an anxiety about the possibility of future sequestration then pension sharing is more secure than a deferred capital payment. A deferred capital payment will be affected by sequestration or simply a lack of assets at the date payment falls due. Pension sharing once implemented following divorce will not.

If your client is the scheme member and wishes to have access to resources at the stage of settlement, it provides a way of justifying a split of the realisable assets.

Disadvantages of pension sharing

If your client receives a pension credit access to the benefit of this by way of lump sum and/or monthly pension will be dictated by your client's circumstances, not the original scheme member's. The consequence may be that no benefit will be available until your client is aged 65.

As mentioned, it may be more difficult to avoid the sale of the matrimonial home for a client who is living there, especially if there are no children.

Factors for legal advisers

With the introduction of pension sharing, there will be more cases where the information provided by the parties will not be sufficient for you to confidently weigh up the options and which will require further specialist advice.

Where the possibility of pension sharing arises it is crucial to advise clients to take financial advice and to record having done so.

Recognise that the regulations dealing with pension sharing were not framed from the perspective of Scottish law. They do not reflect our definition of matrimonial property nor relevant date. In the rest of the United Kingdom, the whole of the pension fund is taken into account at the date of implementing the order which can only be made by way of a percentage of the fund, not by the device of a pension credit for a specific amount. That possibility was introduced for Scotland expressly to address the difficulty created by the failure of the mechanics of pension sharing to allow for our approach of sharing the relevant date value of the matrimonial property. This may lead to difficulty in obtaining a value at our "relevant date" as if the request is made within one year of the "relevant date" the valuation may be calculated at the date of request (S.I. 2000 No. 1048).

There are potential pitfalls in dealing with pension sharing in a separation agreement. It is crucial to bear in mind that pension sharing is implemented on divorce and cannot be implemented by agreement. If a percentage share was set out, that percentage would be applied to the fund value at the date of implementation, not the relevant date value. A specific amount is likely to be more appropriate, but then the issue of interest (addressed later) arises.

The terms of a pension sharing arrangement can be set out in an appropriately worded agreement which is then registered, but the sharing will not be carried out until the divorce is granted and intimated in proper form and within the timescale set out in the regulations.

The unnerving spectre of future catastrophe looms up! Since the divorce itself may well be carried out using the simplified procedure clients may blithely deal with the divorce under their own steam. If you are dealing with pension sharing in an agreement and there are no divorce proceedings either concurrent or to be raised by you immediately the agreement is concluded then you must give absolutely clear, written advice to your client that steps must be taken within a limited time after divorce to trigger implementation of the pension sharing order. Emphasise that if these steps are not taken on time the pension sharing will fall and there will be no means by then to reopen financial division unless the sheriff can be persuaded to extend the time limit in terms of s. 28(10).

Then apply the same stern approach to yourself. If you are involved in a divorce which either triggers pension sharing set out in an agreement or contains a crave for a pension sharing order be on red alert for the timing of the necessary notification to the "pension arrangement" as set out later in this chapter. It is advisable to let the pension scheme have a look at your paperwork in draft form, whichever method of pension sharing is being contemplated prior to more formal intimation. Diary forward to check the progress of the divorce from time to time. Courts can have periods where work is behind. The divorce could be granted without the issue of an extract for several weeks. This could be disastrous to the implementation of a pension sharing order. Check the date of the interlocutor when it arrives and put in a sequence of increasingly strict diary dates to make absolutely sure things are being done on time.

If you are approached by a client who states they only wish help in obtaining a divorce because they have already sorted out the financial aspects it is always advisable to probe further. Now it will be utterly crucial to ask if the arrangements dealt with pension interests and to see a copy of any written agreement which was drawn up in case it did contain provision for pension sharing.

It is also necessary to consider the implications of the possibility, that before implementation, one of the parties dies, the member retires or transfers into another scheme. These possibilities are considered later.

The range of pension interests affected

Remember that pensions in payment can be shared. Bear in mind that if you are acting for the scheme member, his or her income will drop immediately the pension sharing order is implemented. If you are acting for the partner potentially seeking a pension credit make sure that partner understands it will depend on his or her circumstances when the benefit of the fund will be available. It is not the equivalent of splitting the monthly payments.

Remember that pension sharing is available for private pension schemes and SERPS.

There are a very few pension arrangements which cannot be shared. This should come to light if you follow the correct steps in obtaining information.

Pension sharing is not available as well as an earmarking order in respect of the same pension interests.

Pension rights which derived from a pension sharing order can be shared. While by definition such interests could not come within the definition of matrimonial property they are resources which could be used to achieve division of the value of the matrimonial property

Charges

There will almost certainly be costs involved. Many schemes charge for each step. The charges may either be requested as an outlay or be levied within the scheme. Agreement must be reached or an order requested about how those costs are to be shared between the parties.

Procedure

The procedure for pension sharing is complex and, because of the various steps which have to be taken, time consuming.

If you are consulted by a client with pension interests at the time of separation it may be wise to advise them to request a CETV as soon as possible even if there are no negotiations initiated. Remember that if the request is made within a year after the separation the pension arrangement is not be obliged to provide the value at the 1985 Act relevant date. The note to S.I. 2000 No. 1048 creates some ambiguity about the date of valuation the pension arrangement should use if the request is more than one year after non cohabitation but the Regulation itself does refer to the relevant date in terms of the 1985 Act. It has been suggested that you can simply use the flat line formula set out in the Regulations if your client does end up with a CETV later than the 1985 Act relevant date.

If it is decided to use pension sharing for a specific amount (rather than a specified percentage) then the relevant date CETV value is the correct figure to use in the calculation of net matrimonial property and no later value will be required. If pension sharing is being set out in terms of an agreement followed by divorce and there might be some delay before the divorce takes place then it is likely that the issue of having a provision for interest in the agreement will come up. The most obvious approach would be for interest to accumulate at a specified rate on the amount involved. The question which will have to be addressed is whether such a provision, introducing as it does an element of uncertainty about the ultimate amount, stops it being sufficiently specific in terms of the statutory framework. Written confirmation from the pension arrangement that the exact working is acceptable would always be wise and where interest is contemplated, essential.

An alternative way of covering the point is to make separate provision for interest to accumulate and be paid as a separate obligation between the parties rather than as part of the mechanics of pension sharing. This would clearly be the most reliable method provided the member is able to pay interest from his or her available resources.

If the pension sharing is to be by way of a proportion of the fund being shared the position is different. It would still be necessary to have the CETV at the relevant date to allow calculation of the net matrimonial property but if some time had elapsed it may be necessary to have a later CETV to work out what proportion is appropriate for the pension credit which is transferred (with a corresponding pension debit in respect of the transferring spouse). Remember that the proportion will be applied to a CETV calculated at the date of implementation. If the arrangement is being made in terms of a separation agreement then there could be a significant delay before implementation. The proportion then transferred might then be considerably higher than would have been achieved by using a specific amount, even with an interest provision.

Another provision which must be considered if the arrangement is in terms of a separation agreement is against the possibility that one of the parties might die before pension sharing is implemented. The regulations for a court based order would allow implementation even if the member died post divorce during the implementation period. If the pension sharing provision is in an agreement and the member died post agreement but before divorce the surviving spouse's entitlement would depend on the terms of the pension scheme and the provisions in the agreement. It is quite possible that the surviving spouse would receive adequate provision from the pension scheme but it would be essential to check the position. If there was an element of doubt then a contingency clause could be included providing for a specified amount of capital to be paid from the estate of the predeceasing spouse. Not the jolliest of "what ifs" but a necessary part of trying to avoid a serious gap between intention and delivery of financial provision in this minefield.

It is likely that there would be resistance to any attempt to provide for a compensating payment to the transferee's estate if the non member died prior to implementation. Again, it is important to explain that rather grim "what if" to a potential "transferee" client to ensure that informed decisions are made.

A further potential pitfall is the possibility of a pre-implementation transfer out either voluntarily by the member or by the employer. Since any pension sharing provision is directed to a specific pension fund, it could be thwarted by a transfer of the pension interests prior to the divorce being granted. An obligation to co-operate with fresh pension sharing provision and/or an alternative capital payment might be necessary.

The impact of the member retiring pre-implementation would also have to be considered and provided for, since a lump sum will usually have been paid out, affecting the fund. Once in payment, the value of the pension fund will start diminishing rather than increase. This would clearly have a particularly unhelpful impact if pension sharing were to be by way of a proportion rather than a specific amount.

Practical steps

The Welfare Reform and Pensions Act 1999 introduced pension sharing in principle but the detail of the procedure is contained in a cascade of statutory instruments.

They are available online from the Stationery Office website—http://www.legislation.hmso.gov.uk/stat.htm/2000 for United Kingdom statutory instruments and http://www.scotland-legislation.hmso.gov.uk/legislation/scotland/s-stat.htm for the Scottish Executive's regulations.

Preliminary information

Section 23 of the 1999Act and S.I. 2000 No. 1048, regs 2 and 3.

The first step is to obtain some preliminary information. The member is entitled to a valuation of pension rights or benefits (cash equivalent transfer value—CETV), to be provided within three months. The spouse of the member can request that the CETV be sent to the member, though is not entitled to receive the information direct. If this information is not requested, or not passed on, the pension arrangement can be ordered to produce it by the court. If the production of the information is ordered by court or if the pension arrangement have been told it is required in connection with financial provision under the 1985 Act then it is to be provided within three months or such shorter period as the Court may provide.

Motion and specification procedure remains an option but unless there was other information to be recovered it would seem more straightforward to ask the court to order the production of the information in terms of these provisions.

The non-member is entitled to be provided with some general information including details of how the valuations are calculated, whether an internal or external credit is available to the non-member and the scale of potential charges.

In most cases the next step will be to obtain financial and actuarial advice about the implications of potential options. If pension sharing remains a likely option then further communication with the pension arrangement is necessary.

Formal notification that a pension sharing order or provision may be made

S.I. 2000 No. 1048, reg. 4.

The pension arrangement should be notified specifically that a pension sharing order or provision may be made and requested to provide the information set out in this regulation. It includes matters which could have a bearing on the competence of such an order and ensures clarity about what further details are required by the pension arrangement to implement the order. It is vital for the transferee to be satisfied that has been done.

If matters are being dealt with by negotiation the member should give the appropriate notification and receive the relevant acknowledgement and information in response. In those circumstances, it might be preferable for the first overture to the pension arrangement to be by the member and include both formal notification and a request for information in terms of regulations 2, 3 and 4 including the pension value, unless the possibility of pension sharing is remote.

In the context of litigation it would be appropriate to include a crave for notification and the provision of the necessary information under this regulation and the previous one dealing with valuation of pension benefits.

Bear in mind the slightly different procedure for sharing state scheme rights where notification is to the Secretary of State.

Provision in a separation agreement

Sections 28 (1)(f) and (3) of the 1999 Act and S.I. 2000 No. 1051.

Pension sharing can be done by way of provision corresponding to a pension sharing order under the Family Law (Scotland) Act 1985 in an agreement in prescribed form registered in the Books Of Council and Session. A possible style is provided at the end of this book. The specific provisions are to be set out in a "separable annex" to the Agreement. The Agreement must be registered. A registered Agreement includes any annexes in a bound document. It is to be hoped that "separable" can be interpreted as meaning not embedded in the main body of the Agreement rather than as physically separable.

It is likely that the member would wish pension sharing provision in an agreement to be for an amount rather than a proportion since it could be some time before implementation. The non member is likely to seek interest on the amount fixed.

There may be doubt over whether a provision for interest can be considered a sufficient specification of the amount to be transferred to come within the definition of a "pension sharing order" in Scotland. If it was decided that an interest provision was incompetent it would seriously undermine the possibility of using an amount rather than a proportion. Very careful advice and written confirmation from the arrangement would be necessary to have before embarking on provision for an amount plus interest.

A qualifying agreement must contain an appropriate annex (in terms of S.I. 2000 No. 1051) which sets out the information required by the pension arrangement. The annex has to be intimated to and acknowledged by the pension arrangement then referred to in the agreement. The Agreement and the Annex must be separable.

Remember that pension sharing is only implemented once decree of divorce is granted and appropriate intimation made to the pension arrangement (see later).

Pension sharing in court proceedings

A crave for a pension sharing order should cover the provision of any necessary information not yet available or intimation not yet made. The order itself must specify either a percentage or a cash amount (s. 27 of the 1985 Act as amended by s. 20 of the 1999 Act). It may seem appropriate to include interest. Be wary about potential problems with interest provision outlined in the last section. It remains to be seen what rate of interest will be considered appropriate and whether backdated interest should be awarded.

Backdated interest has never been readily granted and has tended to be used to mitigate the impact of a transferor losing the "windfall" increased value of a jointly owned asset. No assumption has emerged from decided cases that interest should automatically be used to allow "relevant date" values of items in the sole name of one party to be "uprated" to the equivalent value at the date of the raising of an action or negotiated settlement. The statutory provisions specifically allow for a specified amount rather than a percentage when pension sharing in Scotland to accommodate the historic "relevant date" valuation of matrimonial property. It does not impose the use of a current proportion. In view of that, there is an argument that interest should not run from the "relevant date". On the other hand, it could be argued that the "fruits" of an asset have been benefiting one party and denied the other for the intervening period. Case law does not provide a clear lead and there seems to be a significant variation in the outcome of negotiation.

Implementation

Ss. 28 and 34 of the 1999 Act and S.I. 2000 No. 1053.

The pension arrangement must receive either a ccpy of the divorce decree including the order and relevant information about the transferee (essentially the information covered in the annex, used with pension sharing provision by agreement) or divorce decree and separate provision for pension sharing (the annex) within two months of the grant of divorce or s. 28 (7) provides that the pension sharing order or provision "shall be deemed never to have taken effect" Although it is reassuring to note that s. 28 (10) does provide that the sheriff may extend that period it would be wise to avoid putting that provision to the test. In view of the importance of the time limit it would be wise to send the appropriate paperwork ("the matrimonial documents") by registered post in good time, just in case there has been a change of address on the part of the pension arrangement. That is more likely if the sharing was set up in an agreement and some time has elapsed. Also check in case there has been a change of address of either party which may need to be brought to the attention of the pension arrangement.

Although that should be an end so far as you are concerned it will be the start of a great deal of activity for the pension arrangement. Four months are allowed for compliance unless notified charges have not been paid or necessary information has not been made available.

"Earmarking"

It is still possible to obtain an order under s. 12A of the 1985 Act (usually referred to as an "earmarking" order) as a means of securing a deferred capital sum instead of a pension sharing order. The use of such an order means that the pension trustees pay over as much of the specified amount of capital (and any interest which has been stipulated) from any lump sum payable to the member on retirement (or to the member's estate on death if this is stipulated). Payment is made direct from the pension trustees to the member's former spouse.

"Earmarking" orders have not been much used. There are a number of potential pitfalls. The scheme member may die before retirement and insufficient death benefit be available to satisfy the capital sum. The member may have the option of electing what amount of lump sum to take and again, there may be insufficient paid out to satisfy the capital sum. The former spouse must keep the pension scheme notified about any change of address.

Despite these drawbacks the order may be of benefit in some circumstances. If a deferred payment is necessary to achieve fair sharing, the amount is not large and payment by instalments not an option then "earmarking" to help secure the deferred payment would be reassuring and a sensible step to take. An important aspect to bear in mind is the potential for sequestration to frustrate a deferred payment. If there were grounds to worry about the payer's future solvency, the impact of sequestration on the deferred capital sum and earmarking order should be explored.

Other options

There are various other ways in which to achieve appropriate financial provision including transfer of property, heritable and moveable, capital payments and periodical allowance. The procedure involved is covered in subsequent chapters.

To achieve a workable combination of elements requires information, energy and flexibility. The possibilities are increasingly complex. Just remember that while you are dealing with the number crunching your client is trying to cope with both practical and emotional challenges.

Keep your "people" skills running in parallel with your legal knowledge.

CHAPTER 5

WRITTEN AGREEMENTS

Introduction

What do clients want?

It has emerged from research (F. Wasoff and others, "Mutual Consent—Written Agreements In Family Law", Scottish Office Home Department Central Research Unit, 1997) that clients look for a number of things in a separation agreement—

—rite of passage

—reliable statement of intent as separated parents

—clear and enforceable directions for financial provision

A significant aim in dealing with matters by negotiation was to avoid bitterness and preserve the best relationships possible.

What do clients get?

The same research disclosed a significant number of clients who felt they had not received enough information about—

—options available

—progress during the negotiations

—cost implications

—topics such as taxation, means tested benefits and the Child Support Agency

Many felt pressurised into agreeing to terms that in retrospect they found unsatisfactory. They believed they had lost out financially. Agreements had often failed to deliver a reliable framework in relation to children or money. Part of the difficulty may arise from unrealistic client expectations but to some extent this should be met by better communication between client and solicitor during negotiations. Communication needs to be geared to helping clients who are going through a particularly stressful time grasp what are complex and unfamiliar concepts of law using a much fuller range of interpersonal skills. Documents should be clear and understandable. They should also be readily enforceable, avoiding room for disagreement about interpretation. How else can advising solicitors close the gap between expectation and reality?

- explain the law clearly
- explore the options fully
- use straightforward language
- The test for the final text should be—

WHAT?

- is the wording clear?

WHY?

- does it deliver what the client wants, does it tie up the loose ends?

WHEN?

- is the timing specified in relation to future provisions?

HOW?

- will it work, is it enforceable?

Range of agreements

Written agreements may cover various circumstances. Separating couples can set down all the arrangements they have agreed covering childcare and financial provision. There may be a need for a restricted agreement covering the sale of a shared home. A young person may want parental support set down in writing. A couple about to marry may wish to record what each bring in to the marriage. Example of these are provided. The most frequently used agreement is between a married couple who have separated. This agreement is examined in more detail.

The legal framework

The starting point for an agreement is that people are free to set down their financial arrangements in written contracts and expect them to be final. The possible flaws are—

—in some limited circumstances the agreement might be open to challenge
—in other cases that finality might prove a straitjacket if possible changes in circumstances are not provided for

It can concentrate the mind when drafting separation agreements to bear in mind the legal tests for possible challenge by an application for variation.

Variation of separation agreements

Section 16 (1) of the Family Law (Scotland (1985) provides that: "Where the parties to a marriage have entered in to an Agreement as to financial provision to be made on divorce the court may make an order setting aside or varying .....(b) the Agreement or any term of it where the Agreement was not fair and reasonable at the time it was entered in to."

If at first glance that appears to allow a fairly general review, look again! It is an uphill task to mount a successful challenge under that provision. The case of *Gillon v. Gillon* (No. 3) 1995 S.L.T. 678 set out the principles to be applied. In it, Lord Weir referred to previous decisions in England and Scotland and observed that he could adopt from those judgments the following principles—

"1. It is necessary to examine the agreement from the point of view of both fairness and reasonableness.

2. Such examination must relate to all the relevant circumstances leading up to and prevailing at the time of the execution of the agreement, including amongst other things the nature and quality of any legal advice given to either party.

3. Evidence that some unfair advantage was taken by one party of the other by reason of circumstances prevailing at the time of negotiations may have a cogent bearing on the determination of the issue.

4. The court should not be unduly ready to overturn agreements validly entered into.

5. The fact that it transpires that an agreement has led to unequal, and possibly a very unequal division of assets does not by itself necessarily give rise to any inference of unfairness and unreasonableness."

In that particular case the Agreement was allowed to stand with the comment that "the Agreement was entered into by the Pursuer in the full knowledge that she had a potential claim on the Defender's pension rights and she renounced that claim in order to achieve what appeared to her to be the immediate and significant advantage of the Defender's departure from the matrimonial home." A familiar motivation for a client's acceptance of proposals which will give her or him significantly less than equal sharing in financial terms.

A similar line was taken in *Inglis v. Inglis,* 1998 Fam. L.R. 73.

The trick is to ensure that the client is helped to truly "walk through" the consequences of the decision to check that the short-term benefits will remain attractive in the long-term. Variation has been allowed in a case where one party was suffering from mental health problems (*Short v. Short,* 1994 G.W.D. 21–1300) and another where both parties had used the same solicitor and were unaware of important information (*Worth v. Worth,* 1994 S.L.T. (Sh.Ct) 54).

Although variation in terms of this provision may be granted in circumstances that fall short of error, fraud, force or fear (*McAfee v. McAfee,* 1990 S.C.L.R. 805), it is very important to avoid the need. Much better to get it right first time!

It is also very important to set out a framework for review where future circumstances might justify another look at any of the financial provisions. This is particularly likely in the case of ongoing financial support. Spousal support before divorce should be described as aliment and after divorce as periodical allowance. A provision for potential variation by the court should be set out. (*Drummond v. Drummond,* 1996 S.L.T. 386 and *Ellerby v. Ellerby,* 1991 S.C.L.R. 608). In the hopefully very rare circumstances where an agreed provision is omitted from the final document in error it may be possible to rectify with a petition to the Court of Session, in terms of section 8 of the Law Reform (Miscellaneous Provisions)(Scotland) Act 1985.

STYLE SEPARATION AGREEMENT

Remember that the object of a separation agreement is to set down all the matters which have been agreed in a way which is clear and self explanatory. The language does need to be precise but should be as understandable as possible to the parties. It can be helpful to avoid using technical legal terms except where normal language would be unnecessarily lengthy or ambiguous. When they are used make sure the client understands their meaning before he or she signs up! What may not seem particularly technical to you may well baffle a client. Provision for interest on arrears has often been taken by clients to mean an automatic increase in aliment. If the transfer of title is part of the Agreement get hold of the titles and take the conveyancing far enough to establish if any serious title problems are looming.

The complete style is printed in the Appendix. What follows is a clause by clause commentary. The commentary notes are in italics. We suggest you consider leaving the headlines shown in capitals as a means of making the agreement more easily navigable.

STYLE & NOTES

Headings in capitals should be retained.
Asterisks denote a choice of phrase has to be made - the asterisks should always be deleted.
Words in bold denote a selection of word/s to be made or word/s to be added.
Words in italics denote instructions and should all be deleted (after reading or implementing)
To insert names instead of "Husband/Wife" the command is "Ctrl F" or "Ctrl G".
[ ] Denote Options

SEPARATION
AGREEMENT
and Schedule

between

Name and Address
(Referred to in this document
as "the Wife")

and

Name and Address
(Referred to in this document
as "the Husband")

Note

Most people like to use "Mr" & "Mrs" or preferably each person's first name and surname. It is recommended that once the full names of any children are established, they are then referred to by first name. There is certainly merit in avoiding the use of the terms "First and Second Party". Both parties (and their solicitors!) are liable to feel disorientated half way through. Careful use of modern technology can allow a "search and replace" for the words "the Wife" and "the Husband" and "the child/children" to substitute your preferred designation! If pension sharing is to be set up then remember that a separable annex must be prepared setting out the details required in terms of the Pensions on Divorce etc. (Pension Sharing) (Scotland) Regulations 2000 No. 1051 (reg. 5)—see previous chapter styles for relevant clauses for pension sharing.

The Wife and the Husband were married at ------**(PLACE)**----- on **(DATE, MONTH, YEAR)** and have *(No.) **child/children**, **(CHILD'S NAME)** born **(DATE, MONTH YEAR)** and

(CHILD'S NAME) born (DATE, MONTH YEAR) and (CHILD'S NAME) born (DATE, MONTH, YEAR) OR no dependent children*. The Wife and the Husband *separated on **Date** /stopped living together as husband and wife on **Date***. Having taken independent legal advice, the parties wish to set out the following agreement in writing—

Note

It is useful to put in the full names of the couple (including the wife's original surname), the place and date of their marriage and the full names and dates of birth of any children involved. It can provide helpful information in subsequent divorce proceedings. It makes it easier to check where provisions in relation to children are age related.

PREAMBLE—ASSETS AND LIABILITIES

Relevant date

If a couple have stopped living together as man and wife before they have separate accommodation the second option can be used to show the accurate relevant date.

(A)   Refer to Schedule
The matrimonial property at the relevant date [and the parties' current income and expenditure] is detailed in the Schedule attached and signed as relating to this document.

(B)   Narrate Assets/Liabilities
It is accepted by both parties that the matrimonial assets and liabilities at the relevant date comprised—
List assets and liabilities

[The Husband has a net monthly income of £   and the Wife has net monthly income of £   together with Child Benefit.]

(C)   No Assets/Liabilities
The parties had no significant capital assets or liabilities at the relevant date. [The Husband has a net monthly income in the

region of £   and the Wife has a net monthly income in the
region of £   together with Child Benefit of
£   .]

*Although it is not a universal practice, it can be helpful to narrate
both the capital assets and liabilities and income and expenditure
to make sense of the terms of the agreement and make it clear
what was taken into account. That information provides a starting
point for any future negotiations about variation of alimentary
provision where that is appropriate. Unless there are very few
assets (and/or liabilities!) it is likely you will already have
assembled a schedule of matrimonial property which can be used
to be attached to the agreement. Otherwise, they can be narrated
using option (B). If pension sharing has to be used the value of
pension interests should be narrated.*

*There can be cases where you are representing one party and
their partner has expressed a degree of accord about a settlement
formula but refuses to take legal advice. Your client's initial
reaction may be of joy unconfined! To moderate their glee not
only do you have to explain the risk of potential variation in terms
of s. 16 but also the need for you to include energetic exhortations
to take independent advice in any correspondence to the other
partner. Clients do usually understand your need to avoid losing
your practising certificate/livelihood! The partner may resist your
encouragement to take advice but indicate a resolve to sign an
agreement you have prepared. Remember to spell out in the letter
sending out the signing copy that the document will be binding
and have legal consequences. The wording in the introduction
should be amended to "Having had the opportunity of taking
legal advice" if there has been no explicit legal representation.*

1.   CHILDCARE ARRANGEMENTS

(A)   *Children Based with One Parent*
        The **child/children**   *(give details)* shall live with **the
        Wife/the Husband**.   **He/She/They** shall have the
        following contact with the **Husband/the Wife**—
        (a) alternate weekends from 6.00 p. m. on Friday until
        6.00pm on the immediately succeeding Sunday (b) the
        first two weeks of the school summer holidays (c) one
        week during the Christmas holiday period (including
        Christmas Day and New Year's Day in alternate years)

(c) one week during the school Easter holidays. These arrangements may be altered if both parents agree.

(B)   *Shared Care*

The parents will continue to share the care of their **child/children (GIVE DETAILS)**. The **child/children** shall live with the Wife ***from (give details) to**   ***** each week and with the Husband for the remainder of the week. The holidays shall be divided as follows— **(GIVE DETAILS)**

(C)   *General Legal Position*

Each Parent shall consult with and take account of the views expressed by the other and where appropriate their **child/children** in any major decision affecting or concerning the welfare, health, education or wellbeing of the said **child/children**. *Either parent has the authority to take the **child/children** out of the United Kingdom without the written consent of the other parent but only for a reasonable holiday period not exceeding **2/3** weeks. OR Neither parent has the authority to take the **child/children** out the United Kingdom without the prior written consent of the other parent.*

Most parents who separate do have their children's welfare as the main priority. That makes it a good starting point. It is important for clients to be made aware that parents are encouraged by the legal Rules to approach arrangements with co-operation and flexibility. You should mention that orders are granted.

It is important to make sure parents are aware that even if a child or children will be residing with one parent the other parent still has parental rights and responsibilities (if that is the legal position). Setting out the legal framework in the agreement can help to underline the position. The ghost of custody and access lingers! Exorcise it!

You must explain the limitations in enforcing arrangements about children. Despite that, it can be very helpful to set down the arrangements in some detail. If contact is likely to prove difficult because emotions are still running high really going into the nuts and bolts such as where the hand-over will take place and responsibilities about feeding and clothing the children could help reduce potential areas of conflict. Putting in a provision that mediation should be attempted in relation to any future difficulties arising from the contact arrangements could allow the parents a mechanism for change if things still remain a bit fraught in the future.

The provision about holiday arrangements is to meet a strict reading of the Children (Scotland) Act 1995, s. 2(3) preventing either parent removing children from the jurisdiction without the consent of the other parent.

2.   HOUSEHOLD CONTENTS

(A)   Transfer to One
The Husband/the Wife agrees to transfer any interest **he/she** has in the furniture and other moveable items in the matrimonial home at **(ADDRESS) ("the home")** to **the Wife/the Husband** [other than *list* which **he/she** will collect from the home within four weeks of the date of the later signature on this document.]

(B)   Sharing/Unspecific
The furniture and other moveable items in the matrimonial home at **(ADDRESS)** have been divided by mutual agreement.

(C)   Specific Division
The parties have agreed to divide the furniture and other moveable contents in the matrimonial home at **(ADDRESS)** in terms of the attached Schedule of Division of Contents. The **Husband/the Wife** will collect **his/her** share within four weeks of the date of the later signature on this document.

*Clients often overestimate the value of household contents because they assume the replacement value of the items should be used. Explain that the valuation should be on a willing seller/buyer basis (*Latter v. Latter, *1990 S.L.T. 805 and* Bolton v. Bolton, *1995 G.W.D. 14–799). Encourage a pragmatic approach! It is usually best if the division of household contents can be done informally. If it is necessary to include details in the agreement make sure that the details are sufficient to identify the items. The arrangements for handover should be spelled out. Many people* *would understandably assume that the word "deliver" implies arranging for an item to be physically delivered to the one receiving it rather than simply handed over. Clarify that point.*

Your original information gathering should have made it should be clear if any of the contents are being bought by way of a loan or subject to hire purchase or credit sale agreements. It is worth double checking if there is any doubt.

If using Option (B) make sure your client understands the division must take place before the Agreement is signed.

3.   MATRIMONIAL HOME

(A)   TENANCY TRANSFER/RENUNCIATION
      The Husband/the Wife agrees to the transfer of the tenancy of the matrimonial home at **(ADDRESS) ("the home")** to **the Wife/the Husband,** and agrees to move out of the home two weeks after the date of the later signature on this document . **He/She** will sign a Form of Renunciation of occupancy rights in the home (in terms of the Matrimonial Homes (Family Protection) (Scotland) Act 1981 as amended) and deliver the Renunciation to **the Wife/the Husband** within two weeks of the date of the later signature on this document.

Remember that the Landlords must consent to the transfer.

(B)   OCCUPANCY RIGHTS/TRANSFER/POSSIBLE SALE/
          JOINTLY OWNED
3.1   **The Husband/the Wife** agrees that the **Wife/the Husband** shall have sole occupancy rights in the [jointly owned] matrimonial home at **(ADDRESS) ("the home")** until the **younger/youngest** of the **child/children** attains the age of **sixteen/eighteen** years. **He/she** shall not during that time take any steps to force the sale of the home.

3.2   At any time until the said child **(NAME OF YOUNGEST CHILD)** attains the age of **sixteen/eighteen** years **the Wife/the Husband** may offer in writing to pay over to **the Husband/the Wife** ******a one half **(or other proportion)** share of the net value of the home at that future date under deduction of the amount of secured loan then outstanding having had the value of the home established by an independent valuer OR the sum of **£Amount** [with interest at **Amount** % a year from the date of the later signature on this document]. ** **The Husband/the Wife** agrees to co-operate with **the Wife/the Husband** to deliver whatever validly signed Deed or Deeds are necessary to convey a good marketable title [so far as affecting **his/her** interests] and to vest the whole right title and interest in the home in the name of **the Wife/the Husband** and to revoke any special destination and (if it is still appropriate to so do) to sign and deliver an Affidavit renouncing **his/her** occupancy rights in the home in exchange for the appropriate consideration. **the Wife/the Husband** shall exhibit and then record in the Land Register or Deed of Variation or Discharge of any standard security in agreed terms validly executed by the creditors discharging **the Husband/the Wife** of all liability and obligations in respect of said secured loan. Prior to settlement the **Husband's/Wife's** solicitors shall show to the **Wife's/Husband's** solicitors a clear Form 10/P16 or 12 Report as appropriate in the property and personal registers in relation to the home. **The Husband's/the Wife's** solicitors shall provide a letter of obligation in the Law Society of Scotland recommended style at settlement.

3.3   At the end of the period of occupation (unless previously transferred to **the Wife/the Husband**,) the home will be sold and **the net free proceeds, after settlement of the outstanding balance of the secured loan, other debts and expenses of sale, shall be divided equally between the Husband and the Wife OR in the following proportion **[State proportion]** OR the **Husband/the Wife** will receive the **sum of £**   plus interest on that figure at the rate of   % per annum from the date of the later signature on this document until payment and the **Wife/the Husband** the balance of the net free proceeds.** Both parties agree they will not exercise any diligence on the free proceeds of sale.

The option of one parent remaining in the family home with the children for a specified time (during which they can purchase the other parent's share at current market value) is not extensively used. It is likely to have the disadvantage of leaving the non-resident parent tied in to a secured loan. His or her borrowing capacity would be restricted. It could leave the resident parent feeling rather beholden. On the other hand, it allows continuity for the children. It is certainly an arrangement which can be requested in litigation (Family Law (Scotland) Act 1985 S. 14 (d)). The length of the potential period of sole occupation could be the main feasibility test. Remember that setting out a specific price with interest running will have income tax implications while capital gains tax has to be considered when stipulating a share of the market value. Advice should be sought from an accountant.

(C)   PROVISION FOR RUNNING COSTS DURING PERIOD
        OF SOLE OCCUPATION

3.4   During the said period of occupation the responsibility for sums due under the secured loan [and related endowment premiums] shall be met *solely by the **Wife/the Husband** OR equally between the Husband and the Wife and if either pay a greater share of said payments during this period he or she shall be entitled to recover from the other such excess over and above one half of the total payments during the same period.* The **Wife/the Husband** undertakes to maintain the home in its present condition. The costs of any structural repairs not covered by insurance will be met *equally between the parties OR solely by the **Wife/the Husband**.* Neither party will increase the borrowing in relation to the home during said period. The **Wife/the Husband** shall be solely responsible for all other outgoings (including Council Tax, fuel and telephone bills and any arrears), decorating and the costs arising from wear and tear.

It is very important to be quite clear where the responsibility lies for outlays during a period of sole occupation. There would seem a reasonable argument for the one remaining in the house to meet everyday costs. It is probably better to keep alimentary provision separate. In the immediate aftermath of the separation it is quite common to find the partner who is not living in the house meeting many or all of the outlays for the matrimonial home. That makes sense in the short term while plans are discussed but is full of potential pitfalls as a more long-term arrangement. The bills are criticised as too high or start being unpaid. Better that each person has a clear budget to work with and a mechanism for review.

(D)   SALE WHERE ONE PARTY SOLE OWNER OR JOINT OWNERS AND HALF SHARE EACH

3.1   Both the Wife and Husband agree that the matrimonial home at **(ADDRESS)** ("the home") will be put on the market within 2 weeks of the date of the later signature on this document. **** The Husband/the Wife** agrees to pay over to **the Wife/the Husband** one half of the free proceeds of the sale of the home (after repayment of the secured loan and all reasonable estate agents and legal expenses). In exchange **the Wife/the Husband** agrees to sign an Affidavit consenting to the sale of the home in terms of the Matrimonial Homes (Family Protection) (Scotland) Act 1981 as amended and any other documentation necessary to effect the sale. **OR** The free proceeds of sale (after repayment of the secured loan and all reasonable estate agents and legal expenses) will be divided equally between the parties. ******

3.2   *By signing this document both Parties authorise and instruct **(DETAIL SOLICITORS ACTING IN SALE)** or any other firm of solicitors instructed in the sale of the home to distribute the free proceeds in accordance with the terms of this paragraph. Both parties agree they will not exercise any diligence on the free proceeds of sale. The property will be put on the market at a price of **AMOUNT**. Both parties undertake to co-operate fully to facilitate a sale of the property. No reasonable offer for the property will be refused. If the property remains unsold at the end of three months the parties will review the price asked to encourage a sale.

If the matrimonial home has to be sold emphasise to the client the importance of having agreement in writing setting out what has to happen to the proceeds before the property is marketed and the offers start pouring in! There seems nothing which encourages offers with early entry dates more than a lack of certainty about division of proceeds. When you first see a client he or she may have assumed it is quite in order to go ahead with a house sale on the basis of equal sharing. Once you have some background information it may be clear that a potential claim for capital could be met from the other person's share of the proceeds. It can be difficult to leave that possibility open without creating a confrontational climate. Correspondence must be very carefully worded and convey a commitment to problem-solving while emphasising the need to look for mutually acceptable proposals that will make sense in both the short and long-term.

(E)   *SALE—JOINT OWNERS—UNEQUAL DIVISION*

3.1   Both the Wife and the Husband agree that the matrimonial home at **(ADDRESS)** ("the home") will be put on the market within two weeks of the later signature on this document. **The Husband/the Wife** shall receive **POUNDS STERLING (£**   **)** from the free proceeds of the sale (after deduction of all reasonable and necessary Estate Agent and Legal expenses) the balance being payable to **the Wife/the Husband** [(unless the free proceeds are less than **(INSERT AMOUNT)** POUNDS STERLING **(£**   **)** in which case the free proceeds shall be divided equally between the Husband and Wife).]

3.2   By signing this both Parties authorise and instruct **(DETAIL SOLICITORS ACTING IN SALE)** or any other firm of solicitors instructed in the sale of the home to distribute the free proceeds in accordance with the terms of this paragraph. Both parties agree they will not exercise any diligence on the free proceeds of sale. The property will be put on the market at a price of *AMOUNT*. Both parties undertake to co-operate fully to facilitate a sale of the property. No reasonable offer for the property will be refused. If the property remains unsold at the end of three months the parties will review the price asked to encourage a sale.

People usually reach an understanding about the proceeds of the sale of a house on the basis of a "guesstimate" of what the house will fetch. It is worth talking through what could happen if the house fetches much less than hoped.

(F)   NARRATION OF OUTLAYS WHEN HOUSE BEING
        SOLD
        Both parties agree that until the date of entry following
        the sale of the home the monthly payments of the secured
        loan will be met by **the Husband/the Wife**, Council Tax
        and other utilities by **the Wife/the Husband**. [In the
        event of a material change of circumstances the
        responsibility for those payments may be reviewed at the
        written request of either party and failing agreement ***be
        determined by Court/OR by an arbiter mutually
        appointed, or, failing agreement, by an arbiter who is
        a Family Law specialist selected and appointed by the
        President or Vice President for the time being of the
        Law Society of Scotland and conducted in accordance
        with the Arbitration Rules of the Law Society of
        Scotland current at the date of appointment of the
        arbiter whose decision will be final and binding on the
        parties.]**

*This can be quite tricky because of the uncertainty of how long it
will take for a property to sell. What makes sense in the first few
months may become unworkable in the longer term. As time goes
on circumstances may change. On the other hand, commitments
to have to be met. Including a provision for variation and hoping
for a buoyant market may be the best compromise!*

(G)   ONE PARTY RECEIVING MATRIMONIAL HOME FOR
        NO SPECIFIC CONSIDERATION
3.1   **The Husband/the Wife** agrees to convey to **the Wife/the
        Husband [his/her** one half *pro indiviso* share in] the
        matrimonial home at **(ADDRESS) ("the home")**and to
        give **him/her** sole occupation. **He/She** shall co-operate
        with **the Wife/the Husband** to deliver whatever validly
        signed Deed or Deeds as are necessary to convey a good,
        marketable title [so far as affecting **his/her** interests], and
        to vest the whole right, title and interest in the home in
        name of **the Wife/the Husband** [alone, and to revoke any
        special destination] together with a validly executed and
        notarised Renunciation of any or all rights available to
        him/her under the Matrimonial Homes (Family
        Protection) (Scotland) Act 1981 (As amended) in respect
        of the home. All this shall be completed as soon as

reasonably practicable, but no later than eight weeks from the later signature on this document.

3.2   In exchange for delivery of said Deed or Deeds of conveyance and Renunciation **the Wife/the Husband** shall free and relieve **the Husband/the Wife** of all obligations in respect of any Standard Security presently secured over the home. **She/He** shall exhibit and then record in the Land Register a Deed of Variation or Discharge of any Standard Security in agreed terms validly executed by the Creditors discharging **the Husband/the Wife** of all liability and obligations in respect of said secured loan.

3.3   Prior to settlement **the Husband's/the Wife's** solicitor shall show to **the Wife's/the Husband's** solicitors a clear search Form 10/P16 or 12 Report as appropriate in the property and personal registers in relation to the home. At settlement, the **Husband's/the Wife's** solicitor shall provide a letter of obligation in the Law Society of Scotland recommended style.

Always check that the one receiving the house is able to discharge the other one from the secured loan. It is wise to seek the lender's formal consent and obtain the title deeds at an early stage. On the other hand, that will probably involve the client in an outlay to the lenders. If their partner refused to agree to the transfer as part of overall settlement and the ultimate decision was for sale or things go on hold the outlay would have been unnecessary. Probably the best timing is when there is reasonable certainty about the possibility of transfer being agreed. Remember never have an Agreement signed before you are sure the lenders will agree to the transfer. For the preliminary stages you should have some idea of how your client would be placed about taking over the loan from your knowledge about his or her income. The client should at least have an informal chat with the lenders before pursuing this option. The disposition must, of course, run in the name of both parties to the disponee to avoid leaving that alarming possibility of an un-evacuated destination! The wording of the agreement should also make provision for the period after the agreement is signed but before it is implemented. It might be wise to consider obtaining a declaration of insolvency.

(H)   ONE PARTY PURCHASING THE OTHER'S SHARE

3.1   **The Wife/the Husband** agrees to convey to **the Husband/the Wife [her/his** one half *pro indiviso* share in] the home at **(ADDRESS)** ("the home") and to give **him/her** sole occupation in exchange for receiving ****£Amount OR** one half of the net value of the home, after deduction of the amount outstanding in terms of the loan secured over the property. The value of the home at that future date will be established by an independent valuer chosen by the parties or, failing agreement, appointed by the Dean of the Faculty of Solicitors for the area in which the property is situated. **OR** in exchange for receiving the capital sum payable in terms of this Agreement**   **The Wife/the Husband** will also be discharged from any liability under any loan presently secured over the home. **The Wife/the Husband** shall co-operate with **the Wife/the Husband** to deliver such validly executed Deed or Deeds as are necessary to convey a good, marketable title [so far as affecting **his/her** interests], and to vest the whole right, title and interest in the home in name of **the Wife/the Husband** [alone, and to revoke any special destination] ** together with a validly executed and notarised Renunciation of any or all rights competent to under the Matrimonial Homes (Family Protection) (Scotland) Act 1981 (as amended).

3.2   In exchange for delivery of those Deeds **the Husband/Wife** shall pay over the consideration due in terms of this paragraph and shall exhibit and thereafter record in the or Land Register a Deed of Variation or Discharge of the Standard Security in agreed terms validly executed by the Creditors discharging **the Wife/the Husband** of all liability and obligations in respect of the said secured loan. The Parties agree that the conveyancing to effect the transfer will be concluded and the money paid over within eight weeks of the date of the later signature on this document. If the titles and conveyancing drafts have been made available by the **Wife's/Husband's** solicitors within four weeks of the date this document receives the second signature and the full consideration is not paid over within eight weeks of the later signature on this document interest on any sum outstanding will be payable by **the Husband/the Wife** to **the Wife/Husband** at 8% per annum until settlement is made in full unless the **Wife's/Husband's** solicitors have failed to return the conveyancing drafts by then. In that case interest will run at 8 per cent per annum from one week after the date of the return of the conveyancing drafts.

3.3   Prior to settlement **the Wife's/the Husband's** Solicitors shall show to **the Husband's/Wife's** Solicitors a clear Search Form 10/P16 OR 12 report as appropriate in relation to the home. At settlement **the Wife's/the Husband's** Solicitors shall provide a letter of obligation in the Law Society of Scotland recommended style.

The comments for paragraph (G) apply.

It may be necessary for your client to check that none of the ongoing commitments are in arrears. If there is any doubt about the matter a provision could be added setting out who is to be responsible for any arrears.

(I)   *NARRATION OF OUTLAYS WHEN TRANSFER AT THIS STAGE*
      The Wife/the Husband will be solely responsible for payment of the secured loan and outlays in respect of the matrimonial home, including Council Tax and utilities from the date of the later signature on this document.

4.   ENDOWMENT POLICY/POLICIES
(A)   *SURRENDER AND EQUAL DIVISION*
      The life **assurance policies/policy number/'s with (DETAILS)** [will be re-assigned to the parties and on re-assignation] will be surrendered, the proceeds to be divided equally between the Parties. The surrender of the **Policy/ies** will be requested within two weeks of ** the date of the later signature on this document OR the date of entry following on the sale of the matrimonial home.**

(B)   *ASSIGNATION TO ONE PARTY*
      The life **assurance policies/policy number/s with (DETAILS)** will be assigned by **the Husband/the Wife**

to **the Wife/the Husband** and said [policy documents and] **assignation/s** will be delivered **together with the Disposition as already referred to OR within six weeks of the date of the later signature on this document**. After the date this document receives the second signature **the Husband/the Wife** will have no liability for premiums on śaid policies payable.

(C)   *WARRANTIES*
The policy/policies are warranted to be free from any restriction or assignation and to be assignable and the premiums up to date. If there are any arrears outstanding at the date this document receives the second signature they will be the responsibility of **the Husband/Wife**.

(D)   *SALE OF POLICY*
(After the date of entry following the sale of the former matrimonial home), An open market value shall be obtained for the policy number **(DETAILS)** with **(NAME OF INSURANCE COMPANY).** [**The Husband/the Wife** shall have the option, within four weeks of the value's being obtained, of paying one half of the open market value or surrender value, whichever is higher to **the Wife/the Husband.** In exchange **the Wife/the Husband** will deliver to **the Husband/ the Wife** within one week an Assignation of **her/his** whole right, title and interest, to the policy and its benefits. Following delivery of said Assignation **the Husband/the Wife** will stop being liable for payment of the premiums on said policy. If **the Husband/the Wife** does not take up said option] **T/t**he said policy will be disposed of at the best sum obtainable and the proceeds divided equally between the Husband and the Wife.

(E)   *MAINTAINING JOINT POLICY*
The policy number **(DETAILS)** with **(NAME OF INSURANCE COMPANY)** [presently used in connection with the loan secured over the matrimonial home] will be maintained in joint names of the parties. **The parties will each pay one half of the relative premiums OR the **Husband/the Wife** will be solely responsible for payment of the relative premiums.** On

maturity the proceeds of the policy [after repayment of the loan secured over the matrimonial home] will be spilt equally between the parties or his or her executors. Neither party will sign any deed or issue any instructions which would affect the other party's right as beneficiary to the Policy either on death or on maturity.

Policy documents seem to have an urge to disappear into the same black hole inhabited by single socks and pens! Now that most lenders leave borrowers with the responsibility for taking care of policies it can be quite difficult to track them down. It is worth alerting clients to the benefits of (and sometimes need for) the actual as opposed to virtual policy document. You must be certain who is the life assured and who is the proposer.

Do make it clear that selling or surrendering policies is unlikely to be a good return for their investment in them and that it would be best for them to seek appropriate financial advice.

(A) *Surrender and equal division*

Remember the caveat about financial advice. Sometimes a client will choose to raise money by cashing in a policy. If the policy or policies have been on the go for any length of time point out the possibility of sale.

(B) *Assignation to one party*

If your client will be receiving the policy do check the whereabouts of the policy document. It is wise to check that the premiums are paid up to date. It is also worth checking it is assignable. Although there is provision in the subsequent clause prevention is better than cure! Remember that the assignation should again run in name of both parties to the assignee.

(C) *Guarantees*

Be cautious about including this if your client is the one granting the assignation!

(D) *Sale of policy*

Again, remember the caveat about financial advice. This should only be used if it has been established that the policy is one which can be sold. There are a number of companies involved in purchasing policies. They can be approached to indicate if the policy has a sale value.

(E) Maintaining joint policy

If your client is considering this as an option he or she will have to be encouraged to think about the gloomy possibility that one of them might die before the policy arrives at its full term. Both of them will have to consider what they really intend to happen. If the policy is being used in connection with a secured loan it is particularly important to be clear what the parties mean particularly because so few policies are now formally assigned.

5.   TRANSFER OF SHARES

The **Husband/the Wife** will transfer to the **Wife/the Husband** his/her interest in **DETAIL SHARES.** He/she will sign the relevant transfer documents and deliver them to **the Wife/the Husband** within 4 weeks of the later signature on this document **The Husband/the Wife** will have no right to benefit from the shares in any way after this document is signed by both parties.

6.   CANCELLATION OF CURRENT INSTRUCTIONS IN HOUSE TITLE OR POLICY DOCUMENT/S

Evacuation of Destination
The parties agree that any survivorship destination contained in the title to the home [or in any joint Endowment Policy] will not operate and the subjects described in the title to the home [or policy]will pass to the respective executors of the parties in the event of either or both parties dying prior to the home [or Policy] being **sold or transferred** as provided for in this Agreement. Both parties, as testified by their signatures to this Agreement, specifically revoke such survivorship destination with the consent and concurrence of the other party.

Continuing the macabre theme, think through what would happen if one of the couple were to die after the document was signed by both but before the terms had been implemented. Sadly, this is not simply academic. It has happened on a number of occasions. It was considered in Redfern's Executors v. Redfern, *1996 S.L.T. (O.H.) 900. In that case it was decided that the terms of the agreement should be upheld despite a special destination. It is better for parties to plan although hopefully for this contingency to prove unnecessary.*

7.   CAPITAL SUM

(A)   IMMEDIATE PAYMENT
      The Husband/the Wife shall pay to **the Wife/the Husband** a capital sum **(of AMOUNT)** within eight weeks of the date this document receives the second signature with interest at the rate of 8% a year on any balance unpaid by that time until payment.

(B)   TIED INTO HOUSE TRANSFER
      The Husband/the Wife shall pay to **the Wife/the Husband** a capital sum of **(Amount)**. Payment shall be made when the transfer of ownership of the matrimonial home is effected on the terms narrated in relation to that provision with interest at the rate of 8% a year on any balance unpaid at the due date until payment.

(C)   INSTALMENTS (NO INTEREST)
      The **Husband/the Wife** shall pay to the **Wife/the Husband** a capital sum of **(AMOUNT IN WORDS) POUNDS STERLING (£Amount)**. The capital sum shall be payable by instalments of **£Amount** per month. The first instalment will be due and payable one month after the date this document receives the second signature. No interest shall be payable except if two or more consecutive instalment payments are outstanding. In that event the whole balance of the capital sum still remaining to be paid shall become immediately due and payable, with interest at the rate of 8% a year on the whole sum or the balance outstanding from time to time until paid.

(D)   *DEFERRED CAPITAL*

The **Husband/the Wife** agrees that the **Wife/the Husband** shall be paid a capital sum of **£**   [with simple interest at the rate of   **% a year** from the date of the later signature on this document on the balance outstanding until payment] by **the Husband/the Wife** or **his/her executor** on **Date,** the retirement or death of the **Husband/the Wife** whichever occurs first.

"EARMARKING"

In the event of divorce proceedings by either party before payment of the capital sum the **Wife/Husband** will be entitled to ask the Court to order payment of a capital sum equal to the capital sum and interest outstanding to the date of the order, together with interest on the capital sum from the date of the order at 8% a year an to make an order in terms of Section 12A of the Family Law (Scotland) Act 1985 requiring the trustees or managers of the pension scheme [provide name and contact address of scheme and any identifying reference number] to pay to the **Wife/the Husband** the whole or such part of the sum due in terms of this clause as can be met from the lump sum which remains payable at the time of divorce in terms of the said scheme on the retirement or death of the **Husband/the Wife.**] Upon the making of such an order **the Husband/the Wife** will no longer be bound to make payment of the capital sum and interest in terms of this agreement.

Most people would prefer a clean break if capital is available but sometimes payment does have to be deferred. Instalment payments might be an option if the capital sum is not substantial and the payer has a reasonable income. So long as the instalments were over a relatively short period it might be appropriate to forego interest. In most cases interest will be a feature. The choice of an appropriate rate of interest will depend on a number of circumstances. If payment is to be made quite soon the interest is really a form of penalty in addition to preserving the interests of the payee and judicial interest is justifiable. Where payment is to be deferred for a lengthy period the object is to allow appropriate and realistic growth. This should obviously be to ensure that the amount on payment has not diminished in real value and may well also be intended to allow an increase in the real value. Pension sharing was considered in the previous chapter. "Earmarking" should only be looked on as one possible way a deferred capital sum might be paid. It is important to set out other means of payment as a fall back if the "earmarking" fails for one reason or another.

8.   FINANCIAL SUPPORT

(A)   *SPOUSAL ALIMENT/PERIODICAL ALLOWANCE*
The Husband/the Wife shall pay to **the Wife/the Husband** the sum of **£**   per **week/month** by way of spousal aliment or periodical allowance payable **until **her/his** death or remarriage OR for a period of **(number)** years from the last date this Document is signed OR until their child **(GIVE DETAILS)** attains the age of **(GIVE DETAILS).****

It is important to word support for a spouse (as opposed to a child) as aliment before divorce and periodical allowance after. In cases where spousal support is justifiable under the Family Law (Scotland) Act 1985, s. 9 (1) (c) because of the burden of childcare the child's attaining the age of 16 is the stated limit on the potential period for payment and the payments could go on until the child reaches a specified age within that range. It is more common to give weight to that provision in considering capital division. Usually ongoing spousal support is considered under s. 9 (1) (d) or, less commonly, s. 9 (1) (e) to prevent serious financial hardship. Although the period of adjustment of up to three years in terms of s. 9 (1) (d) would run from divorce it is usual to accept that the conclusion of a negotiated agreement starts the clock ticking. A longer period under s. 9 (1) (e) might be justified by a lengthy marriage together with some restriction on potential employment such as illness (Johnstone v. Johnstone, 1990 S.L.T. (Sh.Ct) 79 and Haugan v. Haugan, 1996 S. L. T. 321) or to bridge a specific gap longer than three years such as up to retirement (Bell v. Bell, 1988 S.C.L.R. 457). Although there are awards of indefinite spousal support in a few reported decisions (including Johnstone and Haugan) it is not common for this to be a feature in negotiated settlements.

(B)   *ALIMENT*

The **Husband/the Wife** shall pay to the **Wife/the Husband** the sum of **£**   per **week/month** as aliment for [each of] the said **child/children,** for so long as the **child/children is/are** under the age of eighteen, **remain/s** in the care of the **Wife/the Husband** and the **Husband/the Wife remain/s** liable to aliment the said **child/ren** in terms of the Family Law (Scotland) Act 1985 or the Child Support Act 1991 or any subsequent statutory provision amending or replacing same. If an assessment of child maintenance is carried out by the Child Support Agency then ****the Child Support Agency Assessment will supersede this Agreement OR if the Child Support Agency Assessment for the said **child/children** of the marriage is at a rate higher than provided for in this paragraph, the sum due to **the Wife/the Husband** as spousal aliment or periodical allowance as provided for above shall be reduced by an amount equal to the difference between the maintenance assessment and the sum due in terms of this clause and **the Husband's** liability shall be reduced accordingly in respect of aliment or periodical allowance for **the Wife**.

It is still open for parents to set down arrangements for child support in a written agreement. The agreement would become unenforceable if the Child Support Agency carried out an assessment. If the agreement is registered in the Books of Council and Session Commissioner's Case No. CSCS/5/97 1999 Fam. L.R. 37 suggests that the Child Support Agency may lose jurisdiction except in cases involving a qualifying benefit. Since Working Family Tax Credit is not a qualifying benefit (unlike its predecessor, Family Credit) then entering into a written agreement at any time may effectively preclude the involvement of the Child Support Agency (unless Income Support or another qualifying benefit is applied for at some later stage). The decision has been criticised but it does seem that the CSA are following its lead and not taking on such cases. From January 2, 1998, the Child Support (Written Agreements) (Scotland) Order 1997 (S.1. 1997 No. 2943 gives effect to Section 8(5) of the Child Support Act and may allow registration. Any subsequent variation which could not be agreed would be determined in Court or by Arbitration. This will change with the imminent overhaul of the

Child Support provisions which will restore the Child Support Agency jurisdiction in those circumstances at some stage.

(C) *TIMING OF PAYMENT*
The said **sum/s of** [child & spousal] aliment [*or periodical allowance*] shall be payable **weekly/calendar monthly** in advance beginning * as at the last date of signing of this Agreement OR whenever the Husband and Wife separate* with interest at 8% a year on any arrears from the date the arrears fall due until paid.

Make sure everyone is aware of the distinction between calendar monthly and four weekly! A mistake can have quite significant consequences over a lengthy period.

(D) *SCHOOL FEES*
The **Husband/the Wife** undertakes to pay to **(GIVE DETAILS OF SCHOOL)** when requested by them all fees due to them in respect of the attendance of the **child/children** at the school including costs of any mandatory extra curricular activities directly relating to the **child's/children's** education. The **Husband/the Wife** also undertakes to pay for all elective extra curricular activities (providing that the parties agree beforehand that such activities should be undertaken). In the event that the **child/children is/are** removed from that school the **Husband/the Wife** undertakes to make payment of all fees and other outlays as provided for above for such other school as may be chosen by the **Husband/the Wife** in consultation with the **Wife/the Husband (and the child/children** if appropriate) for the **child/children.**

Extra curricular activities can be expensive! Before a client makes a commitment to meeting mandatory extra curricular outlays he or she should check what is likely to be involved. When private schooling is involved parents usually have done quite exhaustive research.

VARIATION
(E)   INDEX LINKING

> The [spousal aliment or periodical allowance for **the Wife/the Husband** and] aliment for the children [other than school fees] payable by **the Husband/the Wife** shall be varied on the First of **Month** of each year in accordance with the percentage increase or decrease of the Retail Price Index published during the preceding month of **Month** in each year.

Although clients are keen to avoid repeated negotiations about the level of aliment and a built-in mechanism to at least keep payments in line with inflation could be attractive it is important for both parties to be clear about how to calculate the increase and that it is automatic.

(F)   MATERIAL CHANGE OF CIRCUMSTANCES

> The child [or spousal] aliment or [periodical allowance] [including liability for school fees and outlays] shall be open to variation on the application of either Wife or Husband in light of a material change in either Wife or Husband's financial circumstances. In the absence of their agreeing the terms of any such variation, application may be made to a Court, Agency or Tribunal of competent jurisdiction for variation or assessment.

Although there is statutory provision for a review by the Court of agreed aliment (the Family Law (Scotland) Act 1985, s. 7 (2)) or periodical allowance (s. 16 (1)) there are important restrictions. A review of agreed aliment cannot be backdated or varied on an interim basis (unlike variation of a court order for aliment). Agreed periodical allowance can only be varied by the court if there is express provision for that in the agreement (it is not sufficient to simply state that the amount is "subject to variation": Ellerby v. Ellerby, 1991 S.C.L.R. 608).

(G)   PROVISION FOR ANNUAL REVIEW & MATERIAL CHANGE—ARBITRATION

> The ****aliment** [for the **Wife/the Husband** and periodical allowance and aliment] for the **child/children** [including liability for school fees and outlays] shall be subject to an

annual review which shall take into account inflation for the preceding twelve months, and the respective financial positions of the Parties involved. The first review shall take place on the first anniversary of the date of the later signature on this document and so forth annually after that until liability for aliment ends as stipulated previously in this Agreement. The revised payment will be effective from the relative anniversary provided that the Party seeking review intimates their intention in writing to the other Party at least four weeks before the relative anniversary. Otherwise the revised payment will be effective from four weeks after the date of giving such notice.

The [child and spousal] aliment [or periodical allowance] [or liability to pay school fees and outlays] shall also be subject to review in the event of a material change of financial circumstances of either Party. The revised payment in that case will be effective from eight weeks after the party seeking the review intimates their intention of this in writing to the other party. Within four weeks of intimation of the request for review the parties undertake to provide vouched details of income and expenditure. In the event of the Wife and Husband failing to come to a mutually agreed sum at any review whether annual or in relation to a material change of circumstances within twelve weeks of intimation that review is sought then the matter will be referred to Arbitration by an Arbiter who is a Family Law Specialist selected by the parties or, failing agreement on the identity of the Arbiter within two further weeks, selected and appointed by the President or Vice-President for the time being of the Law Society of Scotland and conducted in accordance with the Arbitration Rules of the Law Society of Scotland current at the date of appointment of the Arbiter whose decision will be final and binding on the Parties.

This provides a more complex mechanism for review. It may be appropriate if the level of support was quite substantial. Reviewing the level of support can raise quite wide issues and parties would have to be clear they wish to refer future decisions to arbitration rather than the more clearly defined route of litigation. It does allow the possibility of backdated variation, which otherwise would not be competent. Arbitration could be a particularly practical route to resolve disputes over exactly what activities are covered in relation to school fees.

### (H)	CREDIT TRANSFER

Payment of said **sum/s** of [child and spousal] aliment [and periodical allowance] shall be made by credit transfer into a Bank account to be nominated by the **Wife/the Husband** or such other account as from time to time may be designated for this purpose by the **Wife/the Husband**.

A significant amount of friction can be avoided by ensuring that payment is made automatically. The partner receiving the money will be depending on its arrival on time. The one paying may also be working on quite a tight margin. If payment is left to a conscious decision each week or month there is the risk of payment drifting and ill feeling being caused. For more reliable payers automatic payments should simply seem more convenient.

### (I)	POSSIBLE UNEMPLOYMENT OF HUSBAND/WIFE

If the **Husband/the Wife** becomes unemployed no [child or spousal] aliment [or periodical allowance] shall be payable to the **Wife/the Husband during** such unemployment from the date the **Husband/the Wife** intimates a copy of a letter confirming such unemployment from the appropriate government department to the **Wife/the Husband** until the date the **Husband/the Wife** starts work again. The **Husband/the Wife** undertakes to recommence payment immediately on resumption of employment.

### 9.	MOTOR VEHICLES

Both Husband and Wife agree that ownership of the vehicle **(GIVE DETAILS)** will be *transferred **to/retained** by the **Husband/the Wife**. The **Husband/the Wife** will solely make repayment of the related loan agreement **(GIVE DETAILS)** despite the fact that it is in joint names. If the **Wife/the Husband** fails to make the repayments then the vehicle will be sold if it will realise enough to repay the outstanding loan and any free proceeds will be divided equally between the Wife and Husband.]

If one person is going to take on responsibility for a joint loan it is very important for the other one to know that the creditors could still hold either of them liable for the full amount. It is always better for debts to be reorganised to avoid joint debt being one person's responsibility but that is not always possible.

10. SPECIFICATION OF PROPERTY PRESERVED AND APPORTIONMENT OF LIABILITIES
   In addition to the provisions narrated above the Wife will retain the following assets which belong to her—   She will take sole responsibility for the following liabilities—   The husband will retain the following assets which belong to him—   He will take sole responsibility for the following liabilities—
   OR
   All other assets in name of the Husband will be retained by him as his own absolute property. All other assets in name of the Wife will be retained by her as her own absolute property. Each party will be responsible for any debts incurred by him or her in his or her sole name no matter when such debts were incurred.

This may help ensure that all the loose ends are tied up! It also may demonstrate the fairness of a settlement which might otherwise be obscured if assets and liabilities remaining in sole name of one or other were not narrated.

11. SUCCESSION
   Both Parties renounce for all time coming any right to inherit from the other as widow or widower by way of legal or prior rights or by intestate succession. Both parties accept that the terms of this document shall be binding on their executors.[with the exception of liability for payment of aliment OR periodical allowance.]

It is usual for parties to renounce rights of succession but it is important that clients are fully aware of doing this. Clients should be advised that it is wise for them to make a will if they have not already done so or to review any existing will. The consequences of the death of a party who is taking on the responsibility of paying support should be thought through. The viability of insuring the payments or the life of the payer should be explored. The obligation for payment of periodical allowance does not terminate automatically on death (s. 13(7), Family Law (Scotland) Act 1985) and so give thought to whether or not this exception should be made.

12.   DISCLOSURE
       Each Party warrants that he or she has made full
       disclosure of his or her significant financial resources.

Make sure that your client takes on board the implications if it is included.

13.   RENUNCIATION & DISCHARGE OF OTHER
       CLAIMS
       Both Parties in implementation of the terms of this
       Agreement renounce and discharge all and any rights they
       have or may have against the other or against the
       executors or assignees of the other now and in all time
       coming to any capital sum, property transfer order or
       aliment for him or herself or periodical allowance of any
       kind whether under Common Law or Statute either on
       divorce or death and without prejudice to the foregoing
       generality, any claim in terms of the Family Law
       (Scotland) Act 1985 or any amendment or re-enactment
       of that Act other than as set out in this agreement.

It is important to reinforce that there are only very limited circumstances in which an agreement can be varied. Your client should assume that the terms of the document set out his or her full entitlement to financial provision arising from the marriage and with the exception of arrangements for children and ongoing payments such as aliment or periodical allowance must be considered final and binding. Before your client signs the final version it is wise to send out a copy. The accompanying letter should emphasise the final and binding nature of the contract once signed by both, ask the client to read it through very carefully and to let you know if on reflection any of the terms seem unclear or do not reflect his or her understanding of the settlement. If the letter is sending out the signing copy highlight that the client should not sign if there is any doubt about the terms without speaking to you first!

14. EXPENSES

Each Party shall meet his or her own legal costs in respect of the negotiation, preparation and registration of this Agreement [To avoid doubt, each Party shall bear his or her own expenses incurred in relation to the transfer of title to the matrimonial home. The **Wife/the Husband** as transferee will bear all normal conveyancing search and registration outlays with the exception of the Stamp Duty on the Renunciation of Occupancy Rights which will be the responsibility of the **Husband/the Wife** as transferor in the event that a defect in title is disclosed. Parties will share equally any additional costs necessary to achieve a good marketable title.] The **Wife's/the Husband's** solicitor will send the Agreement to be registered and order two extracts, one for each party. The parties will share equally the costs of registration.

OR

The **Husband/the Wife** shall pay the **Wife's/the Husband's** legal expenses in relation to concluding this Agreement as agreed or as may be taxed by the Auditor of the appropriate Sheriff Court.

If the client is receiving Advice and Assistance it is important at this stage to reinforce the recovery provisions. Even if there's a chance that a hardship application might be successful it is better to underline the likelihood of a claw back before explaining the possibility of a discretionary relief from it. You should outline the basis of carrying out work under the Advice and Assistance Scheme at the very beginning, mention it from time to time as you go a long and keep the client informed about the level of expenses as they mount up.

The basis of settlement will be assuming a value for a property on the basis of a marketable title nonetheless, it is likely that asking the transferor to pay any potential costs should there be a difficulty with the title may meet resistance! It is advisable to proceed with the conveyancing in parallel with the preparation of the separation agreement if transfer is part of the picture. That should make it possible to have an idea if complications are likely by the time the separation agreement has to be signed.

15.   ACKNOWLEDGEMENT   OF   FAIRNESS   &
        REASONABLENESS
        The Parties acknowledge that in reaching the terms of this Agreement they have had the opportunity of the benefit of separate legal advice and that having regard to the whole circumstances prevailing at the date of separation and as at the date of this document, the terms of settlement are fair and reasonable. This Agreement shall not prevent either Husband or Wife commencing divorce proceedings and shall remain in force so far as still applicable after any such divorce. [Both Parties acknowledge that they are aware of the implications of the Child Support Act 1991.]

Another clause to emphasise to the client! It is best to assume that clients will tend to concentrate on the parts of an agreement which are clearly to their benefit or detriment. The last few clauses may appear rather less gripping and be more likely to be overlooked.

16.   IMPLEMENTATION CLAUSE
        Both parties undertake to sign all documents necessary to give effect to the provisions of this Agreement.

17.   RECONCILIATION
        In the event that the parties effect a reconciliation before divorce and cohabit continuously for a period of twenty six weeks or more then any terms of this Agreement which remain operative will be considered null and void. In the event of any subsequent separation and divorce the childcare and financial and property arrangements will be considered of new.

And both Parties consent to registration of this document for preservation and execution:

IN WITNESS WHEREOF—

NON MUTUALITY CLAUSE

(It may also be appropriate to add a clause stating that neither party would be entitled to withhold performance of an obligation

in terms of the agreement because of non performance of an obligation owed by the other party in terms of the agreement. If including such a clause take care to specifically exclude linked, mutual obligations from the provision.) Remember that registration not only enables aspects of the agreement to be enforced but also makes it a public document.

The impact of a subsequent reconciliation could be rather unclear (for consideration of cases see Methven v. Methven, *1999 G.W.D. 28–1342). To avoid ambiguity the matter should be discussed and clarified in the agreement.*

COMPARISON

An important point to bear in mind is that word processors will not take into account any changes without human intervention! It remains good practice to mark all potential changes on one copy of the draft Agreement. If the changes become very complex they could be incorporated in an amended draft but in that case the amended draft and original should be sent to the other side for comparison then further changes made to the amended draft and the first one kept out of circulation! The signing copy should always be accompanied to the other side with the draft for comparison (and should be compared by the office preparing the document before the signing copy goes out).

Conclusion

Negotiation will form a substantial proportion of the work of most family lawyers. Separation agreements are the fruits of the process. The negotiation itself may have been quite demanding. Make sure you give as much energy to setting down the outcome in writing as you did in bargaining! It is the written document that has to stand the test of time and is the evidence for all your efforts. Read it through once from your client's point of view. Read it again imagining you were the other solicitor! Pressure of work and demands from emergency cases can make it difficult to set time aside for drafting documents. Discipline yourself to make space by recognising that it does save time overall to get it right first time. Remember that you are setting out a blueprint for your client's future. Make it—

- clear
- comprehensive
- workable
- reliable

CHAPTER 6

PLEADINGS

There is good training available on the general subject of pleadings but the needs of family law actions are distinct. In the dry, relatively emotionless, domain of, say, contract or delict, ongoing relationships may not be important; in family work they usually are. Like it or not, proceedings are steeped in the emotional history of personal relationships. The preservation of ongoing relationships, for example between parents, may be a crucial objective without which any "victory" may feel, and indeed be, worthless. Because of these behind the scenes issues, it is particularly important to reflect on first principles before any drafting is attempted.

What are pleadings for?

Communication

There seems to be, at some level, a belief that the rules of good communication in court are somehow different from those applied elsewhere. That is not the case. The human mind responds positively to good communication and the same qualities make for good communication in court as anywhere else. In court actions the particular difficulty for you is that you are communicating with an audience, ranging from the untutored (your client) to the expert (the Sheriff).

To get what our client wants

We submit our writ to court to ask for something on our client's behalf. The writ is there to persuade and enable a judge to give us what our client wants.

To meet the requirements of the law and court procedure

In order to get what our client wants our pleadings have to set matters out in a manner adequate to meet the requirements of the law and court procedure. Court procedure is intended to facilitate a structured presentation of information meeting legal requirements. The court wants to identify the parties, what they want, the facts supporting them getting what they want with a proposition in law supporting the facts. All these elements interlink. Good pleadings show a clear movement, from request, through facts justifying the request, to the law entitling the client to what is requested.

To provide a foundation from which issues can be addressed

It is self evident that, in meeting other requirements, pleadings can provide the ground work from which issues outwith the court can be addressed and yet it is surprising how often cases are pled in such a way as to provide a decidedly unhelpful basis for resolution.

Who are pleadings for?

The court

Your primary aim is always to satisfy the court that your client should obtain what he or she has asked for. The needs of any other category of participant in the court process are secondary to the needs of the court.

The solicitor

It is ironic that in our desire to cover the relevant bases necessary to satisfy the court we forget the pleadings are our own primary resource. Clear, well laid out pleadings allow us to present our arguments at all stages of a court action in a coherent way. At a proof they allow us to elicit evidence satisfactorily and without omission.

Your client

It is good practice to provide your client with copies of pleadings. It is important that your client should understand what is written. The client is, after all, the person most affected by it. In our style writs we have tried to bear in mind the fact that a client will read the document.

Best practice in most professions has moved away from the use of arcane, exclusive terminology towards straightforward, inclusive language. Where there is no sacrifice in brevity, accuracy or meaning, Latin words should be excluded and shorter/common words preferred. Your client is entitled to expect you to make things simple where there is no compromise of meaning in other directions.

If ongoing relationships are going to be important what you say and how you say it can have a profound effect on those relationships.

The other side

Both the solicitor and party on the other side rely on your pleadings too. If what you say is inaccurate then, on the impersonal piece of paper, the other side is presented with a lie. If you heat up your language with the coals of your clients anger then the other side will be there ready to fan them into flames with their response. If you do not give them fair notice of the facts that matter to your case then they are going to be unhappy at not having the opportunity to provide evidence and arguments to counter what you have said and you should expect them to object to your evidence being led.

What makes good pleadings?

Layout

Common sense and practical experience tell us that all parties can digest and use material best when it is set out in a consistent way with headings and the appropriate use of space and lines. Why is it then that pleadings are so often an unheaded morass of unbroken black type?

The answer seems to lie, to some extent, in a misplaced anxiety about undermining the solemnity of the court process by veering away from some spurious notion of what is "normal" pleading. Pleadings can communicate in a respectful way with a sense of the seriousness of the subject and the forum without being unintelligible to the lay person. The court's solemnity is in no way undermined by the judicious use of headings, lettering and space. What may be perceived to be "normal" presentation is not always what is best for your particular case.

What the Sheriff wants and what should be expected is a layout that eases communication. Communication is made easier if facts about particular topics can be found quickly and if the material relevant to that topic is set out in an easily digested form.

You have the blank sheet of paper on which to make life easier or more difficult by your placing of visual aids such as breaks in numbering. The basic rules and conventions on layout make sense because they provide a consistent format which the court and solicitors pick up easily because they can expect it on every occasion. Beyond that it is a matter of taste and judgement as to how many breaks, headings, numberings assist communication. The human eye is looking for aids to manage and process information without being overloaded by such aids which defeats the purpose of them.

In the style writs that follow in this book we have broken craves into lettered sub-headings where we think it helps the sense of what is said. We have used bold headings to identify topics covered in articles of condescendence. We have used lettering in the course of articles of condescendence if it helps communication. In the book, the headings should be left out as they are there to guide you to the subject matter for which you want a style. You can use headings in your writ above articles of condescendence. In deciding whether to do so make an appraisal of whether they would help or hinder the court, your client, you and the other side in dealing with the case. If you use headings make sure the material under the heading is kept relevant to that particular heading.

If you are narrating in a writ a series of four or five separate incidents involving significant factual detail do not be afraid to make them each the subject of a separate article of condescendence. It is a matter of taste and style as to how far you go with this but it is easier to use a series of numbered paragraphs as a basis for your work than a solid, all incorporating, phalanx of typescript. In an interdict action clear communication might read as follows—

1.   "On about 5th January, 2000 at 8 p.m. the defender attended a party at the matrimonial home. He assaulted the pursuer in the home. He struck her on the head twice. The Police were called and the defender was asked to

leave the home by the Police. The defender left. He returned at about 11 p.m. that evening. He was drunk. He stood at the front door of the house and demanded entry to the house. The pursuer refused to allow him to come in. The defender left at about 11.15 p.m."

2. "On 15th February, 2000 the pursuer was in Gibson Street, Glasgow. The defender approached her in the street and was abusive to her. He threatened to kill her. The pursuer ran away. She was followed by the defender for approximately one hundred yards before he stopped."

The information could just as easily have been presented as one article of condescendence. By breaking it into two articles you provide the reader's eye with a break in space tying in with a break in time. The sentences are short, accurate, unclouded and factual. Any answer on each specific incident can easily be identified and responded to.

In giving details of matrimonial property using lettering within the article of condescendence to show each individual item of property is usually helpful. If you think it would work better be prepared to consider lodging a schedule setting out the extent of the property.

It is useful to show which items are owned by which party. Your schedule might look like this (see over)—

SCHEDULE SHOWING VALUE AND OWNERSHIP OF PROPERTY AT DATE OF SEPARATION

ASSETS	PURSUER	DEFENDER	JOINT
The house at 5 Blinksworth Court			£100,000.00
Royal Bank of Scotland Account 00414883		£2,500.00	
Halifax Account 143841			£1,500.00
Scottish Amicable Endowment	£3,000.00		
	£3,000.00	£2,500.00	£101,500.00

DEBTS

Loan Royal Bank of Scotland			£ 70,000.00
Visacard No.		£2,000.00	
		£500.00	£ 31,500.00

Net value of matrimonial property: £35,000.

The schedule can then be incorporated by reference into your pleadings. You can also put the relevant supporting productions in order in the same inventory as the schedule.

Do not be afraid to use methods of presentation of information that may appear unconventional but serve their purpose. For instance, there's no reason why you should not lodge a chart showing on a one sheet flow chart a complex family set up or set of business arrangements supporting and clarifying your written pleadings.

Make sure events are presented in chronological order. You are then presenting the facts in the way your audience will best understand the history to your client's case.

(b) Accuracy

At each stage in your pleadings accuracy is important in fulfilling all the purposes set out. Veracity and precision can pull in two directions. You want—

- an accurate written representation of the fact given to you by a client
- a precise statement

We have to take what are client has told us and give it its most precise written expression without sacrificing veracity to precision. If the client has told us an event happened on "about the fifth of April 2000" we cannot, for the sake of precision, say it happened "on the fifth of April 2000". The "about" is a necessary sacrifice of precision to veracity. If a client tells us something happened "regularly" we need to establish what he or she means. The word regularly can, after all, mean repeated at uniform intervals (does he mean it happened every year on the December 27 at 12 noon?). The word can mean habitually or customarily with no real sense of frequency (does it mean every minute, hour, day, week?). It is subjective in meaning and therefore imprecise in communication. The client should be interviewed to establish the closest approximate numerical indication he or she can give. If it is once or twice a week the pleadings should say "once or twice a week". If it was about three or four times a month the pleadings should say that. Numbers are objective and precise, adverbs of frequency are subjective and imprecise.

To give an example—

"Between about January, 1991 and December, 1993 the pursuer's parents cared for James after school on two or three days a week from about 3.30 p.m. until 5.30 p.m. During this period James spent every Saturday with the defender."

Communication here is imprecise at the start because veracity requires it. The client cannot recall the exact period during which the arrangement was in place or how often and for how long James stayed with his grandparents. The temptation might be to put the pursuer's parents cared for James "regularly" but that communicates virtually nothing. What is actually written gives as much precision as is possible based on a proper exploration of the witness' recollection. When it comes to the arrangement on a Saturday the client has a good recollection and therefore precision is possible. It is important to check that it was "every" Saturday.

If, for instance, holidays were different then you should say so. If you do not, evidence may be led to show your client has exaggerated and the implication drawn that if he has exaggerated on one point there is every reason to believe he has exaggerated on others.

(c) Plain English

For some unfathomable reason, rather like the characters in Monty Python's "Ministry of Silly Walks", when people put the word "Writ" at the top of a sheet of paper they seem to lose their ability to walk in a straight line. Natural communication patterns go to pot. Tortured syntax and language stumble across the page. The result can be a stilted, ugly, impersonal morass. There is no need for this. If you want everyone, including a client, to understand what you write then simple language should be used. The only excuse for not using simple language is where accuracy would be compromised. On most occasions, both accuracy and simplicity can be attained.

In a world where clients want to fully understand and documents often have to be translated into other languages words such as "crave" and "condescendence", are unnecessary legalisms which could be replaced without any loss of meaning by respectively words such as "request" and "facts founded on". The words are mandatory in terms of the rules (until someone chooses to change the rules!) and we therefore have to use them.

The fact that the rules seem to persist in requiring a few legalisms is no excuse for a continuation of that style of writing into other aspects of the pleadings.

(d) Simple syntax

Craves and pleas-in-law apart, in your pleadings you are stating facts. Those facts can best be grasped if isolated into separate short sentences. Individual factual statements are given a natural boundary and prominence. If you have a proliferation of long sentences, sub-clauses, phrases in parentheses, you are doing something wrong. Take the following sentence—

> "On 5th August, 2000 the defender was going along the garden path when he saw the pursuer with her brother James coming in the opposite direction with a knife, shouting and swearing at the defender."

The sense is lost in the splurge of phrases and commas. It is not entirely clear whether it was the pursuer or James who was shouting, swearing and carrying the knife. An alternative might have been—

> "On 5th August, 2000 the defender was in the garden. The pursuer came into the garden. She was with her brother James Hamilton. She walked towards the defender. She had a knife in her hand. She shouted at the defender. She was abusive to the defender."

The facts are separated out and are not open to misunderstanding.

(e) Concision

Be comprehensive but brief in what you say.

(f) Muted

Your job is to present the facts which will be coloured and fleshed out by what witnesses say. In family actions it is inevitable that there will be reference to emotions such as anger, upset, fear. It is sometimes difficult to see the boundary between the appropriate factual confirmation of emotion experienced and the inappropriate additional emotional overlay. If your client is terrified of her husband then it is fair enough to say so (but be sure you are not "puffing up" a lesser emotion for effect). The word is powerful in itself, more powerful than, for instance, "scared". It is unnecessary to say she is "absolutely" terrified. If your client was angry or upset it is unnecessary to qualify the noun with "very" or "extremely". The flavour of the emotion can be communicated through evidence or, prior to proof, your choice of words in addressing the court (although judges do not like over-coloured submissions either). The courts do not want a glorious technicolour written narration so use your touches of colour with care. Where you use them in a sparing way they will have more weight.

What pleadings have to be

Factual

One of the commonest mistakes in pleadings is to narrate evidence instead of facts to be proved. You do not need to wait too long as a family law practitioner to see pleadings along the lines of—

> "The pursuer called him an "evil monster" and told him she would see to him. The defender ran down the stairs and off down the path on to the street with the pursuer following him with a knife".

Some of this is factual but nonetheless inappropriate. It is the evidence you did not need to plead wrapped around the fact you did need to plead.

If the facts you need to prove are that—

> First, the pursuer was abusive;
> second, she threatened the defender;
> third, she ran after him with a knife,

properly put, the same thing could have been pled—

> "The pursuer was abusive to the defender. She threatened him. The defender ran from the house. The pursuer ran after him with a knife".

In the first example the evidence you hope to elicit from your witness to support your first fact has found its way into the pleadings. The exact words used do not need to be plead. The background information about the parts of the house and garden covered by the chase do not have to be averred as they have no particular significance on this occasion. The averment that both parties were running and a knife was in the Pursuer's possession is important and therefore notice has to be given of it.

Relevant

Having considered what pleadings are for it is really self-evident that if you miss out one of the required elements you are likely to fail. The pleadings have to state a position in fact and law to justify your client getting what is asked for. In other words, if I were to read what you had written I would see that—

- what you have asked for is something you are entitled to ask for and can be translated into a court order.
- the facts narrated, if true, satisfy the legal proposition relied on.
- the legal proposition relied on is properly stated and justifies what is asked for.

Within each of these categories part of what is said may be irrelevant and may invalidate part of the case. If an element necessary to all parts of the case is missing the whole action is irrelevant. "An action will not be dismissed as irrelevant unless it must necessarily fail even if all the pursuer's averments are proved. The onus is on the defender who moves to have the action dismissed and there is no onus on the pursuer to show that if he proves his averments he is bound to succeed", *Jameson v. Jameson,* 1952 S.C. (H.L.) *per* Lord Normand at 50.

Specific

As well as being relevant your case has to be specific. The test of whether it is sufficiently specific is whether it gives other parties fair notice of what facts you intend to prove. In family actions, the problem is that the level of detail required to meet this test by individual sheriffs is variable. The shrieval views range from the widest latitude in allowing evidence in with little or no pleadings to underpin it to a keen determination to limit evidence lead to the facts specifically pled. For the pleader, the situation is unsatisfactory and the only answer is to err on the side of caution and assume a strict approach will be taken. Even where you are used to a relaxed approach from your local sheriff you may find on the day of the proof that a visiting pleadings zealot is there in his or her place. If an incident is referred to give a date and place for it if possible. If not possible, a month, if not possible, a season, and so on. Earlier comments in this chapter on accuracy and the need to avoid pleading evidence should be noted.

The facts pled have to support each remedy sought. Pleadings can be so lacking in specification as to render part or all of the action irrelevant.

Answering averments

We consider the drafting of Defences later on but for both Defender and Pursuer certain basic rules apply to responses made in pleadings. The starting point is OCR Rule 9.7

> "Every statement of fact made by a party shall be answered by ever other party, and if such a statement by one party within the knowledge of another party is not denied by that other party, that other party shall be deemed to have admitted that statement of fact".

In setting out your case you want to have an easy method of reference, as does the court. You should, as Pursuer, state your case and then add to your positive case in the top section of each article of condescendence with your answers to the Defender's position set out in the lower section. With the Defender it is the other way round. The only exception to this Rule is the "general denial" which works best coming at the end of your answer or article of condescendence, so it is easy for you to check it is in The clearer the demarcation between your positive assertion of your client's case and your response to the other side's case, the easier it will be for you and everyone else to work with pleadings in their final form.

The response to the other party's pleadings should always follow the same pattern—

"Admitted"

You admit first what you can admit by putting "Admitted that" followed by the other party's averment. You should as far as possible, repeat their wording. If you can admit every averment made, for instance over jurisdiction, it will suffice to put a one word answer as Defender, "Admitted" but watch for later additions, by adjustment, that you might want to deny.

"Believed to be true"

This will be taken as an admission but cannot be admitted directly by your client because it is outwith his knowledge. Where a party has to prove a ground for divorce, arrangements for a child, that party may still require to prove the averment to the satisfaction of the court. Other than in this type of circumstance, by saying

"Believed to be true" you are removing the need from the other side to prove the particular fact to which you have referred.

"Not known and not admitted"

A fact put forward by the other side that is not within your client's knowledge. Your client is expecting evidence of the fact to be led.

"Denied"

This is an overused term. If only one fact is denied in an article of condescendence, fair enough. The words "Denied that" followed by the other party's averment can be used. However, normally there will be several points to be denied. Sheriffs and other Solicitors are likely to be irritated if you dot your pleadings with "denied" or worse "emphatically" or "specifically" denied. The correct way of handling the situation is to put a general denial at the end of your answer or Article of Condescendence, "The Pursuer/Defender's averments are denied except insofar as coinciding herewith". The normal phrasing often includes *"quoad ultra"* (*"quoad ultra* denied") but the same sense can be given by the above wording without requiring your client to learn some Latin. No further individual denials are needed within that answer. Preparing for an Options Hearing or Proof, you have a useful quick reference point at the end of each condescendence/answer to check you have denied everything you have not covered with any other appropriate form of admission, partial admission or explanation.

"Explained that"

Text books sometimes show the words "Explained and averred that". The word "averred" does not add anything to the sense and is unnecessary. It is useful to use the introductory phrase "Explained that" to mark the movement from answering the other side's position to stating your own. On occasion, the same phrase or "Under explanation that" can be incorporated into your answers on the other side's position where you want to give a slightly different gloss to a fact covered while still admitting it. However, in the interests of keeping your statement of your case separate from answers to the other party's case, this should be done sparingly or not at all.

Expressions to avoid

You are in general trying to avoid superfluous verbiage. Here are some examples of that commodity.

"Averred that"

It is tautologous to say this in an article of Condescendence/Answer. What you say in that context is, by definition, averment.

"Latinisms"

Dispensing with these may be viewed with some suspicion, even disapproval. However, pleadings in family actions are read by the family and most of them will not understand Latin. Most Latin phrases can be replaced with perfectly adequate and equally brief English equivalents. If the aim is communication then words which are understood by all the parties should, so far as possible, be preferred. On that basis, out go *"brevitatis causa"*, *"et separatim"*, *"esto"*, *"quoad ultra"*, and in their place come respectively "for the sake of brevity", "separately", "be it that", "otherwise".

"The said"

As part of the "Ministry of Silly Walks School" of pleading comes this favourite verbal "tic". Sometimes the phrase is necessary to avoid ambiguity but it is unnecessary where there can only be one house, child or whatever being talked about. For the client who may already be having some difficulty in seeing his or her child as a human being for whom he should be doing the best regardless of any stated or unstated desire for possession, constant references to "the said child" will be particularly unhelpful. If a particular pension or item of property is to be referred to frequently and there is the possibility of doubt it is good practice to put after the first mention of the pension or item of property "hereinafter referred to as ….."

Conclusion

Your pleadings can be a pivotal aid to the resolution of family problems or a principle obstacle to achieving that resolution. There is nothing intrinsically difficult in making them former rather than the latter. All that is required is time, thought and the holding in mind of what they are there for.

CHAPTER 7

DRAFTING THE INITIAL WRIT—BASIC CASES

It is not our intention to cover the elements of a writ in the type of detail that can be obtained just as easily in seminal works such as Macphail's *Sheriff Court Practice*. Our aim is to give you the essentials with a particular emphasis on the concerns of the family law practitioner and his or her clients.

This chapter is intended as a quick reference, reminder or refresher for those who have been there before and an introduction for those venturing in to court for the first time. It deals with the basic elements in a straightforward case. More specialised elements and situations are dealt with in the next chapter. If there are any unusual elements to the particular case, for instance over capacity, jurisdiction, potential additional parties for service and the like, take care to have a look at Chapter 8.

The elements of the initial writ

The ordinary course rules are brief about the form for an initial writ. OCR 3.1 sets out the rules for all Sheriff Court actions but does not apply in its entirety to family actions (see OCR 33.2 and 33.6). The rule states that Form G1 is the form for the initial writ and that gives the basic layout we follow. The initial writ must be on A4 size paper of durable quality. It is not backed. It has to be signed by the pursuer or his solicitor. It has to move through a progression—

- Heading
- Description
- Instance
- Craves
- Condescendence
- Pleas-in-law

Within the prescribed form each element of the writ has to be properly framed we look at each element in turn.

113

The heading

Each writ is headed with the name of the Sheriffdom and the place of sitting of the Court in which the action is raised such as "Sheriffdom of Lothian and Borders at Edinburgh".

The description

Under the heading, the name of the document is given, for example "Initial Writ" or "Minute".

The instance

Below the description of the writ you put the description of the parties. You start by saying "in the cause" followed by the full name and address of the person bringing the action. You then have the word "against" and the full name and address of the person against whom the action is being taken.

In the case of a married couple full names mean first name, all middle names, maiden name, names under a previous marriage and married name in that order. For a woman the husband's surname (or husbands' surnames, if she has been married more than once) are added as an alternative ("Mrs Alexandra Jane Quinn or Jones or Smith" where Quinn is the maiden name, Jones the first married name and Smith the current married name). The marriage certificate tells you the correct names and you or your secretary should check your instance against it.

If a person has legal aid the words "Assisted Person" are added after their name. If these words are not added it can create problems over expenses at a later stage. The same words should appear in every subsequent part of the process. If a person is not initially legally aided but becomes so the words can be added later.

Where a person is appearing in an action in a specific capacity that specific capacity must be disclosed in the instance.

Craves

The crave has to have three elements—

- it must say what is sought
- it must be competent
- it must be enforceable

What the Court is looking for is something that it is possible to frame easily and quickly as an interlocutor. The qualities looked for are—

Precision

An imprecise crave may be unenforceable The wording should leave no room for doubt as to exactly what is sought. The only qualification to this is that in actions for aliment or for financial provision on divorce it is usually not possible to be absolutely accurate with the figure sought. You can only get an award of a figure as high as you have craved. Because of this it is better to err on the side of caution by craving a higher figure and amending the figure later if necessary. A grotesquely exaggerated figure however can cause unnecessary friction between the parties. An overstated figure can also have implications on expenses. Common sense needs to be applied. The client needs to be fully informed as to why a particular figure has been chosen so that false hopes are not raised.

Alternative craves

If an alternative is sought in the event of, for instance, a request for residence being refused the alternative should be set out with clear averments in the articles of condescendence to support the primary and alternative positions stated.

Where you need to identify what you want by reference to a statute, it makes sense to include that reference here (otherwise the inclusion can be in the plea-in-law).

Interdict craves

Where an interdict is sought the crave must be directed to the specific actions complained of. Remember that the order is going to be served on an individual who may well not have or get legal advice. It is particularly important to lay out what is prohibited in the most precise, clear and simple way you can.

Interim orders

If an order is to be sought on an interim basis that must be made clear in the body of the crave.

Warrants for intimation

Remember to check that the crave covering the relevant warrant is included where appropriate.

Condescendence

This is the statement of the facts on which your client's claim is based.

It should set out the facts on which your case relies. Remember the law is in your pleas-in-law, the evidence comes from your client. You should links your facts to the pleas-in-law by reflecting in your narration of facts the terminology of the relevant law.

For example your client may have told you that she wants to seek a periodical allowance from her husband so that she can maintain herself after divorce. Your facts are going to have to hit a few targets. Dependence to a substantial degree, insufficiency of capital to meet her claim for ongoing support and the like. If your language wanders away from the legal proposition you want to link up to you can easily find that your own understanding of the relevant test and the evidence required will do the same thing.

The articles of condescendence are set out in consecutively numbered paragraphs. As mentioned in the chapter on pleadings, you should not be afraid to set out your facts in a series of short articles of condescendence if that makes your communication clearer. Such a course is infinitely preferable to the confused and confusing long central condescendence. The groupings for your articles of condescendence in a divorce action might be along the following lines—

1. Background

Basic non contentious information about the parties.

- confirmation of their addresses.
- date of marriage.
- full names and dates of birth of children.
- date of separation.
- reference to the marriage and birth certificates being lodged

2. *Jurisdiction*

Covering the points required under OCR 3.1 and 33.2 as appropriate. A number of the provisions of OCR 3.1 are inapplicable, for instance parties cannot prorogate jurisdiction in divorce so no averment on this goes in.

3. *Grounds of divorce*

Potentially contentious facts about the marital breakdown.

- the marriage has broken down irretrievably.
- the breakdown is established on a particular basis - narration of incidents. If the facts are complex use separate articles of condescendence for separate incidents or logically coherent groups of facts.

4. *Grounds for interdict/exclusion order etc.*

These may follow on from the grounds of divorce.

- a narration of facts bringing the situation within the terms of the relevant legislation.
- a narration of the effects on the pursuer can be set out in a separate article of condescendence.

5. *Facts in relation to children*

Again, if factually complex or numerous elements need to be averred consider using separate articles of condescendence. There is no reason why facts about housing, health, education, relationships, day to day care arrangements, finance should not be set out as separate articles if that makes for better communication.

6. *Financial provision*

An article of condescendence narrating the extent of the matrimonial property.

In more complicated cases a further article can narrate the facts relevant to the case covering arguments under, for instance, Section 9 (1)(a) to (e) of the Family Law (Scotland) Act 1985.

7. Interim aliment/periodical allowance

Where you are seeking periodical allowance it may make sense to include your relevant arguments under Section 9 in this article of condescendence along with details of the parties' income and expenditure, earning capacities and other circumstances of the case relevant to an award for interim aliment. Remember very different considerations apply to periodical allowance from interim aliment.

Pleas in law

The idea is to set out a distinct legal proposition specifically applicable to the facts of the particular case. Each crave must be supported by an appropriate plea in law. Each plea in law in turn must be supported by averments of all the facts which the law says are necessary to make the plea in law successful. If the relevant averments are not there then the crave linked to the plea-in-law may be removed at debate or, in a proof before answer, refused after proof. It is useful for you and the court to have the appropriate statutory section in as an aide memoire to the statutory authority for orders sought (where relevant). Usually it is better to have this in the plea in law unless it is easier to identify what you want in the crave by reference to the statute in which case it may make sense to include it in there.

Drafting the initial writ

Which court ?

Before you draft anything you need to consider—

 (a) should the action be brought in the Sheriff Court or the Court of Session?
 (b) if it is to proceed in the Sheriff Court which Sheriff Court has jurisdiction?

The Court of Session or the Sheriff Court?

This book does not deal with Court of Session procedure and most family lawyers will have their cases dealt with in the Sheriff Court. However, that does not obviate the need to consider whether the matter would be best dealt with in the Court of Session or indeed has to be dealt with in the Court of Session. If a matter is of particular complexity or high value there may be good reasons for proceeding in the Court of Session. If in doubt seek the opinion of an advocate before proceedings are raised.

For the purposes of this chapter we assume the action to be pursued is for divorce or a more straightforward action relating to children both in the sheriff court.

Jurisdiction

Establishing jurisdiction for divorce and ancillary orders

The basic rules on jurisdiction for family actions are governed by the Domicile and Matrimonial Proceedings Act 1973.

Brussels II (Regulation) ("E.C. No. 1347/2000 of May 29, 2000 on jurisdiction and the recognition and enforcement of judgements in matrimonial matters and in matters of parental responsibility for children of both spouses") which came into force on March 1, 2001 made important changes to the rules (see also the European Communities (Matrimonial Jurisdiction and Judgements) (Scotland) Regulations 2001, at Clause 2). We discuss the wider impact of the regulation in Chapter 8. For the purposes of the straightforward writ the ground of jurisdiction can be habitual residence of both parties. However, before drafting you should weigh up the choice of jurisdiction questions presented by the other jurisdictional options under the regulations and note the issues over choice and delay dealt with in Chapter 8.

Section 8(2) of the Domicile and Matrimonial Proceedings Act 1973 gives the Sheriff Court jurisdiction to entertain an action of divorce or separation if the Scottish Courts have jurisdiction under the regulation. The first ground of jurisdiction referred to in the regulation lies with the "Member State" in whose territory the spouses are "habitually resident" (the old requirement that went with habitual residence of having been habitually resident for one year before the action was begun, in this basic situation, has gone). The requirement of 40 days' residence ending with the date when the action is begun (s. 8(1)(b)(i)) or having been resident in Scotland for not less than 40 days, ending not more than 40 days before the action was begun with no residence in Scotland at that date (s. 8(1)(b)(ii)) appears to remain (although the word "and" at the end of the original subsection 8(2)(a)(ii) is not there in the amended version after Brussels II).

We discuss the implication of the lack of distinction between Scotland (part of the United Kingdom and part of the "Member State") and the United Kingdom (the "Member State") in Chapter 8. For normal purposes where both parties are habitually resident in Scotland you can proceed.

Jurisdiction for orders ancillary to divorce

Brussels II confirms that, where a Member State has jurisdiction to deal with a divorce or legal separation under the Brussels II regulation then the State also has jurisdiction to deal with parental responsibility over a child of both spouses where the child is habitually resident in that Member State (Article 3.1; see also the European Communities (Matrimonial Jurisdiction and Judgements) (Scotland) Regulations 2001 at Clause 4).

Where the child is habitually resident in a different Member State from that of the court, the court still has jurisdiction if—

—the child is habitually resident in one of the Member States;

—at least one of the spouses has parental responsibility in relation to the child; and

—the jurisdiction of the Court has been accepted by the spouses and is in the best interests of the child.

The above regulation does not, thankfully, alter section 10(1) and 1(A) of the Domicile and Matrimonial Proceedings Act 1973 as amended by the Children (Scotland) Act 1995, Sched. 4, para. 20 which states that, where an application is made to the Court of Session or a Sheriff Court for—

—the making;
—variation; or
—recall

of an order which is ancillary to an action of divorce or separation (whether the application is made in the same proceedings or separately or before or after decree in the action) then if the court had jurisdiction to entertain the action of divorce it also has jurisdiction to deal with the ancillary matter (s.10(1)).

Put at its simplest, the ancillary order follows the jurisdiction of the divorce action in most cases. Indeed s. 11 of the Family Law Act 1986 makes it clear that the jurisdiction of the Court to entertain an application for a Part 1 Order based on habitual residence is circumscribed by the idea that where matrimonial proceedings are "continuing" in a court in any part of the United Kingdom in respect of the marriage of the parents of the child the application for a variation or recall of a Part 1 Order has to be made in those proceedings.

The definition of "continuing" in section 42(2) and (3) of the Family Law Act 1986 for matrimonial proceedings is given as being until the child concerned attains the age of 16 unless the matrimonial proceedings have been dismissed or Decree of Absolvitor has been granted. What is unclear is how this will link up with Brussels II Article 3.3 which refers to jurisdiction under Article 1 as ceasing as soon as

"(a) the judgement allowing or refusing the application for divorce, legal separation or marriage annulment has become final; or

(b) (in those cases where proceedings relating to parental responsibility are still pending) a judgement in those parental responsibility proceedings has become final; or

(c) the proceedings referred to in (a) and (b) have come to an end for another reason."

Jurisdiction for children (not ancillary to divorce)

The law on this is complex. Our intention is to cover the basics. Chapter 8 has a fuller discussion of jurisdiction in relation to children. Where orders relating to children are not ancillary to a divorce action, jurisdiction is mainly governed by the Family Law Act 1986. The Act sets out the type of orders it covers, described as "Part 1 Orders".

What is a Part 1 Order?

A Part 1 Order in Scotland means—
Family Law Act 1986, section 1

"(a) a section 8 Order made by a Court in England and Wales under the Children Act 1989, other than an order varying or discharging such an order.

(b) an order made by a court of civil jurisdiction in Scotland under any enactment or rule of law with respect to the residence, custody, care or control of a child, contact with or access to a child or the education or upbringing of a child, excluding—

(i) an order committing the care of a child to a local authority or placing a child under the supervision of a local authority;

(ii) an adoption order as defined in section 12(1) of the Adoption (Scotland) Act 1978;

(iii) an order freeing a child for adoption made under section 18 of the said Act of 1978;

(iv) an order giving parental responsibilities and parental rights in relation to a child made in the course of proceedings for the adoption of the child (other than an order made following the making of a direction under section 53(1) of The Children Act 1975);

(v) an order made under the Education (Scotland) Act 1980;

(vi) an order made under Part II or III of the Social Work (Scotland) Act 1968;

(vii) an order made under the Child Abduction and Custody Act 1985;

(viii) an order for the delivery of a child or other order for the enforcement of a Part I;

(ix) an order relating to the guardianship of a child."

(See section 1(1)(c) to 1(6) for minor additions/exceptions to the above.) In other words the vast majority of cases you will deal with involving children but not divorce will come within s. 1(b). It is fair to say that "Part I Orders" all come within the ambit of s. 11 of the Children (Scotland) Act 1995 but s. 11 in fact covers a wider range of possible orders than those under "Part I" of the Family Law Act 1986.

Section 9 of the Family Law Act 1986 states—

"Subject to s. 11 of this Act, an application for a Part I Order otherwise than in matrimonial proceedings *may* be entertained by—

(a) the Court of Session if, on the date of the application, the child concerned is *habitually resident* in Scotland;

(b) the Sheriff if, on the date of the application, the child concerned is *habitually resident* in the Sheriffdom."

"Child" is defined under s. 18(1) as meaning "a person who has not attained the age of 16".

"Matrimonial Proceedings" are defined under s. 18(1) as meaning "proceedings for divorce, nullity of marriage or judicial separation".

"The date of the application" is defined under s. 18(2) as meaning, "where two or more applications are pending, the date of the first of those applications; and, for the purposes of this subsection, an application is pending until a Part I Order or, in the case of an application mentioned in section 16(1) of this Act, an order relating to the guardianship of a child, has been granted in pursuance of the application or the court has refused to grant such an order".

Jurisdiction over aliment for children

The Child Support Act 1991 means that most claims for aliment are dealt with through the Agency. Wilkinson and Norrie, *Parent and Child* at p.449, 14.13 helpfully narrates occasions where the courts keep jurisdiction. The courts retain jurisdiction where—

"(a) a child claims aliment from his or her step-parent (s. 3(1)).

(b) a child claims aliment from an adult who has accepted him or her as a child of that adult's family (s. 3(1)).

(c) a child claims more aliment than that assessed by the CSA (s. 8(6)).

(d) a claim is made for education or training expenses for the child (s. 8(7)).

(e) a claim is made for expenses related to certain disabled children (s. 8(8)).

(f) a child claims aliment against the parent with care of the child (s. 8(10)).

(g) a child claims aliment where the parent with care, absent parent or child is habitually resident outside the United Kingdom (s. 44).

(h) a child over 19 claims aliment (s. 55(1)).

(i) a child is over 16 but under 19 and receiving full-time education (which is not advanced education) in certain specified circumstances (s. 55(1)(b)).

(j) a child is over 16 but under 18 and who does not come into category (i) but meets prescribed conditions of Child Support Act 1991 (s. 55(1)(c)).

  (k) a child claims aliment where he or she has been married (s. 55(2)) (includes void marriage or marriage where there is a Declarator of Nullity.)"

A sheriff court has jurisdiction for a separate action of aliment if the defender is domiciled in the sheriffdom (Civil Jurisdiction and Judgements Act 1982, Sched. 8, r. 1). Aliment can also be sought as an ancillary matter in divorce proceedings following the jurisdiction of those proceedings.

Jurisdiction over Interdict

In an action for interdict, jurisdiction is in terms of the Civil Jurisdiction and Judgements Act 1982; basically it is the place of domicile of the defender or the place where it is alleged the wrong is likely to be committed (r. 1and Sched. 8, para. 2(10)).

In an action under the Matrimonial Homes (Family Protection) (Scotland) Act 1981 jurisdiction includes the sheriff with jurisdiction in the district where the matrimonial home is situated.

Special Rules for Family Actions (Chapter 33 OCR)

Is this a "family action"?

(OCR 33.1)
With the Sheriff Court special rules apply to actions defined as "family actions" within the rules.

The definition of a family action is given in OCR 33.1. The rule is so important it is worth setting out in full. "Family action" means—

  "(a) an action of divorce;
  (b) an action of separation;
  (c) an action of declarator of legitimacy,
  (d) an action of declarator of illegitimacy;
  (e) an action of declarator of parentage;
  (f) an action of declarator of non parentage;
  (g) an action of declarator of legitimation;
  (h) an action or application for, or in respect of, an order under section 11 of the Children (Scotland) Act 1995 (court orders relating to parental responsibilities, etc.), except—

(i) an application for the appointment of a judicial factor mentioned in section 11 (2) (g) of the Act of 1995 to which Part One of the Act of Sederunt (Judicial Factor's Rules) 1992 applies; and

(ii) an application for the appointment or removal of a person as a guardian mentioned in section 11 (2) (h) of the Act of 1995 to which paragraph 4 of the Act of Sederunt (Family Proceedings in the Sheriff Court) 1996 applies;

(i) an action of affiliation and aliment;

(j) an action of, or application for or in respect of, aliment;

(k) an action or application for financial provision after divorce or annulment in an overseas country within the meaning of Part IV of the Matrimonial and Family Proceedings Act 1984;

(l) an action or application for an order under the Act of 1981;

(m) an application for the variation or recall of an order mentioned in section 8 (1) of the Law Reform (Miscellaneous Provisions) (Scotland) Act 1966".

In other words the specialised rules set out in Chapter 33 of the Rules apply to most, but not all, family actions. If in doubt, check the rule.

Information about other proceedings (remembering exclusivity of jurisdiction)

(OCR 33.2.) This confirms the information about other proceedings to be provided in actions of divorce or separation or other "continuing" proceedings. OCR 33.1(3) confirms that proceedings are "continuing any time after they have commenced and before they are finally disposed of".

The situation will have a different flavour "post Brussels II" because now, where one party from a member state raises proceedings in the court of a member state, that court has exclusive jurisdiction. Any proceedings subsequently raised in any other member state have to be sisted, or stayed, with only a few exceptions.

The rules require the parties to the action to tell the Court about any proceedings continuing outwith Scotland which are in respect of the marriage or capable of affecting its validity or subsistence (*i.e.* "concurrent proceedings"). The machinery by which the duty is discharged is set out in OCR 33.2. The rule sets out the information about the proceedings you require to include.

The rules provide for what are called "mandatory" and "discretionary" sists by the Scottish Court where there are concurrent proceedings elsewhere. The rules are set out in Schedule 3 to the Domicile and Matrimonial Proceedings Act 1973. MacPhail's *Sheriff Court Practice* at 22.27–22.31 explains how the rules work.

The duty to tell the court of any concurrent proceedings continues while the action is pending and until the proof in the action has begun.

Where section 11 orders are sought

(OCR 33.3) For actions where a section 11 Order under the Children (Scotland) Act 1995 is sought OCR 33.3 has to be complied with.

For actions of divorce or separation averments are required giving particulars of other proceedings in Scotland or elsewhere which relate to the child in relation to whom a Section 11 Order is sought. Critically the information covers not just continuing proceedings but "concluded" proceedings (OCR 33.3(1)(a)).

In other family actions (in addition to the aforementioned averments) you are required to give particulars of continuing proceedings which relate to the marriage (OCR 33.3(1)(b)).

Where the Pursuer omits the appropriate averments or includes incomplete or incorrect information other parties to the action have a duty to include the relevant information (OCR 33.3(2)).

Whereabouts unknown

(OCR 33.4) "In a family action, where the identity or address of any person referred to in rule 33.7 as a person in respect of whom a warrant for intimation requires to be applied for is not known and cannot reasonably be ascertained, the party required to apply for the warrant shall include in his pleadings an averment of that fact and averments setting out what steps have been taken to ascertain the identity or address, as the case may be, of that person".

Maintenance orders

(OCR 33.5) "In a family action in which an order for aliment or periodical allowance is sought, or is sought to be varied or recalled, by any party, the pleadings of that party shall contain an averment stating whether and, if so, when and by whom, a maintenance order (within the meaning of section 106 of the Debtors (Scotland) Act 1987) has been granted in favour of or against that party or of any other person in respect of whom the order is sought."

Certain family actions with links to the Child Support Act 1991

(OCR 33.6)

OCR 33.6 deals with averments in—

—Family actions with craves relating to aliment to which sections 8(6), (7), (8) or (10) of the 1991 Act (top up maintenance orders) apply (33.6.2).
—Family actions with craves relating to aliment where the court retains jurisdiction and which sections 8(6), (7), (8) or (10) of the 1991 Act do not apply (33.6.3).
—Actions for declarator of non-parentage or illegitimacy (33.6.4).
—Family actions where a decision has been made in any application, review or appeal under the Act of 1991 relating to any child of the parties (33.6.5).

The different requirements for such actions are listed in the rule and should be noted.

Forms

(OCR 33.7)

Forms for intimation in actions of divorce or separation

OCR 33.7 sets out the rules for intimation in family actions. The easiest way to deal with the possibilities is to have a list of particular forms for particular types of actions with the relevant forms on computer disk.

Basic requirements

OCR 33.10 and 33.11

> **Form F14**—Warrant of Citation (provided by the Court attached to the principal Initial Writ)
> **Form F15**—For citation of defender (note OCR 5.6 where address of person is not known)
> **Form F16**—Certificate of Citation (attached to the principal Initial Writ. Note comments below on mentioning additional forms)
> **Form F26**—Notice of Intention of Defend

Subject to the exception governing service where the address of a defender is not known every intimation includes at least a copy of the writ and Forms F14, F15 and F26. In addition particular types of actions have extra forms.

The requirements under OCR 33.8 where an improper association is averred should be noted.

Additional Forms Divorce/Separation

OCR 33.14

> 2 Year with consent divorce—**Forms F19 and F20**
> Action of separation—**Forms F21 and F22**
> Non cohabitation for 5 years divorce—**Form F23**
> Non cohabitation for 5 years Separation—**Form F24**

It is a specific requirement that the Certificate of Citation states which notice or form relating to the ground of divorce has been attached to the Initial Writ (OCR 33.14(2). It is useful to narrate in the body of the certificate all the forms sent with it so that there can be no doubt what was included.

Productions at warranting

(OCR 33.9)
OCR 33.9 specifies that—
> Unless the Sheriff otherwise directs—

"(a) in an action of divorce, a warrant for citation shall not be granted without there being produced with the Initial Writ an extract of the relevant entry in the register of marriages or an equivalent document; and

(b) in an action which includes a crave for a section 11 Order, a warrant for citation shall not be granted without there being produced with the Initial Writ an extract of the relevant entry in the register of births or an equivalent document."

Style writs

How to use the style writs

1. Look out the type of writ you want.

2. Look for the subject you want. Follow through the writ linking the craves, condescendences and pleas-in-law relevant to the subject you want.

3. Note that throughout the styles, the following assumptions are made—

    (a)   The Pursuer is a female with the use of *"her"* for alteration as appropriate.

    (b)   Children are referred to in the masculine singular. The use of *"him"/"child"* for alteration as appropriate.

    (c)   The styles proceed on the assumption that the first occasion the child's name appears in the condescendence, the child is referred to by his full name followed by ("hereinafter referred to as *First Name*").

    (d)   Where reference is made to giving details of behaviour and the like, you should consider on each occasion whether the information would be better given in separate articles of condescendence or can be contained within one article.

    (e)   We have avoided giving too much by way of style averments to be incorporated on the basis that that will risk an inappropriate or incomplete narration of a client's position. Each case has to be considered on its own merits and links made between the three elements of the pleadings. Our elements in bold are intended only as a starting point for your consideration of what facts need to be averred.

CHAPTER 8

THE INITIAL WRIT—COMPLEX SITUATIONS

Our aim in Chapter 7 was to provide you with the basics for drafting an Initial Writ. However, on many occasions there will be unusual situations that need to be addressed. This chapter is not intended to be an in depth analysis but rather a pointer and introduction to some of the circumstances that may arise.

Capacity

On occasion in our eagerness to resolve matters for our client we forget to ask ourselves the essential initial questions on capacity. As part of your initial investigation before drafting you have to ask yourself—

- Can my client sue?
- Can my client sue the proposed defender?

Can your client sue?

Mental Incapacity

You have to consider whether your client has the capacity to give instructions (*Gibson v. Gibson and Another,* 1970 S.L.T. (Notes) 60). If your client is mentally incapacitated to the extent that he or she is incapable of giving instructions or receiving advice then he or she cannot raise proceedings. It is incompetent to raise proceedings in his or her name (*Moodie v. Dempster,* 1931 S.C. 553, *per* Lord Clyde at 554–5). The rules on the appointment of a curator *ad litem* to a defender (see hereinafter) do not apply to a pursuer.

If a client's ability is in doubt the medical position should be clarified prior to raising proceedings.

If a client cannot give instructions but an attempt to secure divorce is still considered necessary the appointment of tutor dative for the sole purpose of beginning and conducting divorce proceedings could be considered, although there is no past precedent for this. From April, 2002, section 53 of the Adults With Incapacity (Scotland) Act 2000 will allow a sheriff to authorise the start of divorce proceedings and authorise someone to conduct them for an incapacitated person.

Can you sue the proposed defender?

Under OCR 33.16, it is stated that, where it appears to the court that the defender is suffering from a mental disorder, the Sheriff must appoint a curator *ad litem* to the defender (OCR 33.16(2)(a). Again, the question is whether the client is able to understand the issues in the case and deal with the proceedings whether by instructing a solicitor or acting in person. There is a presumption of sanity and therefore a person would be presumed to be able to deal with an action until the contrary was shown to be the case. Where the defender does not meet the criteria to enable him to give instructions, OCR 33.7(1)(c) provides for intimation to relatives and a curator bonis (if one has been appointed).

Under OCR 33.16(2)(b), where a divorce is sought on the basis of a two-year non cohabitation and consent, and it appears to the court that the defender is suffering from a mental disorder, the court has to make an order for intimation of the ground of the action to the Mental Health Welfare Commission for Scotland and to include in the order a requirement that the Commission sends the Sheriff Clerk a report indicating whether in its opinion the defender is capable of deciding whether nor not to give consent to the granting of decree.

The specialities of further procedure in such cases should be noted (OCR 33.16 and 33.7(1)(c)). If the Defender is resident in a hospital or other similar institution the rules for citation under OCR 33.13 should be noted. To serve proceedings in the wrong way on a vulnerable individual in hospital could have devastating consequences for that person.

Which court can have jurisdiction?

Before committing yourself to a particular choice between the Sheriff Court and Court of Session, and facing the embarrassment of finding you are in the wrong place, check matters out. MacPhail, *Sheriff Court Practice,* p. 50 at 2.56–2.64 is a good starting point for establishing what actions are appropriate to the sheriff court.

Jurisdiction—"Brussels II"

We mentioned this in Chapter 7 in discussing jurisdiction in basic cases. A broader knowledge is needed to deal with more complex situations.

What it covers

The regulation makes important changes to jurisdiction rules.

The regulation covers—

"(a) Civil proceedings relating to divorce, legal separation or marriage annulment;
(b) Civil proceedings relating to parental responsibility for the children of both spouses on the occasion of the matrimonial proceedings referred to in (a)" (Article 1(1)).

Who it covers

The regulation covers—

- a national of; or
- person habitually resident; or
- person domiciled in
- another member state of the EC (Denmark has not adopted it and therefore is excepted).

What it amends

This is a directly applicable EC regulation and requires no legislation in the United Kingdom to implement it. The European Communities (Matrimonial Jurisdictions and Judgements) (Scotland) Regulations 2001 S.S.I. 2001 No. 36 make the relevant adjustment to the Domicile and Matrimonial Proceedings Act 1973, Child Abduction and Custody Act 1985, the Family Law Act 1986 and Children (Scotland) Act 1995.

Brussels II Separation and Divorce.

As with the old form of the Domicile and Matrimonial Proceedings Act, the regulation puts habitual residence and domicile at the heart of jurisdiction. However, the slant is different in significant ways. Section 8(2) of the Domicile and Matrimonial Proceedings Act 1973 now states—

"s. 8(2) The Court shall have jurisdiction to entertain an action for separation or divorce if (and only if)—

(a) either—

(i)   the Scottish courts have jurisdiction under the Council Regulations; or

(ii)   the action is an excluded action where either party to the marriage in question is domiciled in Scotland at the date when the action is begun.

(b) either party to the marriage—

(i)   was resident in the sheriffdom for a period of not less than 40 days ending with that date or

(ii)   had been resident in the sheriffdom for a period of not less than 40 days before the said date and had no residence in Scotland at that date."

Article 2 of the Regulation in turn states—

"1. In matters relating to divorce, legal separation or marriage annulment, jurisdiction shall lie with the courts of the member state—

(a)   in whose territory

— the spouses are habitually resident, or
— the spouses were last habitually resident, in so far as one of them still resides there, or
— the respondent is habitually resident, or
— in the event of a joint application, either of the spouses is habitually resident, or

— the applicant is habitually resident if he or she resided there for at least a year immediately before the application was made, or

— the applicant is habitually resident if he or she resided there for at least six months immediately before the application was made and is either a national of the member state in question or, in the case of the United Kingdom and Ireland, has his "domicile" there;

(b)   of the nationality of both spouses or, in the case of the United Kingdom and Ireland, of the "domicile" of both spouses.

2.   For the purpose of this regulation, "domicile" shall have the same meaning as it has under the legal systems of the United Kingdom and Ireland."

In other words, a new range of options has been brought in to found jurisdiction. In Chapter 7 we followed the idea of both spouses being habitually resident in Scotland and meeting the rule requiring forty days residence within the relevant Sheriffdom. Now we see that jurisdiction can be obtained in a variety of different but equally valid ways in the Member state where—

Option 1   The spouses are habitually resident

Option 2   Both spouses were last habitually resident if one of them still lives there, so that if one spouse runs off to Spain leaving the other in Scotland, the spouse in Scotland can raise proceedings straight away.

Option 3   The Defender is habitually resident. In other words a spouse can run off to Spain but still seek a divorce in Scotland if the other spouse is still in Scotland.

Option 4   A joint application is made with either spouse habitually resident in Scotland.

It is difficult to give a context in Scotland for this based on previous practice and requirements so it will be interesting to see what happens to this rule within Scotland, bearing in mind that under the law as it currently stands it is simply not possible.

Option 5   The Pursuer is habitually resident if he or she lived in the Member State for at least a year immediately before the application is made. In other words, once an individual has lived in any Member State for a year he can raise proceedings.

Option 6   The Pursuer is habitually resident if—

He or she has lived in the Member State at least six months immediately before the application was made;
and
He or she is a national of the particular State (or in the United Kingdom if domiciled there).

It was nice of the Council to keep things simple! What this means is that nationality/domicile can still matter. If a Spanish husband returns to Spain from Scotland, lives there for six months and wants to raise proceedings in Spain he can after the six months. His wife, whatever her nationality, can raise proceedings in Scotland straight away if she is habitually resident there. The spouse in Scotland has to decide whether she wants to negotiate without raising proceedings in the knowledge that if she does not raise proceedings she could find herself facing an action in Spain after six months.

Option 7   A further twist is given by the final subsection 2(b) which allows the spouses to raise proceedings in the territory where they are nationals, or in the case of United Kingdom and Ireland, domiciled.

In other words if our Spanish spouse is married to a Spanish wife with whom he lives in Scotland he could run off to France and after one year, if his wife was still in Scotland, have a choice of three different jurisdictions! Spain based on nationality, Scotland based on habitual residence of his wife and France based on his residence there for one year. We look forward to instructing lawyers in two other jurisdictions to allow us to compare the rights of three different jurisdictions over financial issues on divorce!

Exclusivity of jurisdiction

Once a particular Member State is "seized" of jurisdiction a second Court in which proceedings are raised will have to sist them (Article 11) with only very limited exceptions. A Court is deemed to be "seized" of jurisdiction either

—when the Initial Writ is lodged with the Court provided proper service is made afterwards (*i.e.* the date of warranting where service is achieved), Article 11.4(a); or

—on the date a document is received by the authority responsible for service where service has to take place before lodging provided the Pursuer takes the necessary steps to lodge the writ with the Court thereafter. Under current Scottish legislation, this would have no application to proceedings raised here.

Having read the above you may well be desperate to find situations where Brussels II does not apply! If Brussels II does not apply then the laws of the particular State apply (Article 8). The European Communities (Matrimonial Jurisdiction and Judgements) (Scotland) Regulations 2001 define an "excluded action" as meaning an action "in respect of which no court of a contracting state has jurisdiction under the Regulation and the defender is not a person who is—

(i) a national of a Contracting State (other than the U.K. or Ireland); or
(ii) domiciled in Ireland."

In other words few people are going to be excluded. Where a person is excluded, section 8(2)(a)(ii) of the Domicile and Matrimonial Proceedings Act 1973 gives the Scottish Courts jurisdiction "where either party of the marriage in question is domiciled in Scotland at the date when the action is begun". (Compare Brussels II, Article 8(2)(b) which gives jurisdiction in the territory where both parties are domiciled.)

An additional question

The regulation does bring up a question particular to the United Kingdom. By referring to a "Member State" the implication is that a person habitually resident in England could raise proceedings in Scotland because the person's habitual residence of the United Kingdom covers both jurisdictions. Article 41 of "Brussels II" appears to cover this issue by saying that where two legal systems operate in a Member State the references to Member State are to be taken as referring to the "territorial unit" of the particular legal system.

Domicile

E. Clive, *Husband and Wife*, pp. 572–574 at 28.002 to 28.011 gives some succinct and useful information about the concepts of domicile and habitual residence. He confirms that domiciled in Scotland means, very roughly, settled in Scotland on a more or less permanent basis. As a practical matter, in broad terms, an adult who has lived all his or her life in Scotland (apart from occasional absences) and intends to go on living in Scotland indefinitely is domiciled in Scotland. An adult who comes to Scotland with the intention of settling here for the rest of his or her life, or at least for a lengthy indefinite period, and not just for a limited time or particular purpose, will acquire a domicile of choice in Scotland on arrival here.

Habitual residence

"Habitual residence" is not defined in the Domicile and Matrimonial Proceedings Act 1973. It tends to be an easier concept to pin to the practicalities of an individual's living arrangements. It means more than residence alone and requires both residence and some sort of settled intention to remain in the particular place.

The Lord President in *Dickson v. Dickson*, 1990 S.C.L.R. 692, at p. 703b-c states "It is enough to say that in our opinion a habitual residence is one which is being enjoyed voluntarily for the time being and with the settled intention that it should continue for some time".

With the European flavouring provided by Brussels II interpretations used by the European Court of Justice will no doubt be given significance. Habitual residence there has been described as the place where a person had established, on a fixed basis, his permanent or habitual centre of interests. Both the Scottish and European Courts have looked to all the relevant facts for the purpose of deciding whether there is a habitual residence in the particular case.

Unusual situations over jurisdiction for children (not ancillary to divorce)

Section 10 of the Family Law Act 1986 states "subject to section 11 of this Act, an application for a Part I Order otherwise than in matrimonial proceedings *may* be entertained by—

    (a) the Court of Session if, on the date of the application, the child concerned—
        (i)   is *present* in Scotland; and

(ii)   is *not habitually resident* in any part of the United Kingdom;

(b) the Sheriff if, on the date of the application,—

(i)   the child is *present* in Scotland;

(ii)   the child is *not habitually resident* in any part of the United Kingdom;

(iii)   either the pursuer or the defender in the application is *habitually resident* in the Sheriffdom.

Section 10 is there to give jurisdiction to make Part I Orders over children who are not habitually resident in the United Kingdom and for children for whom the emergency jurisdiction mentioned hereinafter would not be appropriate but over whom jurisdiction is required.

The most important point to note is the application "may be entertained" in other words the court is not obliged to accept jurisdiction on this ground. The action could be turned away or sisted.

Emergency jurisdiction

This is covered by section 12. Basically it grants a residual jurisdiction to both Court of Session and the Sheriff Court based on the presence of the child if there exists an emergency making it necessary for the protection of the child to make a Part 1 Order. What constitutes an emergency to justify the use of section 12 is a matter within the discretion of the court.

Duration, variation, enforcement and recall of section 11 orders

Actions of divorce and separation

OCR 33.44 covers actions of divorce or separation. It is made clear that where a variation or recall of a section 11 Order is wanted the request should be made by minute in the process of the action to which it relates. The same applies to the enforcement of a section 11 Order.

Actions other than actions of divorce and separation

OCR 33.65 covers applications for variation or recall of section 11 Orders in family actions other than divorce. The requirements are almost exactly the same as for divorce actions except that, for some reason, the rule does not cover enforcement of a section 11 Order. It is unclear what the reason for this is, but our suggestion is that the Minute procedure should probably still be used.

What is clear is that, for most purposes, where a variation is sought, a minute in the original process is the appropriate mechanism. That continues to be the case even if the original basis of jurisdiction has ceased to exist (provided there are no matrimonial proceedings continuing in a United Kingdom court and the order continues to be effective) (Family Law Act 1986, s. 15(2)). The Family Law Act 1986 give a further gloss on this. The full terms of sections 11 and 15 of that act should be paid attention to.

The primacy of matrimonial proceedings

The wide definition of continuing matrimonial proceedings as being until a child (over whom the court has jurisdiction in those proceedings) reaches 16 or the proceedings have been dismissed or decree of absolvitor granted. (Family Law Act 1986, s. 42(3)) is important.

Subject to the important caveat or the lack of clarity on the impact of Article 3.3 of Brussels II, it appears discussed in the last chapter the jurisdiction of a court to entertain an application for a Part 1 order under sections 9, 10 and 15(2) of the 1986 Act is excluded if proceedings are continuing in any part of the United Kingdom in respect of the marriage of the parents of the child (Family Law Act 1986, s. 11(1)) subject to certain qualifications under section 11(2). Broadly put, you are giving the court dealing with primacy, matrimonial proceedings in dealing with children whether orders have been made about them elsewhere before or not.

Declining jurisdiction

The above interpretation of "continuing" as lasting potentially several years can throw up problems. Under the Family Law Act 1986, s. 13 (6) this is catered for by allowing a court with jurisdiction in relation to matrimonial proceedings to decline jurisdiction to make a Part 1 order under section 11(1), where it would be "more appropriate" for matters to be dealt with in another court which would have jurisdiction but for section 11(1).

Unusual situations over service

Service where the defender's whereabouts unknown (OCR 33.4, 33.11 and 5.6)

Specific averments are necessary where the identity or address of a person is not known as we mentioned earlier on. The citation still includes Forms F15 and F26. OCR 5.6 states that where the address of a person to be cited is—

— "not known" and
— "cannot reasonably be ascertained"

the Sheriff shall grant Warrant for Citation or service upon that person either by:

Newspaper Advertisement

—"by the publication of an advertisement on *Form G3* in a specified newspaper circulating in the area of the last known address of that person" (OCR 5.6(1)(a).

(if citation has been by way of newspaper advertisement a copy of the newspaper containing the advertisement is lodged with the Sheriff Clerk by the Pursuer's solicitor (OCR5.6(4).)
or

Display on walls of court

—"by displaying on the walls of Court a copy of the instance and crave of the Initial Writ, Warrant of Citation and a Notice in *Form G4*" (OCR 5.6.(1)(b).

(where a display on the walls of Court is required the pursuer's solicitor supplies the Sheriff Clerk a certified copy of the instance and craves of the Initial Writ and any Warrant of Citation (OCR 5.6.5).)

The period of Notice fixed by the Court runs from the date of publication of the advertisement or display on the walls of Court as the case may be (OCR 5.6).

Where service takes place on this basis the pursuer's solicitor lodges a service copy of the Initial Writ and a copy of any Warrant of Citation with the Sheriff Clerk (OCR 5.6(2). They can be uplifted by the person for whom they were intended.

Extra Forms and People for Intimation

OCR 33.7(1) narrates a whole series of situations where there are additional requirements for services. We simply list the circumstances and the rule to cover them.

(a) Defender's Whereabouts Unknown and not Reasonably Ascertainable

(OCR 33.7(1)(a))

(b) Allegation of Adultery

(OCR 33.7(1)(b))

(c) Mental Disorder

(OCR 33.7(1)(c)) (Note the specialities of service under OCR 33.13)

(d) Marriage Under Law Allowing Polygamy

(OCR 33.7(1)(d))

(e) Certain cases where a section 11 Order may be made

(i)   Child in Local Authority care (OCR 33.7(1)(e)(iii))
(ii)   Child who is the child to one party of the marriage and has been accepted as the child of the family by the other party of the marriage and is liable to be maintained by a third party (OCR 33.7(1)(e)(ii)
(iii)   Were a third party exercises care and control (OCR 33.7(1)(e)(iii)

(f) Action where the pursuer craves a section 11 Order

(OCR 33.7(1)(f))

(g) Actions where the pursuer craves a Residence Order and is not a parent of the child and is resident in Scotland when the Initial Writ is lodged.

(OCR 33.7(1)(g)) The requirements of service under OCR 33.12 should also be noted.

(h) Intimation to child affected by a crave for section 11 order ' who is not party to the action

(OCR 33.7(1)(h)) N.B. the child is *not* sent a copy of the Initial Writ, only the Form F9 with wording appropriate to the age and maturity of the child. The aim is to inform while creating the least possible upset. Note also the possibility to dispense with service (OCR 33.7(7)).

(i) Applications for transfer of property (under Section 8(1)(aa) of the Act of 1985

(OCR 33.7(1)(i))

(j) Avoidance transactions (applications under section 18 of the Family Law (Scotland) Act 1985)

(OCR 33.7(1)(j))

(k) Certain applications under the Matrimonial Homes (Family Protection) (Scotland) Act 1981

(OCR 33.7(1)(k))

(l) Earmarking Orders (under Section 8(1)(b) of the Family Law (Scotland) Act 1985)

(OCR 33.7(3))

Actions where the Pursuer craves a Residence Order in respect of a child, is not a parent of the child and is not resident in Scotland when the Initial Writ is lodged for warranting

(OCR 33.7(4))

Actions where the address of a person mentioned under OCR 33(7)(1) (b), (d), (e), (f), (h), (i), (j), (k) or (l) above is not known and cannot reasonably be ascertained

(OCR 33.7(5))

Where the identity or address of a person to whom intimation of a family action is required becomes known during the course of the action

(OCR 33.7(6))

Dispensation with service on a child

(OCR 33.7(7))

Intimation where improper association

(OCR 33.(8))

Service in cases of mental disorder of Defender

(See OCR 33.13). (N.B. The further requirements in such cases under OCR 33.16 should also be noted.)

Orders by the Sheriff for intimation or to dispense with intimation

As well as the above provisions a Sheriff may at any time order intimation to be made on "such a person as he thinks fit" or postpone intimation which he considers "such postponement is appropriate". In that case the Sheriff may make such order in respect of the postponement "as he thinks fit".

The Sheriff can dispense with intimation where he considers such dispensation is appropriate. (OCR 33.15).

CHAPTER 9

INTERIM HEARINGS AND INTERIM STEPS

Introduction

Any interim steps are an unforgiving test of your preliminary
information gathering! If you are thorough and patient with your
client from the beginning you will be less likely to launch into
dire emergency mode in situations where time and support could
defuse what initially appears to be a crisis. Equally, you would be
less likely to be caught wrong footed and ill prepared by a full
scale life, child or property threatening scenario.

Full information and insight into a client's emotional state are
both required to be able to do realistic risk assessment. If you
make a move for protective remedies which are not required or
realistic it will heighten tension and lower your and your client's
credibility. If you fail to secure your client's position in the short
term he or she may be significantly prejudiced in the long term.

The joys of being a family lawyer!

The first thing to recognise is that you are there to advise the
client, not to tell him or her what to do. You should summarise
each option, assess the possibility of success, the consequences of
failure and the cost implications. You will often find the
experience of doing that will make it fairly clear what the next
step should be without any agonies over decision-making.

Many interim steps are purely procedural. They still require
accurate and full information.

If you are consulted by a defender always remember to check
the warrant immediately in case it gives intimation of an interim
hearing.

Interim hearings

Preliminary preparation

It's essential to have a good grasp of the facts and law you're
relying on. Know which of the court rules are relevant, know

where in the articles of condescendence the relevant facts lurk and have copies of any relevant cases available for yourself, the other side and the Sheriff. If you are dealing with an intimated hearing check that you've returned the writ or your updated pleadings to court along with any affidavits, productions and relevant cases. (Remember OCR 9.4 directs each party to send updated pleadings to court not later than 2 days before the hearing). Send copies to the other side if you know who is instructed. There's no point producing things at the last moment in a triumphant flourish —all that will happen is that you'll be faced with a continuation (inevitably, to a time you are due to appear at court in the opposite direction!).

It can be handy to use a ring binder for interim hearings and opposed actions. It can contain—

- a chronology setting out in shorthand a list of key dates and events
- the pleadings
- copy precognitions and affidavits
- copy productions
- copy authorities

all kept under control by appropriately labelled dividers!

A **chronology** can be an invaluable map through what would otherwise be confusing terrain. If you prepare one at the outset it will throw up inconsistencies or gaps in your knowledge and understanding of events before this becomes a problem. It can be amended and expanded as matters develop. A chronology can be a most efficient way of ensuring you cover the appropriate ground at any interim hearings, in your pleadings and subsequently at proof. All you need is a list in date order narrating main events such as when the couple met, married, had children, fell out, fell in, fell out again, parted, tried contact arrangements, fell out again, tried again, failed. Specific incidents which will be mentioned in the pleadings should be referred to in shorthand.

Using a highlighter to pick out the relevant part of your pleadings and affidavits can also help you navigate the raw material.

It is useful to have a record of court attendances and also a court attendance sheet. Examples are given at the end of the book. You can use the back of a court attendance sheet to summarise the points you wish to make and note the counter arguments put forward at the hearing. The outcome is noted on the front. It should also jog you to diary forward any continued hearing.

Be aware of the wide range of approaches taken by different courts to interim hearings. Always check the form with the Sheriff Clerk and, if possible, a local agent if you are going to an unfamiliar court. Most courts would not expect the parties to be in attendance or to participate, if represented but some Sheriffs believe in involving the parties as soon as possible. The hearing will almost certainly be of crucial importance to your client. It is a good idea to suggest that your client be available in case something crops up.

Pre-warrant hearings

The most common orders requested before service are interdicts. The writ itself will contain the crave. Each court will have a different procedure. Some courts will deal with pre-warrant motions in chambers, some in open court. Either way, be ready to point to the precise parts of the pleadings supporting the need for an interim order. If the hearing is in chambers you may have to function with no helpful props such as a desk or table in front of you so it is particularly useful to have your papers accessible in a clear order in a folder rather than in random fashion in a file ready to launch themselves like confetti given a moment of inattention!

The interdict might be to prevent molestation, removal of children, removal of furniture or disposal of some other asset. Remember that you need an intimated hearing before a power of arrest can be added to a matrimonial interdict.

Intimated hearings

While the period of notice is running, or at later stages in a defended action there may be intimated hearings.

Protective orders

If you are trying to obtain protection in the short-term against a client's abusive former partner there is a range of possibilities. For married couples or unmarried couples where you are also seeking an occupancy order you could try for an exclusion order and power of arrest. For couples married or unmarried an interdict against molestation remains a possibility or the newer option of a non-harassment order under s. 8(5) of the Protection from Harassment Act 1997.

Confusion has arisen over the stage at which a non-harassment order may be granted. In *Furber v. Furber,* 1999 S.L.T. (Sh. Ct) *26* the Sheriff Principal in Glasgow upheld the granting of an interim non-harassment order. It was stated that such an order could be granted at an early stage on the basis of statements or affidavits, preferably at least affidavits. Over on the east coast things have developed differently! In *Heenan v. Dillon,* 1999 S.L.T. (Sh. Ct) 32 Sheriff Morrison refused to grant an interim non-harassment order finding that such an order is a determinative order and cannot be made without the Defender having had an opportunity to be heard. There is an article considering these different approaches *(Glasgow v. Edinburgh,* Fam. L.B. 39–7). Sheriff Principal Risk followed the line of thinking that an interim non-harassment order is incompetent in *Alexandra v. Murphy,* 2000 G.W.D. 4–153.

The safest way is to seek interim interdict initially and have a crave for non-harassment to be triggered to replace the interim interdict in the final decree. Just remember that you can't have both! You would have to crave dismissal of the interim interdict in your final minute for decree craving the non-harassment order.

Another uncertainty is that the legislation does not set down what to do with your non-harassment order. It seems appropriate to intimate to the police in a similar way to an exclusion order and examples of correspondence are provided.

Remember that if you have intimated a power of arrest you must let the police know if the order is subsequently recalled or superseded for example by decree of divorce.   If your involvement with the case ends while the power of arrest is still in place you should write to the client making the existence of the order and need for the police to be told if the situation changes utterly clear. If you have taken steps to intimate a non-harassment order it would be wise to take the same precaution.

Interim orders re children

Some courts will be inclined to encourage the use of child welfare hearings to tackle any short-term issues to do with children but there can be occasions when an intimated hearing may be fixed to deal with questions of contact or residence. Practice varies. Some courts will deal with those matters mainly on the basis of oral submissions, some by a mix of affidavits and oral submissions and some by reference to a report from a solicitor or social worker. Again, it is important to check with the Sheriff Clerk or a local agent what usually happens. It is wise to sound out a local agent about the climate of an unknown court before you make rash promises to your client!

Interim aliment

Prepare a Schedule of Income and Expenditure. Provide vouching for as much as is realistically necessary. Have copies of the Schedule and the vouching available for the Bench and other Solicitors. Check the information provided, both your client's and his or her partner. Make sure it tallies.

Specific issues orders

These are likely to be quite urgent but not strictly interim since the granting or refusal of the order may well be determinative. Since it is competent to dispose of matters at a child welfare hearing one approach is to frame a writ for a specific issues order in such a way as to trigger a brief period of notice and an early child welfare hearing. The approach of seeking a shortened period of notice and early Child Welfare Hearing could be used for having other urgent specific issues, such as differences over medical treatment or selection of school sorted out.

Affidavits

This is one area where practice varies wildly from court to court and indeed from Sheriff to Sheriff within one court. Some Sheriffs seem allergic to affidavits, some addicted! It is always safer to have affidavits available. They will be necessary for orders under the Matrimonial Homes (Family Protection) (Scotland) Act 1981 and are likely to be of some help in child related matters.

Remember, though, that the affidavits are then part of the process as sworn evidence from your client and witnesses. Any departure from that earlier account of things is likely to be remarked on. The contents will certainly be pored over and broadcast to a wide public. An exchange of affidavits is likely to generate some of the fall out usually associated with a proof, often in the very early stages when everyone involved is particularly polarised and florid in their interpretation. Make sure anyone who signs an affidavit is aware that it will become a public document.

Prognosis

Your client will want to know the likely outcome of the hearing. It is hard to predict even if you know which Sheriff will deal with the hearing, almost impossible if you don't. It's at the stage of interim hearings that the huge disparity in shrieval attitudes is particularly clear. The facts alone will rarely deliver an answer. Once decisions are explained in terms of the evidence, underlying attitudes of the decision maker can be masked but the discrepancies in attitude shine out at the interim stages. This is particularly true in relation to contact. Some courts will energetically try to foster contact from the earliest stage except in the most desperate cases. Some will recoil from over much involvement in the minutiae of family life.

Remember to instruct service and to check if the order needs to be intimated. There is not much point struggling away to get an exclusion order with power of arrest only to receive a frantic message from your client that the police have no record of such a thing.

Next steps

While any preliminary matters are being dealt with the Sheriff Clerk's office will quietly be getting on with the more decorous procedural aspects of the case. A letter will be issued setting out the dates for defences, adjustments, Child Welfare Hearing (if appropriate) and Options Hearing. Remember to ensure a reliable system to diary all those dates. It's best to do that even if the case is likely to be sisted. Then you have to remember to undiary them all again! Also, let your client in on the secret! A suggested letter is provided. If you keep separate appointment and court diaries remember to have any away fixtures put in both.

Motion to sist

After the hectic flurry at the beginning of the action you may wish to draw breath! Equally importantly, your client may need his or her legal aid application processed. If you are off your mark quickly or if you have a motion to sist endorsed as unopposed by the other solicitor this could be dealt with before the defences have to be lodged. If there is a risk you won't achieve that or if you are just too close to the deadline remember that once the timetable is issued you will be covered by the S. U. 2 procedure for lodging defences.

Some courts consider it self evident that by sisting the case any hearings fixed will be cancelled but other courts take a different view. An example setting out a request for a sist for legal aid and the cancellation of any hearings fixed is provided.

Disclosure

It may be necessary to enlist the court's assistance to obtain information or documents your client needs.

Whereabouts of a child

One of the most poignant steps to have to take is to ask the court to order disclosure of the whereabouts of a child under the Family Law Act 1986 s. 33 (1) and O.C.R. 33 .23. The information can be provided by way of affidavits or by personal appearance. If the source of the information is official an affidavit may well be sufficient.

Financial information

Yet again, the importance of good preparation is underlined if it becomes necessary to seek forced disclosure of financial information from the other side. Any request you make must tie in with your pleadings. You can only make the request if you have obtained full enough information from your client to recognise there is a gap which has to be filled.

Section 20 Motion

The benefit of a motion under s. 20 of the Family Law (Scotland) 1985 is simplicity. The drawback is that it is not a vehicle for an inquiry into the extent of the disclosure and in terms of s. 27 (1) only extends to the disclosure of "present and forseeable resources", not relevant date values. Details, not valuations, are to be provided (*Nelson v. Nelson,* 1993 S.C.L.R. 149*).* This procedure has a clear benefit in connection with craves for aliment or periodical allowance. It, unfortunately, does not come close to making Motion and Specification procedure redundant.

It could be worth using s. 14 (2) (b) of the Family Law (Scotland) 1985 to precipitate the valuation of a specific asset such as business interests and setting out exactly what information is required.

Motion and specification

This procedure is frustratingly expensive and cumbersome but must be used if there is an important gap to be filled about information or documentation. An example is given. You must have enough in your pleadings to support the request which must not be over wide. Remember to make the appropriate intimation if requesting hospital records (though not if seeking recovery of information from a G.P.). Remember that a shorthand writer must be booked for the next stage if the Motion is granted and the commissioner fixes a Hearing.

Other procedural steps

Minutes of amendment

There may be a number of reasons to ask the court for permission to change your pleadings.If ancillary matters are resolved during the course of a fault based divorce you might wish to change the basis of the action to two-year non-cohabitation. Just remember—

— the two years must have elapsed by the date of amendment (*Duncan v. Duncan,* 1986 S.L.T. 17)
— you will then need to re-serve an amended writ with the appropriate consent notice

An example is provided of such a minute and the related motion.

Joint Minutes of Admission

Make the most energetic possible efforts to identify evidence which can be agreed and set down in a Minute of Admissions. It will restrict the expense of a Proof and earn you Brownie points with the Bench! An example is given.

Joint minutes

The prospect of drafting a Joint Minute can puncture the sense of achievement in having the practical issues resolved by agreement! An example is given to help you continue to enjoy the process of resolving matters on an agreed footing.

The main thing is to be systematic—check that all the craves are dealt with (and in the way your client expects!). Consider if any remedies might be more suitable for a Minute of Agreement. Although it is reassuring to have an order for sale in a Joint Minute, implementing such an order is a very expensive way of disposing of a house. No cut-price conveyancing on offer in those circumstances! A belt, braces and piece of string approach would be to include an order for sale in the Joint Minute but also make provision for the mechanics of sale in a Minute of Agreement stating that the order for sale in the decree would only be enforced if there was non compliance with the agreement.

Double and treble check the details of any insurance policy. If you have not established by now where the policy document is do so before everything is signed! Make absolutely sure you have checked the timing of any aspects of the eventual decree.

Let your client have a look at both documents. Explain that he or she will sign the Minute of Agreement but that the solicitors will sign the Joint Minute.

The object is to ensure that you and your client are equally happy with the outcome!

CHAPTER 10

CHILD WELFARE HEARINGS AND DECISIONS ABOUT CHILDREN

All family lawyers have a strong responsibility to help clients make wise decisions about their children. Separating out the hurt and confusion clients feel arising from the failed adult relationship from their responsibilities as parents is painfully difficult. It is one step which could make all the difference for their children. You will have to use your "people skills" energetically to help them take that step. It is useful for you to have some knowledge about research into how children react to parental separation to pass on to your client in helping him or her assess any problems arising. A referral to mediation can also ease the transition from a former couple to separated parents. Sometimes things cannot be sorted out by agreement. Court proceedings might be necessary and court proceedings affecting children are the subject of this chapter.

Proceedings affecting children

A significant proportion of court time is devoted to deciding issues about children. Although no matter could be more deserving of attention that does make it all the more important to ensure the best use of the resources available. Many Sheriffs express disappointment and even impatience when confronted by parents who are unable to make co-operative decisions about their children. Without a doubt, joint decision making by parents is preferable to a decision imposed by the court. On the other hand, having their parents locked in unresolved conflict over arrangements about them can be a source of extreme stress for young people. An objective decision made by a third party should improve the situation.

The majority of parents do sort things out either entirely under their own steam or with the assistance of advising lawyers or mediators. Those cases which do end up in court tend to represent extremes of either pathological breakdown in communication or suspected or actual bad behaviour in respect of one or both parents. Although it is always appropriate for the Bench to remind

155

parents of how helpful it is for the children to see their parents able to co-operate the fact that it has reached this stage suggests that a direction to advising lawyers to "knock heads together" is unlikely to prompt immediate settlement!

Legal framework

The legal framework introduced by the Children (Scotland) Act 1995 has certainly helped promote the idea of continuity of parenting patterns rather than a power struggle between the parents. In general, avoiding the need for a young person to feel ashamed of or rejected by one parent is a reasonable objective. Having some knowledge of both parents will in most cases help a young person in building his or her own identity. Sometimes these aims cannot be met. The pleadings should make clear the basic nature of the problem to enable the right approach to be taken in dealing with the action.

Focus of pleadings

Violent or drug taking parent

Although in general the difficulties in the adult relationship may well not be relevant in assessing child related issues there are some exceptions. If it is suggested that there is a history of violence by one parent against the other or drug taking by a parent or abuse of the child and this is denied, the factual basis for these allegations must be clearly set out. The emphasis should be to achieve adjudication on the factual issues just as soon as possible. It may be inappropriate for contact to take place or appropriate for contact to happen only on a supervised basis in the interim and so it is crucial to have the facts explored at the earliest possible opportunity.

Contrite parent

If a degree of bad behaviour is admitted but stated to be in the past, evidence of this reform would obviously be necessary to satisfy a sheriff and the means to do this may in some cases reassure the other parent enough to facilitate an agreed outcome. It is important to encourage clients who may have had a drug or alcohol dependency to recognise this as a source of legitimate concern to the other parent and to put some effort into acknowledging the past problem and meeting current anxieties.

Hostile parents

Sometimes acute hostility and conflict has only arisen at the time of separation. Sometimes each parent has such a different view of the other's parenting abilities that you might think they come from entirely different families! In both cases the pleadings should try to highlight what is important from the child or children's point of view. Housing, the division of responsibility when the parents were together for practical tasks, the quality of parent/child relationship, the child or children's current progress at school, important leisure activities and any health problems should be outlined. The proposed arrangements including the nature of the future involvement of the other parent should be set down. It is an important exercise to focus your client's mind on these aspects. The information should be the building blocks for decision-making.

In these cases, appropriate intervention from the Bench at a reasonably early stage can defuse rather than inflame the situation. Each parent may have become dependent on making sense of the situation by blaming the other parent. They may have lost sight of the value of the other parent to the child or children. A courteous and sympathetic but firm approach from the Bench could help put things back on track. If the parents feel that the difficulties of the situation have been recognised in an even handed way, any unacceptable behaviour identified and the decision making process started they may feel it possible to continue the process themselves. If they feel they have had a row or that the sheriff has not understood the realities of the situation their level of co-operation is likely to be minimal.

Interim hearings and child welfare hearings

Although some urgent steps about young people are dealt with by submissions at interim hearings it is now more common for arrangements to be considered in the presence of the parents at a Child Welfare Hearing reflecting the emphasis in the Act on the involvement of the parents in the Act.

With effect from November 1, 1996, OCR 33.22A introduced the requirement in a family action for a Child Welfare Hearing to be fixed automatically where a section 11 order is opposed or sought by a defender or in any other circumstances by decision of the sheriff. A "family action" is defined in OCR 33.1 and includes an action of divorce, separation, declarator of legitimacy, illegitimacy, parentage, non-parentage, legitimation or affiliation and aliment, an action or application for an order in respect of a section 11 order (with some non-standard exceptions), aliment, or under the Matrimonial Homes (Family Protection) (Scotland) Act 1981.

Even if a Child Welfare Hearing is fixed the parties can still make requests by way of motion (OCR 33.22 A (3). Unless the subject matter of the motion was extremely pressing it is likely that the court would prefer matters to be canvassed fully at the Child Welfare Hearing. The motion might well be continued.

The parties must receive intimation of the Child Welfare Hearing. All parties are expected to attend the Child Welfare Hearing personally. That includes any child who has indicated he or she wants to attend the Hearing. Remember to let your client know he or she must attend unless you are able to persuade the court there is good cause for non-attendance. Most parents are keen to attend. Inform your client in writing.

Preparation

Information and affidavits

OCR 33.22 A (6) stipulates that "It shall be the duty of the parties to provide the Sheriff with sufficient information to enable him to conduct the Child Welfare Hearing". Make sure that your information is completely up-to-date. Major developments by the minute are the rule rather than the exception in family law cases. Practice about the provision of affidavits varies from court to court. O.C.R. 33.27 provides that "The sheriff *may* accept evidence by affidavit at any hearing for an order or interim order". It is usually best to have affidavits available from your client and the witnesses. They should be submitted ahead of the Hearing and copies delivered to the other solicitor. The drawback is that the sheriff may choose to ignore the affidavits while the other party does the very opposite! The affidavits will represent the sworn evidence of your client and witnesses and could lead to challenge if, with the passage of time, variations crop up should they need to give the evidence in person.

Adjusted pleadings

Remember that in terms of OCR 9.4 you must submit a copy of your adjusted pleadings not later than two days before the hearing. Although a Child Welfare Hearing is likely to take place early in the process and there is understandable encouragement to avoid unnecessary "mud slinging", your client is likely to feel let down if factors which are of importance are difficult to get across because there has been no prior warning in the pleadings.

Prepare your client

Make sure your client is aware of what is likely to happen in terms of procedure. It can be difficult to predict because of the very different approach taken by each sheriff even within one court but some indication should be given. Arrange to meet your client at court fifteen minutes early. Be there on time! Remember just how important the hearing is to the parties involved.

If you are representing a young person arrange to show him or her round the court before the day of the Child Welfare Hearing. Explain what is likely to happen in clear language and check that the information has been understood. Give plenty opportunity for questions.

If you are representing the parent remember that only a child who has indicated he or she wishes to attend need be at the Hearing. You should talk through the practicalities of various possible outcomes in case a child in your client's care goes to live with the other parent after the Hearing or a Contact Order is made. It can be difficult but is necessary to explore that possibility in case prior fixtures could potentially cause practical problems.

Views of children

In the past, custody and access actions were mainly straightforward wrangles between parents adjudicated by the sheriff. The decision usually delighted one parent and horrified the other. The adults blamed one another and/or the sheriff and/or the advising lawyers for outcomes which displeased them. The process was neither educational nor civilising. It did not encourage a direct input from the child or children concerned. Neither, however, did it open the possibility of the child or children being blamed for the outcome.

In view of OCR33.19 (3) the sheriff must give "due weight" to views expressed by the child, having due regard to his age and maturity were the child involved has, either by returning Form F9 or made his or her views known in some other way. It is clearly essential for the views of any child involved to be taken into account. This provision, however, can lead to children being pressurised to express views which amount to a choice between parents or to express views which make sense to them at the time but may not be the best long-term option. Such views may be given decisive weight.

OCR 33.20 sets out how any views which are expressed should be recorded. Although OCR 33.20 (2) provides that the Sheriff *may* direct that such views shall be marked "Views of the child—confidential" and be available to a sheriff only such confidentiality cannot be guaranteed in advance. Even if such a direction is made it could be open to challenge. Although in *Dosoo v. Dosoo,* 1999 S.L.T. 86, the decision was that confidentiality should be respected except in compelling circumstances a different line was taken in *McGrath v. McGrath,* 1999 S.L.T. (Sh. Ct) 90. There is a significant tension between the principle of openness and the right to confidentiality intensified by ECHR considerations. The matter has been considered in a number of other cases including *Ross v. Ross,* 1999 G.W.D. 19–863; *Oyeneyin v. Oyeneyin,* 1999 G.W.D. 38–1836 and *Grant v. Grant,* 2000 GWD 5–177. The reality is that even if the views of child were not explicitly revealed in the process the decision itself would by implication give a very strong indication of their nature. It is crucial for any young person who is considering expressing their views in a formal way to be warned clearly that their mum or dad might get to know what they are saying.

Explanation and advice

You must obviously explain to clients the significance of their children's views. It is important to do so in a way which highlights how helpful it is to explore the children's priorities in a practical way. Talking over arrangements which recognise the children will spend some time with each parent and looking for workable solutions is an entirely different discussion from asking a child which parent they would rather live with.

Clients who are still feeling very hurt and distressed by the separation may be inclined to encourage their children to "tell the Sheriff" they do not wish to see the other parent where contact arrangements have been difficult and the children seem unwilling to go. It is very important to talk through the possibility that although the children may well be upset and perhaps angry, taking the step of rejecting the other parent might be damaging rather than healing in the long term.

Conduct of hearing

In terms of OCR 33.22A (4) the hearing may be held in private and most courts follow that practice. Having only the parents and their advising solicitors present does create a much better climate than picking over private details of family life in front of various lawyers and other litigants. The remainder of the rule gives the sheriff a wide discretion in dealing with matters.

Exercise of discretion

The practice of each court and indeed each sheriff varies so much in relation to the conduct of a Child Welfare Hearing that parents swapping experiences might wonder if they are talking about different legal systems! The Child Support Act has highlighted how impossible it is to achieve uniformity. A wide element of discretion should lead to creative and flexible outcomes but the result in practice can seem arbitrary and unfair.

At one end of the spectrum the experience for some parents may be very similar to watching the hearing of an interim motion in open court with perhaps the added dimension of being at the receiving end of a general tirade against the breakdown of the fabric of society in general and their failure as parents in particular. At the other end, other parents could find themselves listened to carefully in chambers, their child or children might have a helpful chat with the sheriff and the information elicited fed back diplomatically.

Good practice

One factor which has emerged is the desirability of having a sheriff who is able to take on an inquisitorial role, has some knowledge of child development and children's reaction to separation and who can communicate sympathetically to the parties (and any child involved in the Hearing) yet still maintain the authority of the Bench. Quite a tall order!

The Child Welfare Hearing does provide an opportunity to emphasise the importance of contact in most cases and the need for courtesy and co-operation from both parents.

Possible disposals

Although any order in the short-term is likely to be extremely significant for the long-term disposal the possibility of a final disposal at the Child Welfare Hearing was flagged up in *Hartnett v. Hartnett,* 1997 S.C.L.R. 525. In that case the Child Welfare Hearing was continued to allow proof to be heard and a decision made after submissions at the continued Child Welfare Hearing. An appeal was allowed only because there was no shorthand writer.Otherwise, the general approach met with approval. In *Morgan v. Morgan,* 1998 S.C.L.R. 681 a decision to grant a residence order at a Child Welfare Hearing on the basis of affidavits was upheld on appeal. *McCulloch v. Riach and Sumpter,* 1999 S.C.L.R. 159 confirmed that the rules permit a final order to be made at a Child Welfare Hearing provided there is material before the Sheriff which provides a basis for a decision even as to disputed facts.

Reports and reporters

Appointment and cost

In terms of OCR 33.21 the sheriff can appoint either a local authority or another person to "investigate and report to the court on the circumstances of a child and on proposed arrangements for the care and upbringing of the child". In practice the reporter will be either a social worker or solicitor in most cases. A solicitor is likely to be able to provide a report more promptly but there are cost implications! Remember, in terms of the rule, if the sheriff calls for the report him or herself the cost in the first instance is the responsibility of the pursuer or minuter. Otherwise, the initial responsibility for costs lies on the party requesting a report. If your client has applied for legal aid it is important to submit an SU2 if the application has not yet been granted. The opinion was expressed in one case that a firm of solicitors should not be personally liable for the fee for a report as they were agents for a disclosed principal (*Catto v. Lindsay & Kirk,* S.C.L.R. 1995 541). If your client would be responsible for the cost of the report and does not have legal aid it would be wise to alert the court to the position unless you are in funds to cover the cost.

Remember that if the matter still goes to proof the report itself will have no evidential value (*Kristianson v. Kristianson,* 1987 S.C.L.R. 462 and *Oliver v. Oliver,* 1988 S.C.L.R. 285). Despite that, in some courts, reports do seem to be taken into account at proof.

Experienced family lawyers are quite often appointed as reporters. It is a very responsible task. A reporter has been described as "the eyes and ears of the court". This makes sense where the disagreement is over the family dynamics. It can make all the difference to have an objective assessment from first hand observations. It is less obviously appropriate where there is a significant dispute over past factual matters of relevance which should really be a matter for the court to decide rather than delegate.

It is the responsibility of the party seeking the appointment of a reporter or, where the court makes the appointment of its own motion, the pursuer or minuter to instruct the local authority or reporter (and also to intimate details of the local authority or reporter to any local authority to which intimation of the family action has been made).

Curator

If it has become clear that there is a conflict of interests between the child and one or both parents or if it is felt for any other reason that it would be appropriate a curator may be appointed. This will usually be an experienced family lawyer. In some cases the curator's involvement will be restricted to the preparation of a report. In others, the curator may become involved as a party to the action. The interlocutor should state who will be responsible for the costs in the first instance (usually the pursuer or minuter). If the curator decides to become involved as a party he or she can apply for legal aid on the basis of the child's means. The curator's role is to make an objective assessment of what is in the child or children's best interests. The curator is not there as an advocate for the child. Obviously, if you are appointed as curator you will take the child or children's expressed views into account but you need not follow them if they seem detrimental to the child in the long-term. It is very important to explain this to the child in language which they can understand.

Mediation

OCR 33.22 allows a referral to family mediation in any family action in which an order in relation to parental responsibilities or parental rights is in issue. The referral must be to a mediator accredited to a specified family mediation organisation. If the referral is to a mediator accredited by CALM (Solicitor Mediators) and your client is on legal aid the cost of your client's half share will be met by the Legal Aid Board. Although there must be a child related issue for a mediation referral to be made it is quite appropriate for financial and child issues to be tackled during mediation.

Supervised contact

If there are serious concerns about parenting skills or high conflict between the parents which does not preclude the possibility of a workable parent/child relationship contact supervised by the social work department is a possibility in terms of OCR 33.25. Before that can be done intimation does have to be made to the Chief Executive of the local authority (unless the local authority is already involved in the action).

Specific issues orders

Because of their nature, you might wish to aim for a resolution of a specific issues order application at a Child Welfare Hearing. If the issue is a particularly urgent one you could show cause to shorten the period of notice in terms of OCR 3.6 (2) and request that if a notice of intention is lodged the Sheriff should direct that a Child Welfare Hearing be held on an earlier date than after the usual 21 day period as provided in OCR 33.22A (1). This procedural approach could be relevant for tackling health or education issues.

Representing young people

Since young people are entitled to become involved in litigation concerning them (now specifically covered in the Children (Scotland) Act 1995, s. 11 (3) (a) and (5)) you could find yourself representing a child. In terms of 1995 Act a child of 12 or more is presumed to be of sufficient age and maturity to form a view (s. 11 (10)). Remember that is just a presumption. You might find a 13-year-old did not appear to have sufficient understanding of what it meant to instruct a solicitor. Equally, you might be asked to act for a mature and articulate 10-year-old and feel confident in their grasp of the situation.

It is very important to be able to assess both the young person's capacity to become involved and your own capacity to act. Representing young people is a particularly demanding role Unlike a curator or reporter you are bound by the child's instructions. While, as with an adult, you will help your client anticipate the consequences of any decision you might find it harder to remember that the responsibility lies with the client. It can be hard to avoid slipping into parental rather than solicitor mode!

For a young person to become involved in an action as a party puts them in direct and very open conflict with at least one of their parents. Although that could be a liberating experience, it could also become a heavy burden. It is certainly important to talk through other ways of getting their views across. It is equally important to avoid giving a young person the impression that their opinion is not of value. Listening to adult clients with kindness and understanding is important, doing the same to young clients is crucial.

CHAPTER 11

KEY STEPS TO THE OPTIONS HEARING

An action having been raised and preliminary matters having been addressed, the next stage can go forward in two ways by undefended procedure or defended procedure.

Undefended actions

The rules for this are set out under OCR 33.28 and OCR 33.29. OCR 33.28 states:

"(1)This rule—

(a) subject to sub-paragraph (b) applies to all family actions in which no notice of intention to defend has been lodged, other than a family action—
  (i)   for a section 11 order or for aliment;
  (ii)   of affiliation and aliment;
  (iii)   for financial provision after an overseas divorce or annulment within the meaning of Part IV of the Matrimonial and Family Proceedings Act 1984; or
  (iv)   for an order under the Act of 1981;
(b) applies to a family action in which a curator *ad litem* has been appointed under rule 33.16 where the curator *ad litem* to the defender has lodged a minute intimating that he does not intend to lodge defences;
(c) applies to any family action which proceeds at any stage as undefended where the sheriff so directs;
(d) applies to the merits of a family action which is undefended on the merits where the sheriff so directs, notwithstanding that the action is defended on an ancillary matter.

(2) Unless the sheriff otherwise directs, evidence shall be given by affidavits.
(3) Unless the sheriff otherwise directs, evidence relating to the welfare of a child shall be given by affidavit, at least

> one affidavit being emitted by a person other than a parent or party to the action.
>
> (4) Evidence in the form of a written statement bearing to be the professional opinion of a duly qualified medical practitioner, which has been signed by him and lodged in process, shall be admissible in place of parole evidence by him."

The most common type of undefended action is divorce. This rule makes it clear that in taking forward any undefended action the primary form of evidence is usually going to be affidavits.

Undefended divorce

By definition, if you are not proceeding by way of the *pro forma* divorce application based on a two year or five year separation mentioned later, there must either be children of the marriage under the age of 16 or financial issues to be resolved. Affidavits evidencing the facts pled to justify divorce will have to be obtained. Clients often assume that if, for instance, they both want a divorce, both accept one spouse has committed adultery and are both prepared to swear affidavits to that effect then they must be able to get a divorce. That is, of course, not the case. Section 8(3) of the Civil Evidence (Scotland) Act 1988 provides that the evidence required—

> "shall consist of or include evidence other than that of a party to the marriage."

This is to avoid collusion. The evidence of one witness, without any evidence from the spouses, could in theory suffice if that witness was not one of the spouses. In practice the pursuer would normally give evidence by way of Affidavit. The Civil Evidence (Scotland) Act 1988 allows the Lord Advocate to provide that Section 8(3) will not apply to certain types of actions (s .8(4) and (5)). The Evidence in Divorce Actions (Scotland) Order 1989 (S.I. 1989 No. 582) provides that these above requirements do not apply to actions that meet all of the following conditions—

— they are undefended
— based on the two year or five year separation

— the pursuer confirms there are no other proceedings pending in any court which could have the effect of bringing the marriage to an end
— there are no children of the marriage under 16 years of age.
— neither party is applying for financial provision on divorce.
— neither party suffers from a mental disorder, within the meaning of section 1(2) of the Mental Health (Scotland) Act 1984

hence the *pro forma* application used for these types of divorce.

Affidavits about children where no section 11 order sought

The question of whether or not Affidavits should be produced in these circumstances has generated a lot of discussion.

Section 12 of the Children (Scotland) Act 1995 states that in any action for divorce, judicial separation or declarator of nullity of marriage the Court has a duty to consider, in the light of such information as is before the Court, whether to exercise powers under section 11 (orders relating to parental responsibilities, etc.)and 54 (referral to Principal Reporter) of the Act in relation to any child of the family under the age of 16. However, it has no obligation to be satisfied about the arrangements for children before divorce is granted.

Where the Court is of the opinion that the circumstances of the case "require" or are likely to require it to exercise a power under section 11 or 54 it can postpone its decision (s. 12(2)).

As is so often the case you should know or find out the practice in the Court to which you are applying and proceed accordingly. In broad terms it can be do no harm to give some basic information about the welfare of the children where you have it and to provide evidence of facts to indicate that there is no need for the Court to exercise its powers under section 11 or 54.

Once the necessary evidence is available an application can be made by Minute in appropriate form supported by the Affidavits and relevant productions (OCR 33.29 and Form F27) and supported by the appropriate fee. Extract decree is issued no earlier than 14 days after the divorce has been granted (OCR 33.30).

Affidavits about children where a section 11 order is sought

The rules under OCR33.28 and 33.29 still apply but are added to by OCR 33.31 which states—

> "(1) Where no notice of intention to defend has been lodged in a family action for a section 11 Order, any proceedings in the cause shall be dealt with by the sheriff in chambers.

> (2) In an action to which paragraph (1) applies, decree may be pronounced after such inquiry as the sheriff thinks fit."

The procedure for these situations varies from court to court but you should be ready, and expect, to lodge affidavits covering the elements set out in the Sheriff Principal's practice note for affidavits. In our view you should set out facts confirming that it is better that an order be made than that no order be made (to meet the terms of the Children (Scotland) Act 1995, s. 11(7)(a)). The need to take account of the views of a child where appropriate (S.11(7)(b)) should have been met by service of the Form F9.

Defended actions that become undefended

Later on an action may become undefended. The options for how the undefended action can be dealt with are laid out in OCR 33.37. Depending on the type of action you could get decree, have an undefended proof (for instance where the action becomes undefended on the day of the proof and witnesses are present) or proceed by affidavit evidence as set out above.

Defended actions

Where an action is defended the terms of OCR 33.34 to 33.72 should be considered for their applicability to the particular type of action you are involved in. The use of Minutes for particular categories of interested parties and others should be noted. Our aim is simply to cover key steps on the way from the service of the Initial Writ to the Options Hearing.

Notice of intention to defend

This must be lodged where the intention is to oppose any crave to seek an order, to make a claim or challenge jurisdiction (see OCR 33.34). The notice is in Form F26.

Timetabling

The court issues a note to the parties on receiving a notice of intention to defend giving—

— the last day for defences
— the last day for adjustment
— the date of the Options Hearing

These dates should be given to your client with a clear explanation as to what defences, adjustments and an Options Hearing are and what they need to do. Remind the client of the need for the parties to attend the Options Hearing (OCR 33.36).

Defences

OCR 33.34 states that where a defender seeks—

"(a) to oppose any crave in the Initial Writ;

(b) to make a claim for—

(i) aliment;
(ii) an order for financial provision within the meaning of section 8(3) of the Act of 1985; or
(iii) a section 11 Order; or

(c) an order—

(i) under section 16(1)(b) or (3) of the Act of 1985 (setting aside or varying agreement as to financial provision);
(ii) under section 18 of the Act of 1985 (which relates to avoidance transactions); or
(iii) under the Act of 1981

(d) to challenge the jurisdiction of the court."

then he sets out in his defences—

—"craves;
—averments in the answers to the condescendence in support
   of these craves;
—appropriate pleas-in-law."

Where a section 11 Order is sought by the defender, which
would have required a warrant for intimation if it had been sought
in the Initial Writ, the defender includes a crave for intimation or
to dispense with intimation (OCR 33.34(3)). This is done on the
same basis as set out under OCR 33.7.

When to lodge defences

The defences have to be lodged within 14 days after the expiry of
the period of notice in the action (OCR 9.6(1)). Beyond what is
stated above the defences are in the form of answers in numbered
paragraphs corresponding to the articles of condescendence with
pleas-in-law for the defender at the end (OCR 9.6(2)).

The terms of OCR 9.6(3) suggest that no crave or averments
are needed in the defences to support any order under section 11
of the Children (Scotland) Act 1995. This directly contradicts
OCR 33.34 (1) and (2)(b). The best course is to put in craves and
averments under OCR 33.34 but, the terms of OCR 9.6(3) should
be remembered if objection is taken to a claim for a section 11
Order where you do not have supporting craves or averments. The
object is, presumably, to achieve the right outcome for children
where that outcome is not actually craved and to give the Court a
flexible fallback rule on which they can base a judgement that
does not reflect what is craved.

Drafting defences

The same principles applied to drafting mentioned in Chapter 6
should also be applied to drafting defences. Have a consistent
structured approach to what you do.

Adjustment

Adjustment of the pleadings is allowed up to 14 days before the
Options Hearing or any continuation of it (OCR 9.8(1)).

Adjustments are exchanged between agents, but not lodged in
process (OCR 9.8(2)) although be careful to lodge adjusted

pleadings prior to hearings taking place before the Options Hearing (OCR 9.4).

Changes to the instance and craves

OCR 18.1 makes it clear that "any sum sued for" in a cause of the initial writ can be changed before the closing of the record by "amending" the crave and intimating the amendment to every other party. Notwithstanding the use of the word "amending" the implication is that the procedure could be dealt with by a note of adjustments as OCR 18.2 refers to a formal minute of amendment being required to adjust the sum sued for after the closing of the record (implying it is not required before the record is closed).

The distinction between amendment and adjustment prior to the closing of the record has, in practice, become blurred probably because of an imprecise use of the word "pleadings". Sheriff MacPhail (*Sheriff Court Practice*, p. 263 at 9.01)defines "pleadings" as "the written statements by the parties of their grounds of action and defence which, when finally adjusted, form the Closed Record... The first written pleading is the Initial Writ, which embodies the Pursuer's claim."

The definition implies that the word "pleadings" could include the instance and craves of the Initial Writ in which case OCR9.8(1) would allow alteration of the crave and instance by adjustment as being "pleadings". However, Sheriff MacPhail suggests that, in fact, they can only be altered by amendment (*Sheriff Court Practice,* p. 309 at 10.01). OCR 18.2(2) (a) and (b) specifically refer to the power of the Sheriff to allow amendment of the craves and instance, although it could be argued that the rule is intended to cover the wider situation of changes after the Record is closed.

The bottom line is your client probably does not want you to be the pioneer of change to the interpretation of the finer points of the rules. On that basis any alteration to the instance and craves of the Initial Writ should be by way of Minute of Amendment with other changes by adjustment prior to the closing of the Record.

Implied admissions

Remember you have to answer every statement of fact made by every other party. If a statement by one party within the knowledge of another party is not denied by that other party the other party is deemed to have admitted the fact (OCR 9.7).

Entering the process by minute over section 11 orders and aliment

Where an application is made by a person other than the pursuer or defender for a section 11 Order or any order for aliment for a child that is done by Minute (OCR 33.39). A style minute is provided in the Appendix.

Child welfare hearings and other interim steps

See Chapter 9.

Making mistakes

We all make mistakes. Remember OCR 2.1 allows you relief from the consequences of a failure to comply with rules where the failure is due to "mistake, oversight or other excusable cause". Also remember that the relief is at the discretion of the sheriff so do not bank on it being exercised every time.

Where the adjustment period is over you can seek to amend before and even during proof (OCR 18.2) but remember this is again a discretion. The later you are the more difficult it is to get a favourable exercise of the discretion.

No options hearing required

The adjustment to OCR 9.2 dealing with Options Hearings made by OCR (1A) and (1B) should be noted.

"(1A) where in a family action—

(i) the only matters in dispute are an order in terms of section 11 of the Children (Scotland) Act 1995 (court orders relating to parental responsibilities etc.) (b) or
(ii) the matters in dispute include an order in terms of section 11 of that Act

there shall be no requirement to fix an options hearing in terms of paragraph (1) above in so far as the matters in dispute relate to an order in terms of section 11(2) of the Children (Scotland) Act 1995.

(1B) In paragraph (1A) above "family action" has the meaning given to it in rule 33.1(1)".

This is presumably because disputes over parental rights and responsibilities are focussed at the Child Welfare Hearing instead of the Options Hearing.

The options hearing

Much was expected of the Options Hearing when it was introduced under the current ordinary cause rules. It was going to be the moment when the judiciary got hold of cases and agents and metaphorically, if not quite literally, shook them into a semblance of streamlined order.

The intention has not been matched by the reality. In most jurisdictions too little time is allocated to the process in busy court timetables. The hearing tends to veer toward formality rather than interactive investigation. The opportunity to push unfocussed proceedings in the right direction is nevertheless welcome. Used properly an Options Hearing can be an opportunity to move your case forward in a constructive way.

The rules are laid out in OCR 9.12. The only apparent difference between a family Options Hearing and any other in terms of the rules is that all parties are required to attend a family Options Hearing except on cause shown (OCR 33.36). It is odd, but worth noting, that it is not a default if a party fails to appear personally (OCR 33.37). However the court will be likely to be deeply unimpressed if a party fails to appear and has sufficient general powers in the context of the hearing to make a failure to appear extremely unwise.

Procedure prior to the options hearing

The Options Hearing is automatically fixed on the lodging of a notice of intention to defend for "the first suitable court day occurring not sooner than ten weeks after the expiry of the period of notice" (OCR 9.2) (the "period of notice" being that within which the intention to defend has to be intimated).

The date for the hearing is intimated in form G5 along with the timescale for lodging defences and for adjustment. As mentioned previously it is a good idea to have a standard letter sent out to your client on receipt of the G5 explaining the timetable, what defences and adjustments involve, the significance of the record and what the Options Hearing is for. Most importantly the letter can confirm the need to attend.

Over the weeks leading up to the Options Hearing you are adjusting to provide any extra detail needed for your clients case to take account of information coming to hand and averments from the other side. One of the more irritating things that can happen within the procedure is the lodging of a last-minute set of adjustments. Made by the other side at about one minute to five on the last date for adjustment you have no time to respond within the adjustment period. We have all received them and, I suspect, most of us have on occasion lodged them. If you do lodge them late the minimum courtesy required is to tell the agent on the other side that you'll have no objection to their late adjustments in response to the specific points raised by you.

Procedurally the situation is slightly tricky in that the rules require the lodging of a record that reflects the pleadings up to the last date allowed for adjustment. It may be that the particular sheriff court has a standard accepted practice in such situations, in which case try and find out what it is and follow it. Otherwise in the above situation it would be unwise to assume that it is okay to lodge an updated record including late adjustments. A common approach is to lodge two records one to the correct date and one incorporating the late adjustments with a covering letter to the sheriff clerk explaining that a joint motion will be made to the court to allow the up-to-date record to be received in place of the earlier record. This will usually be allowed if both agents want it. In any event the sheriff can order that a closed record including late adjustments be lodged within seven days of the Options Hearing under rule 9.12 (6) (b).

If you find yourself having to amend as a result of late adjustments then you have the remedy of seeking the expenses entailed from the other side.

The lodging of the open record

The pursuer has to lodge a certified copy of the record in process not later than two days before the Options Hearing (OCR 9.11 (2)). Proceed on the basis that two days is two full days and you will not go wrong. In other words if the Options Hearing is on the Friday lodge it by 5 p.m. on the Tuesday at the latest.

Lodging rule 22 notes

Remember that if you intend to insist on a preliminary plea your rule 22 note has to be lodged not later than three days before the Options Hearing (OCR 22.1 (1)).

It is now only "on cause shown" that a party can raise matters in addition to those set out in the Rule 22 Note at Debate or Proof before Answer (OCR 22.1(4)). It is therefore essential that your Rule 22 Note is rigorously thought through to ensure it covers all the debate points you wish to make.

Appearing at the options hearing

Your experience may be that, in your court, an Options Hearing is over in seconds and dealt with in the most perfunctory manner. No matter what the past experience you should still try and make the hearing work for your client.

OCR 9.12 (1) states—

"at the Options Hearing the sheriff shall seek to secure the expeditious progress of the cause by ascertaining from parties the matters in dispute."

If "expeditious" (and expeditious is pretty much another word for quick) progress is to be made then facts need to be specifically pled, documentary evidence produced and real issues clarified. If this has not been done before, due to a failure on the other side, this is a vital opportunity to get orders to ensure it is done now. The incidental orders available under section 14 of the Family Law (Scotland) Act 1985 should be considered. Along with the more specific incidental orders available the terms of section 14 (2) (k) allow to be made "any ancillary order which is expedient to give effect to" the principles set out in section 9 and orders under section 8 (2) of the Act. In some Courts such orders would require a written Motion, in others they can put forward by verbal Motion at the Options Hearing—check the approach taken in the court you are attending.

Do not be afraid to look for—

— orders for valuations of matrimonial property to be produced within a specified period (the Family Law (Scotland)Act 1985 s. 14(2)(b).)

— details of resources to be produced within a specified time (the Family Law (Scotland)Act 1985 section 20)

— clarification of whether the divorce crave is actually to be defended at proof or whether that aspect can be disposed of by affidavit evidence

— admissions to be considered for inclusion in a joint minute of admissions

— a remit to mediation under OCR 33.22 where children are involved or, perhaps, to CALM for all issues mediation on the basis of the sheriff's general authority to make orders, as he thinks fit, on matters other than the extent of the proof, the lodging of a joint minute of admissions or agreement (OCR 9.12 (3) (a))

— confirmation as to whether residence is still in dispute where there is perhaps only limited contact taking place under an interim order and a residence award is unlikely

— an order for a report by a psychologist or other expert. A report ordered by the court may be more likely to persuade parties than a report from an expert instructed by one party.

— a proof on the merits of the divorce alone if the merits of the divorce are still challenged, with any proof on the financial provision postponed (OCR 29.6). There is no point in going to the expense of a proof on financial issues where those financial issues actually depend on a ground for divorce being proved and there is some doubt as to them being proved.

The above is not an exhaustive list simply illustrative. Always seek a time limit for any disclosure or valuation to be dealt with. The powers given under OCR 9.12 taken with the powers available under the Family Law (Scotland) Act are such that you should be able to find a way of justifying requests you need to make to push matters forward.

Preparation

OCR 9.12 (2) states—

"it shall be the duty of parties to provide the sheriff with sufficient information to enable him to conduct the hearing as provided for in this rule."

that means knowing the elements of what you want, what your legal propositions are for getting them and the main facts supporting those propositions. It means knowing the key issues for your client, the admissions he or she is prepared to make, and the admissions you hope to obtain from the other side.

OCR 9.12 (3) to (5) gives the sheriff various possible disposals—

— proof
— orders as to the extent of proof
— orders as to the lodging of a joint minute of admissions or agreement
— making such orders as he thinks fit
— proof before answer
— debate
— additional procedure under OCR Chapter 10
— a continuation of the Options Hearing on one occasion only for a period not exceeding 28 days or to the first suitable court day thereafter.

From this you can gather that the sheriff has the widest powers in seeking the expeditious progress of the cause. You need to know which option you want him or her to take and why. If a Debate is sought then you need to be ready with an outline of your arguments in support of your rule 22 Note.

You will have gathered from the above that, under nearly all circumstances, you should attend the Options Hearing yourself if you are the principal agent. If you do not your correspondent should have sufficient instructions to allow him to give your client exactly the same level of service as if you had attended.

Whoever conducts the Options Hearing your client needs to be told where to sit before the case calls, what to do when the case calls and reminded what happens when the case calls. The practice varies widely from court to court. Your responsibility is to know what happens in this particular court.

The continued options hearing

Exactly the same criteria apply to a continued Options Hearing as applied to the original Options Hearing. Remember that an

Options Hearing cannot be continued a second time (OCR 9.12 (5)).

Additional optional procedure

OCR9.12(4) states—

> "At the Options Hearing the sheriff may, having heard parties—
>
> (a) of his own motion or on the motion of any party, and
> (b) on being satisfied that the difficulty or complexity of the cause makes it unsuitable for the procedure under this chapter,
>
> order that the cause proceed under the procedure in Chapter 10 (additional procedure)."

The procedure is rarely used in the Sheriff Court and should be reserved for cases where, for instance, there are complex factual elements to be clarified, over business interests and the like.

OCR Chapter 10 sets out the rules for additional procedure. The case is initially continued for 8 weeks for adjustment OCR 10.1(1) with the same rules for the exchange of adjustments as applied prior to the Options Hearing for the normal procedure.

The record can be closed within the period of adjustment if parties seek it jointly or of consent (OCR 10.3(1)).

An extension of the adjustment period can be sought under (OCR 10.3(2)). At the end of the adjustment period the record is closed without any steps being required from the parties and a hearing termed a "Procedural Hearing" is fixed (OCR 10.5).

At the Procedural Hearing the Sheriff, as with the Options Hearing, seeks to "secure the expeditious progress of the cause under OCR 10(6)(3). He can—

(a) Fix a proof and make such other orders as he thinks fit
(b) Fix a proof before Answer (having considered any rule 22 note) and make such other orders as he thinks fit
(c) Fix a Debate (having considered any rule 22 note) and being satisfied there is a preliminary matter of law justifying it.

There is no provision under the rules for a continuation of the Procedural Hearing.

Conclusion

The journey to the Options Hearing and the Options Hearing itself can provide opportunities to put your case in order, and to resolve and clarify issues. Alternatively, it can be a series of pointless stopping places on the way to an ill focussed, expensive proof. Your responsibility is to make it, as much as possible, the former rather than the latter.

CHAPTER 12

DEBATES AND APPEALS

The Debate

What is it for?

As we discussed earlier on, each party is entitled to expect certain basic elements from the other party—

- A competent action
- A relevant action
- Sufficient specification

A Debate is an opportunity to challenge the other side's written statement of their position on the ground that it is deficient in one of these areas. More detailed information about Debates can be found in I.D. MacPhail, *Sheriff Court Practice,* at p. 407 onwards Our intention is simply to look at the bare bones of particular relevance to family law practice.

When can they happen?

Debates are comparatively rare in Family Law actions because clients and solicitors usually find that the advantages of proceeding to Debate are outweighed by the disadvantages. There is an erroneous, but strongly held, current of opinion that somehow the standards for family actions are different from other actions. It is true to say that many sheriffs will be reluctant to send family cases to Debate but the fact of the matter is the same requirements of fair notice, relevancy and competency apply to family actions as apply to any other civil action. The difficulty is of course that you cannot insist on a Debate at the Options Hearing, it is a matter for the sheriff to consider based on the information presented to him (see Chapter 11).

There are occasions when a Debate should be sought. A client who denies the truth of grounds given for divorce is just as entitled as any other defender in civil proceedings to proper specification of the grounds given. There is no reason why someone seeking a divorce based on unreasonable behaviour should be excused the need to set out specifics of the nature and timing of behaviour resulting in the claim for divorce (but see our comments on when to seek a Debate below). The behaviour must be linked causally to the fact that the pursuer cannot reasonably be expected to cohabit with the defender (*Findlay v. Findlay,* 1991 S.L.T. 457 but see also *Smith v. Smith,* 1994 S.C.L.R. 244 and Clive, at 381).

On financial issues there can be substantial gaps or a lack of detail in what is averred about the financial position of a particular party, there may be no averments to support a particular plea-in-law. A Debate may be useful to force clarification, the removal of unspecific averments or the unsupported plea-in-law.

When to seek a debate

Before asking for a Debate always consider what benefit there will be to your client. Is it going to be helpful to your client to spell out the deficiencies in the other side's case?

Do remember that by asking for specifics on divorce, your client may get more than he or she bargained on in terms of blackening detail. He or she may end up wishing the divorce element had allowed to drift through in an unspecific but less damaging way.

A Debate involves effort, time and expense. If you can successfully attack another party's pleadings at a Debate and they see that you are right, or are given a nudge by the Sheriff, they will seek leave to amend. You may get the expenses of the Debate but they will put their case in order. If the parties have limited overall funds an award of expenses will simply reduce the resources available to the other party to meet your client's claims.

There might have been a far better outcome if the other party were left to go to Proof or Proof before Answer and be limited in the evidence they were able to lead by the paucity of averments there to support evidence (see *Ross v. Ross,* 1997 S.L.T. (Sh. Ct) 51 and *Knox v. Knox,* 1993 S.C.L.R. 381).

On the other hand where sweeping statements of an unspecific nature are made about your client in a contact action there may well be reason to challenge them rather than let your client's ability to look after his child be attacked through a welter of unspecific and therefore unanswerable allegations which would allow the other side to produce any number of surprise bits of evidence at proof. Ultimately the circumstances of the individual case have to be looked at and, advantages and disadvantages of going to Debate weighed up.

How is it obtained?

In order to obtain a Debate a relevant plea in law has to be in place in your pleadings. A note of the basis of your preliminary plea has to be lodged in process not later that 3 days before the Options hearing a copy of it has to be intimated to every other party (OCR 22.1). As mentioned in chapter 10 matters not mentioned in your Rule 22 Note can only be raised "on cause shown" (OCR 22.1(4)). The down side of this is that you need to be rigorous in thinking through your debate points before drafting the Rule 22 Note. The upside is that you should have full notice of the Debate points your opponent intends to make. If not, he will only be able to introduce them if he can show why they were not canvassed in the original Rule 22 Note.

Where an Options hearing is continued and a preliminary plea is added by adjustment the party intending to insist on the plea has to, again not later than three days before the date of the continued Options hearing, lodge a note of the basis for the plea and intimate a copy of it to every other party.

At the options hearing

If the Sheriff has closed the Record he or she is still bound by the primary aim of seeking to "secure the expeditious progress of the cause" (OCR 9.12 (1)). If you ask for a Debate the Sheriff has a choice of fixing a Proof, a Proof before answer or a Debate. A Debate is fixed if the Sheriff is "satisfied that there is a preliminary matter of law which justifies a Debate" (OCR 9.12 (3)(c)).

The party wanting the Debate has to satisfy the Sheriff that there is a preliminary point of law justifying it (see *Blair Bryden Partnership v. Adair*, 1995 S.L.T. (Sh. Ct) 98).

It is important to note that the Options hearing is only to decide whether a Debate should be ordered and not to make a decision on the issues to be canvassed at the Debate. (See *Ritchie v. Cleary*, 1995 S.C.L.R. 561).

Preparation

Once a Debate has been fixed you need to prepare for it.

Timing

There is a great temptation to leave preparation for a Debate until the last day or so before it is due to happen. The result is that you discover, disconcertingly late, either that your proposed Debate point is not quite as strong as you had thought or that the other side's Debate point is really rather good. You are left scrabbling for a discharge of the Debate with the knowledge that, at best, you may have to concede the expenses of the Debate to the other side, at worst, you are going to have to make a verbal motion at the Debate to have it discharged to allow you to lodge a Minute of Amendment.

Because of Court timetabling Debates are usually fixed a considerable time after an Options hearing. The best time to prepare for the Debate is as soon as possible after that Options hearing. Certainly you should aim to have done your preparation at least 14 days in advance of the Debate. The usual experience is that you set aside two or three hours for preparation and then find that, as a result of your preparation, you need to read several cases and that the preparation time required expands.

There are different elements to what happens at a Debate. You have to be ready for what you are going to say, what the other side are going to say and what the Sheriff is going to say.

What to prepare

Preparation is possibly best done in stages. If it is your preliminary plea—

- prepare what your arguments are going to be
- put your opponent's shoes on and consider his or her arguments
- revise your argument in the light of those arguments
- if it is your opponent's preliminary plea again put on his or her shoes and consider the arguments to be advanced
- prepare your counter arguments

It is necessary to have to hand in written form something sufficient to allow you to remember and, if necessary, show the development of the particular legal proposition in question from originating statute/case law to date.

Having grasped the law you then need to see how the particular facts plead, craves and pleas-in-law inserted in the case fit in with the general legal principles you have established to meet arguments on competency, relevancy and specification.

Many Debates are discharged after preparation simply because one or other party realises that he or she is going to have problems at the Debate and agrees to amend prior to it. Having made your analysis of the relative merits of each sides position it is helpful to telephone the other side to confirm the points to be raised by him or her and by you. The expense of many a Debate has been avoided by a phone call made in advance.

Remember each solicitor is limited to taking points mentioned in the note of the basis of preliminary plea other than "on cause shown" (OCR 22.1 (4)). If the other side tries to introduce new matters be prepared to argue that there is no cause shown for the introduction. Where new matters are allowed to be raised you may have a remedy in expenses.

In preparing remember that, for the purposes of the Debate, each parties averments are to be taken as true. An action can only be dismissed if it must, of necessity, fail (*Jamieson v. Jamieson,* 1952 S.L.T. 257).

The Court will usually only dismiss an action on the grounds of relevancy in the most exceptional circumstances. Even where an action is dismissed at first instance on many occasions a party will be allowed back in if they appeal and turn up to the appeal with a beautifully worded Minute of Amendment.

Lodging authorities

Most Courts have a practice note confirming when lists of authorities should be lodged. Usually it is at least the day before the diet although it can be longer. You should send a copy of your list of authorities to your opponent as a matter of courtesy.

Conduct of the debate

Structure

Where only one party has stated a preliminary plea or pleas that party's solicitor opens the Debate. Where both parties have stated a preliminary plea the defender starts. This is because, if his plea is sustained, there will be no need to consider his defence.

An exception to this might be where the defender has only a limited plea to, for instance, the relevance of particular averments by the pursuer while the pursuer has a general plea to the relevancy of the defences. In that situation a possibility of reversing the order of speaking should be canvassed with the other solicitor and if appropriate proposed to the Sheriff at the beginning of the Debate.

After the opening speech the other solicitor makes a speech in reply and may present an argument in support of his plea. Usually the first speaker would then reply with the second speaker making a final response but really you have to be guided by the practice of the particular Sheriff in the particular court.

The opening speaker gives a brief description of the case and confirms which pleas are to be Debated.

Usually the Sheriff will have read the Record before the Debate. If you are the first speaker you should check that that is the case and if not, the Record may have to be read out loud in open Court, although this once common practice, is now extremely rare.

Having established the content of the Record the opening speaker presents his or her arguments. A good way is to

—confirm the pleas-in-law you wish to have sustained or repelled;

—give a short listing of the arguments to be made;

—give the structure within which you intend to make them

—make your arguments;

—conclude by summarising your position if appropriate.

If you are attacking the relevancy or specification of particular averments draw the Sheriff's attention to them.

In presenting your case you should have a plea in law supporting your argument. If there is no plea in law then the other side will be likely to object.

There can be a degree of fluidity about Debates. It is sometimes the case that one party seeks the leave of the Court during the Debate to make a minor amendment to their pleadings subject to any provisos about expenses and the possible adjournment or discharge of the Debate. If it is clear you need to amend be prepared to ask the Sheriff for leave to amend rather than battling on to the end of the Debate with no benefit, but more expense, to your client.

After the initial arguments have been presented against the responding party's pleadings it makes good sense as the respondent to first counter the arguments put forward and then move on to attacking the other side's pleadings. A sensible way forward is to confirm the plea-in-law you wish sustained or repelled, give a short listing of the arguments you intend to make, your structure within which you intend to make them and then make your arguments, again summarising at the end if appropriate.

Watching the shrieval reaction

Some Sheriffs will maintain a poker face throughout a Debate, others will positively overflow with heavily weighted comments and sighs suggesting directly or indirectly that one party might like to take their pleadings away and change them. If you can get an insight into how the Sheriff is thinking you can save yourself time and embarrassment by conceding gracefully where necessary, concentrating your strongest arguments in countering a perceived weakness in your position, or pushing a position that is finding favour.

The decision

Often decisions following Debates are taken to *avizandum*. Prepare your client for a delay in knowing the outcome

Expenses

If you have been successful at Debate remember to seek expenses of the Debate and any other expenses directly related to the other side's failures, which precede or follow on (for instance related amendment procedure).

Appeal (after debate)

If an action or part of an action has been dismissed think about an appeal. You need to decide whether the failure in the pleadings is remediable, in which case an appeal may be the way forward, or irremediable, in which case there is no benefit to you or your client in banging heads off brick walls. The Sheriff Principal is unlikely to see an action or part of an action lost simply through a pleading mistake. If a mistake is remediable you have a reasonable prospect of being allowed to make the necessary amendment on appeal to allow you to move forward.

Appeals

Appeals are not that common in family actions primarily because many of the decisions made are discretionary in nature and therefore unlikely to be overturned other than in exceptional circumstances. We simply want to give a brief overview of what is involved. For a more comprehensive consideration of appeal procedure ideally MacPhail *Sheriff Court Practice,* at page 569 onwards, should be your starting point.

While mentioning the basics of the appeal procedure we want to highlight any of those elements which are of particular significance to the family law practitioner.

The methods of review

Appeal, reduction, suspension and the exercise of the *nobile officium* are the four normal methods of review available for Sheriff Court decisions. The latter three all take place in the Court of Session leaving only the conventional appeal being within the remit of this book.

What can be appealed against

Broadly speaking appeals are possible against—

1. Final judgement
2. Particular types of interlocutors
3. Other types of interlocutors against which leave to appeal is required

Final judgements

A final judgement is defined in section 3(h) of the Sheriff Court (Scotland) Act 1907 as being—

> "an interlocutor which, by itself, or taken along with previous interlocutors, disposes of the subject matter of the cause, notwithstanding that judgement may not have been pronounced on every question raised, and that the expenses found due may not have been modified, taxed or decerned for."

(For a fuller interpretation of this definition see MacPhail, *Sheriff Court Practice* at p. 580.)

Remember that you cannot challenge any of the findings in fact unless the shorthand writers notes have been extended. If necessary get them extended.

Appeals without leave

These include—

— Interim interdict (although the interim interdict is binding until recalled).
— Interim decree for payment of money other than expenses.
— Interim orders for payment of specified sums other than aliment. (*Irving v. Irving,* 1998 S.C.L.R. at 373 and *Wilson v. Wilson,* 2001 S.L.T. (Sh. Ct) 55 should be noted.) The issue in both cases was whether leave was required to appeal against a decision on an application under section 2(4)(b) of the Matrimonial Homes (Family Protection) (Scotland) Act 1981 for a contribution towards mortgage repayments. Sheriff Principal Kerr in *Wilson* decided leave was needed on the basis that it was an order to provide interim financial support to the family and was so close in type to interim aliment that leave was required.
— Orders *ad factum praestandum.* (including orders to appear at the bar, awards of contact or residence to which an order for delivery is attached but not an award of interim contact without an order for delivery) (see *Black v. Black,* 1991 S.L.T. (Sh. Court) 5).
— Orders to sist

— Orders allowing, refusing or limiting the form of proof

Appeals with leave

A sheriff can grant leave to appeal either of his own volition or on the motion of a party. If the sheriff is granting the leave of his own volition then that should be noted in the interlocutor against which the leave to appeal is given.

The party seeking leave to appeal makes a motion to the sheriff and has to do so within seven days of the date of the interlocutor against which leave to appeal is sought (unless it has been extracted early following a motion under OCR 30.4(2)) (OCR 31.2(1)).

Where leave has been granted the appellant then has a further seven days within which to mark the appeal (OCR 31.2 (2)).

Matters that are appealable with the leave of the sheriff include—

— awards of interim aliment
— allowing a minute of amendment to be received or granting leave to amend
— granting or refusing a commission and diligence
— refusing a sist
— interim decisions governing residence and contact. The terms of OCR rule 31.9 should be noted—

"where an appeal is marked against an interlocutor making an order under section 11 of the Children (Scotland) Act 1985 (Court orders relating to parental responsibilities, *etc.*) or in respect of aliment, the marking of that appeal shall not excuse obedience to or implement of that order unless by order of the sheriff, the sheriff principal or the Court of Session, as the case may be."

It should be noted that where one part of the interlocutor would require leave to appeal if stated on its own and the other would not the appeal can proceed without leave.

The basis on which leave to appeal is granted or refused

The sheriff uses his discretion in deciding in the particular circumstances of each case whether leave should be granted. The type of factors that can come into play are set out in Macphail, *Sheriff Court Practice,* at p. 588, 18.50 to 18.51.

Time limits for appeal

We have already mentioned the time limits for motions where leave to appeal is required. Other interlocutors that can be appealed—

> "may be appealed within 14 days after the date of the interlocutor unless it has been extracted following a motion under rule 30.4(2) (early extract)" (OCR 31.1).

The most important thing to remember is inform the client of the right to appeal and time limit for it. Make sure the last date for appeal is in your diary.

Marking an appeal

OCR Rule 31.4(1) confirms that the form for the note of appeal is form A1.

The form A1 leaves space in which the statement of the grounds on which the appeal is to proceed have to be included. In terms of OCR 31.4 (3) it is stated—

> "The grounds of appeal in a note of appeal shall consist of brief specific numbered propositions stating the grounds on which it is proposed to submit that the appeal should be allowed or as the case may be."

A copy of the appeal has to be sent to every other party (OCR 31.4(4)).

The appellant can change the grounds of appeal at any time up to fourteen days before the date of the hearing of the appeal. If that is done a copy of the amendment is sent to every other party (OCR 31.4(5)).

In the Form A1 there is provision for the solicitor to ask for a "note" from the sheriff. If the request is made then the sheriff has to write a note giving the grounds on which he has proceeded.

Abandoning an appeal

Remember an appeal can not be abandoned unless with the consent of all the other parties or with leave of the sheriff principal (OCR 31.11).

Preparation

The same kind of approach recommended for a debate applies to an appeal. Most sheriff principals will appreciate it if you can produce a short summary or skeleton layout of your submissions. It helps you check your arguments in advance, it can also save time and ensure that the sheriff principal has an accurate record of your basis for your position. The trick is to put enough in to show the line of your argument but not too much so as to overwhelm with detail and to deny you proper flexibility in presenting your argument.

Know your sheriff principal is as important a maxim as know your sheriff. If you do not already know, find out if you can, his or her approach to appeals.

Remember most jurisdictions will have a rule requiring the authorities to be lodged usually at least 48 hours in advance of the appeal. Remember also that, by definition, you are more likely than usual to be dealing with an important point of novelty or controversy. An understanding of the law applicable to the points in issue is all the more essential.

Conducting the appeal

The appellant

The person who is taking the appeal speaks first giving the sheriff principal a short explanation of what the case is about and relevant details of its history.

The next step is to confirm what the sheriff's decision was and those parts of the interlocutor which are being appealed against. You should highlight the issues you consider arise. As appropriate refer to the relevant pleadings and productions.

You should advise the Court how the issues were dealt with referring to the sheriff's note and findings in fact.

You should indicate the terms of the order you are looking to the sheriff principal to pronounce.

Finally indicate where the sheriff has erred and why. If factual findings are being challenged you will need to refer to the relevant passages of evidence with an explanation of why they should not be accepted

Burden on appellant

Do remember that the original interlocutor appealed against will be regarded as correct until the appellant shows why it should be altered. Even if the respondent does not oppose or come to the appeal hearing the appellant still has to show why the appeal should be allowed.

The respondent

The respondent speaks after the appellant. The best way for a respondent to present the counter-argument is less clear-cut but, assuming the appellant has taken a logical progression through his or her grounds of appeal, it makes sense to follow the same order.

After the respondent's speech the sheriff principal will usually give the appellant's agents an opportunity to respond.

If the respondent has appealed him or herself then he or she would normally divide the speech into two parts. He would answer the other side's appeal first and put forward his own appeal second. Obviously the other party would then have an opportunity to answer the appeal made by the other side.

The principles applied on appeal

It is beyond the scope of this book to go into the relevant principles. The comments of Sheriff MacPhail *Sheriff Court Practice,* at p. 612, 18.100 to 18.114 should be noted. Sheriff MacPhail's comments at 18.111 and 18.112 on the rationale for intervention in discretionary decisions are particularly relevant. At its simplest you can say discretionary decisions are unlikely to be overturned on the basis that:

"it is of the essence of a judicial discretion that on the same material different minds may reach widely different decisions, any one of which may reasonably be thought to be the best, and any one of which, therefore, a judge may make without being held to be wrong".(MacPhail, *Sheriff Court Practice,* at p.613 at 18.111).

However discretionary decisions can be overturned where they are, for instance, plainly wrong, or unreasonable, or where the sheriff failed to take into account relevant considerations, erred in balancing material facts, acted in a manner which was manifestly inequitable. The terminology is subjective and leaves scope for appeal notwithstanding the fact that different judicial minds can reach widely differing decisions. If you are challenging a discretion you need to identify early on the specific basis for the challenge you have in mind.

Be sure that the judgment in question is a discretionary one (see for instance *Osborne v. Matthan (No. 2)* 1998 S.C. 682 at 688 to 689 where the Lord President observed that a decision by a judge on parental rights may "be better described not as a matter of discretion but as a matter of judgment exercised on consideration of the relevant factors").

Human rights legislation

The human rights act will undoubtedly increase the scope and number of appeals. (See Chapter 16)

Powers of sheriff principal

A succinct summary of the relevant powers is provided by MacPhail, *Sheriff Court Practice,* at p.600, 18.78 to 18.86. These include—

— dispensing power. The sheriff principal can exercise the same powers as the sheriff under OCR 2.1 (1)
— amendment of pleadings
— back to the sheriff. The sheriff principal can send the case back to the sheriff for specified steps to be taken or for the case to proceed in the normal way.
— further options hearing. Where the appeal has been made before or at an options hearing a further options hearing can be fixed. The sheriff principal has the same powers as the sheriff at the original options hearing to make "such other order as he thinks fit"(OCR 31.8).
— further proof. This can be allowed on the motion of one of the parties (*LRC v. S.*, unreported, Edinburgh Sheriff Court, February 14, 1991)
— refuse the appeal. In other words adhere to the sheriff's decision

— recall the judgment. In other words grant the appeal replacing the original decision. In this context the judgment can be recalled on the basis of the circumstances in place at the time of the appeal as being, for instance, premature

— part refuse/vary. The sheriff principal can grant part and refuse the rest of the appeal or adhere to the original decision with specific variations

— dismiss. If the appeal is abandoned or incompetent it is dismissed

— award expenses. The Sheriff Principal has discretion to decide what expenses if any are to be awarded

Appeal to the Court of Session

You are less likely to be involved in appeals to the Court of Session. Before taking such an appeal counsel's view should normally be canvassed and the form for the appeal should be noted (OCR 31.3).

CHAPTER 13

THE PROOF

Most solicitors tend to have a love/hate relationship with proofs. There is an immediacy to them that is both exciting and anxiety inducing. There's nothing better than feeling you put your client's case smoothly and effectively with a sense of approbation emanating from all corners of the court. However when something goes wrong you would happily disappear.

The person who made the perfect preparation for and presentation of a proof does not exist. This chapter is not intended as a large stick with which to beat yourself for failures. It is intended to give some guidance on how cases should be prepared if we lived in an ideal world.

A great deal is written and said about the mystique of the able advocate, of his or her brilliance on his or her feet, "uncanny insight", "understanding of the law". Some people do have an aptitude for court presentation but it is an aptitude based on hard work that can only function satisfactorily when supported by many elements that have nothing to do with genius or natural talent and everything to do with appropriate attention to detail and preparation at each stage of a case. Where you have prepared well you will have a path to return to in moments of crisis. You will have a clear idea of where you are going and what you want to see and hear on the path. Your presentation will have a coherence and logic. You will almost certainly find that the moments of approbation from the court and your clients far outweigh those of disapprobation.

Preparation

Always prepare

The biggest mistake you can make is to assume a proof will settle and therefore not prepare. If you do not prepare you are weakening your bargaining position with every passing day and increasing your exposure as a professional through lack of preparedness. No matter how sure you are that a case will settle you have to continue to prepare on the assumption that it will not.

Which sheriff/which court?

A proof is, in a sense, a conversation. You may know the law and the rules of court but you need also to know, as far as you can, the peccadilloes of the particular Sheriff you are conversing with and the particular court you are talking in. As with any other conversation you need to try and understand the person you are speaking to and the context in which you are expected to speak. You need to get the Sheriff to listen and to do that you need to present information, as far as possible, in the way he or she wants and will respond to.

The best sources of information are a friend, correspondent, sheriff clerk or someone similar. If the particular court has more than one Sheriff you may find that, even without knowing which Sheriff your going to have, you can get some useful guidance as to the "culture" operating within the court.

In a sense it is regrettable that these things matter so much but they do. Even at the most elementary level different Sheriffs can take widely different views. One Sheriff may consider pleadings almost a tiresome irrelevance in family actions and allow pretty much any evidence in. Another Sheriff may be rigorous in the application of the rules on fair notice. You need to have some idea of what to expect.

A caveat to this is that, even where you think you are getting a Sheriff who pays little attention to the pleadings, you need to be able to present your case to meet the most rigorous application of the rules. On the day of the proof you cannot guarantee you will get the Sheriff you expected. The information on the expected Sheriff is obtained to alert you to potential difficulties and legal points for which you need to be prepared.

The early stages

In essence what you are preparing for is very simple. Your client wants something. You are asking what your client wants in a document (the Writ, then the Record). You produce evidence to prove facts set out in the document to justify your client getting what he or she wants. You point to the legal proposition on which your client's request is based. In other words you need a document, witnesses, productions and a law to get what your client wants. From your own point of view you need to be paid.

To achieve your end the preparation starts from day one with the foundation stone of your precognitions, initial writ and the various further building blocks on the way to the Options Hearing, which we have already discussed. When the proof is fixed certain practical considerations kick in.

Witnesses

You should have checked on availability of witnesses as far as possible before the Options Hearing. Straight after the Options Hearing you should write to all your potential witnesses confirming the proof date and asking them to let you know immediately if there are any difficulties over their attendance. You should confirm that you will be sending them a formal witness citation nearer the time.

You should diary ahead a date three or four weeks before the proof to send out the formal citation. Remember the requirement to send the other side your witness list not later than 28 days before the Proof and to lodge a copy of the list in Process (OCR 9.14). The old version of this rule was usually ignored and yet information about the other side's witnesses may have a profound impact on your client and influence his decision on whether to proceed. If a list has not been produced do not be afraid to write asking for it and even to consider a motion to force it out if you think it is going to be important.

Productions and affidavits

Remember that OCR 29.11(1) in its latest form requires productions and affidavits to be founded upon at proof also to be lodged not later than 14 days before the proof. With the revisal of old OCR 29.3 affidavit evidence must now be admitted for what it is worth by virtue of section 2(1) of the Civil Evidence (Scotland) Act 1988.

Shorthand writer

If you act for the pursuer you should book a shorthand writer for the proof (OCR 29.15).

Funding

On the funding side of things you need to be careful. If your client is a private client this is an important moment to take stock, consider rendering an interim account, give an estimate of the costs of going to proof, give some indication as to the prospects for success at proof. When a client knows the outer and inner limits for his or her own costs and the possible costs for his or her opponent it can concentrate the mind wonderfully on the advantages and disadvantages of going to proof. If a client does not know it can easily lead to dissatisfaction with you when events do not go as he or she had hoped.

If your client is legally aided made sure they are aware of the clawback provisions. Make sure you have obtained sanction for any expert witnesses, have lodged a legal aid certificate and that that legal aid certificate covers all the craves you have included.

Productions

Your productions should all be lodged and numbered. The last date for lodging productions and affidavits to be referred to at proof is 14 days before the proof (OCR 29.11(1)). You should remember you will need to lodge numbered copies of documentary productions for the use of the Sheriff (OCR29.12). You should have a file containing—

- the record
- your productions
- the other sides productions
- your witness list
- your precognitions
- a section for authorities and notes on submissions
- other relevant documents such as copy affidavits and the like.

Each section should be separated by a divider. The better your system for managing paperwork the more time and effort you will be able to give to good presentation of your case, the more easily you can get back on track if things start going wrong.

Section 20 motion/commission and diligence

You should have thought of using these before and considered addressing shortcomings at the Options Hearing but if you are still not satisfied a full disclosure has been made strike now. Remember that a motion under section 20 of the Family Law (Scotland) Act 1985 and commission and diligence are not procedures for compelling the production of valuations (that should be done under section 14 of the act). Section 20 compels the other party to produce information and documents. A commission and diligence compels the other party and third parties to produce documents.

Amendment

Remember that the Sheriff can allow amendment at any time before final judgement (OCR 18.1). The types of amendment allowed are set out in OCR 18.2. The requirements of OCR 18.3 should be noted. Adjustments to Minutes of Amendment and Answers are exchanged between the parties and not lodged in process. The parties have to maintain a record of adjustments made and the date of their intimation. No adjustment is allowed after the period of adjustment allowed except with leave of the Sheriff. Most importantly both parties require to lodge no later than two days before the hearing fixed on the minute and answers (OCR 18.3(2)) a copy of their Minute of Amendment or Answers as adjusted with all adjustments made to them in italics, bold type or underlined (OCR 18.3(6)).

It makes sense to diary ahead for key dates other than the proof diet. The dates we would suggest are a four week, two week, one week, day before preparation opportunity.

Having fulfilled these basic "housekeeping" chores you can focus on ensuring that the fundamentals of your case are in place.

First stage of preparation—checking the fundamentals

A useful way of doing this is to start, even at this early stage, to sketch your proposed submissions. In pulling together the links between your craves, the facts and your pleas in law in a family law case the most important element is the legal basis for your case.

The Family Law (Scotland) Act includes a deceptively simple looking set of principles under section 8 and 9 on financial and property issues which are then fleshed out by other sections and the case law—

— Have you considered all the relevant statutory possibilities?
— Have you framed your craves and pleas in law properly?
— Have all relevant facts that might key in to the statutory possibilities been elicited in interviews with your client and are they in the pleadings?
— Has a full disclosure of relevant financial and other information been obtained from the other side?
— Have up to date values of policies and other property been obtained. This information may be crucial in questions over resources, contributions made since separation and the like
— What do you need to prove?—How will you prove what you need prove?

Remember you may need experts to prove the value of the house, contents, pension, company, etc. if values have not been agreed

— have relevant productions been lodged?
— is their scope for a joint minute of admissions/notice to admit?
— would a motion for the defender to lead at proof be helpful?
— is any evidence to be taken on commission?
— do you have funding for all aspects of the case?
— have you explained the position on expenses to your client in writing?
— has any offer in settlement been considered and put in writing as a marker in any question of expenses
— has your client been given a copy of the record? Does he know what it is for and what "fair notice" means in broad terms?

It is surprising how often possible arguments remain only partially explored or not explored at all even at this relatively late stage. For instance averments about economic advantages suffered/advantages gained may need more detail. There may be new arguments that have only just emerged about resources available to meet a claim. Issues relating to tax and interest may not have been properly considered. Have you averred how the award sought can be met? If you have made a mistake or there is an omission you can, hopefully, put it right now by way of amendment. If you delay you may not be allowed to.

Notices to admit

As part of the above process you have inevitably identified areas of dispute/admission. One of the most frustrating elements of family law practice is the inclusion of unnecessary denials on the part of the opposition which force you to unnecessary expense on the part of your client in producing evidence. You may wish to address what is admitted by way of a joint minute of admissions but still find that you are getting little cooperation. There is a little used mechanism for getting round this called a notice to admit. With the notice to admit you are effectively calling on your opponent to admit for the purposes of the particular cause only—

"(a) such facts relating to an issue averred in the pleadings as may be specified in the notice;

(b) that a particular document lodged in process and specified in the notice is—

(i) an original and properly authenticated document; or
(ii) a true copy of an original and properly authenticated document" (OCR 29.14).

Where the notice has been intimated and the other party does not admit a fact so specified or does not admit or seeks to challenge the authenticity of a document specified in the notice that person has to, within twenty one days after the date of intimation of the notice, intimate a notice of non-admission. That notice of non-admission has to state the fact or document challenged. If this is not done then that party is deemed to have admitted the fact or document specified in the notice to admit for the purposes of the proof. It should be noted that "on special cause shown" the Sheriff can direct otherwise. Where the party receiving the notice to admit does not intimate a notice of a non-admission within twenty one days after the notice to admit that party is liable to the party intimating the notice to admit for the expenses of proving the fact or document specified in the notice if ultimately required unless the Sheriff, on special cause shown, otherwise directs.

The party serving the notice to admit or the notice of non-admission has to lodge a copy of it in process (OCR 23.14(5)).

This rule has been tempered by the addition of OCR 29.14(7) and (8). OCR 29.14(7) says the Sheriff may, at any time, allow a party to amend or withdraw an admission made on such conditions as the Sheriff thinks fit. OCR 29.14(8) allows a party at any time to withdraw, in whole or in part, a notice of non-admission by intimating a notice of withdrawal. A style Notice to Admit is included in the Appendix.

Second stage four weeks before the proof—starting your final preparation

The proof may seem a long way away. However our view is that at this stage you should be preparing your submissions in detail and reviewing the case law. This gives you an opportunity to revisit your productions, record and precognitions to see whether any final re-precognosing of witnesses or minor amendments are required.

One of the difficulties with family law cases is that, particularly where children are involved, the factual situation can be changing right up until, literally, the day of the proof. The fact that this happens and that some sheriffs take a relaxed view towards pleadings in family law cases does not mean that you can count on getting one of those sheriffs and therefore fail to follow the normal rules on providing fair notice of your client's position. If things have changed and you do need to amend there is still time for you to seek to do so by minute of amendment.

Our comments later on in this chapter about court craft and preparation for examination of witnesses should be noted.

Two weeks before the proof—completing your preparation

Different people work better with different systems for the presentation of a client's case at proof. For most of us a consistent method of headings/colour/layout is useful.

Especially where there is a complex interrelation of statutory provisions on financial issues there is a lot to be said for producing a typed basis for your final submissions for the sheriff. The art is in putting enough down so that the document can act as a useful *aide memoire* to the sheriff while leaving enough room for manoeuvre for it to fit in with what actually happens in court. Where complex maths are involved sheriffs are usually particularly grateful to have something typed in front of them (as you probably will be!) but do not over elaborate. Keep it simple and clear.

Make sure all your productions and affidavits have been lodged (remembering that they should have been lodged "not later" than 14 days before the date of the proof OCR 29.11(1)).

One week before proof

You should submit your list of authorities both to the court and the other side. You should ensure your list of witnesses has not changed since lodging it and if it has, have it typed up for the court with a copy for the Sheriff, bar officer and shorthand writer. Check you have lodged the copy productions for the use of the Sheriff (OCR 29.12). It is good practice to also provide the Sheriff with an extra copy of the record for his or her own use.

The last meeting with a client is an opportunity to run through the practicalities of what happens in court, giving information about the participants, order of witnesses, how witnesses are questioned. If appropriate give your client some advice about what he or she might wear.

In larger courts it is extremely useful to find out which sheriff is likely to be dealing with your case. If you do not know the type of approach taken by the individual in question find out if you can.

The day before—refreshing your memory and checking your administration

This is the time to refresh your memory, check all previous steps have been dealt with and check that you have your papers, text books, rules, pens and gown to hand.

The proof

Many solicitors are anxious at the start of a proof. If you are anxious imagine how your client feels. You have already given your client an explanation of what is involved but when you get to the court you should remind them, playing down, rather than up, the intricacies of the process. Even if you are nervous you have to radiate calm.

Arrive early

If you have got to the court 30 minutes early you have time to—

— compose yourself
— check the layout of the court room
— make sure your witnesses are there and in the right place
— check the shorthand writer is there
— check your case is going ahead
— check the process with numbered productions and copy productions for the sheriff are there
— make a final check that your papers and pens are in order
— relax your client as far as possible
— go to the toilet
— introduce yourself to the other solicitor and make sure that you each understand the other persons position on any procedural matters to be dealt with prior to the proof.

Arrive late!

If you arrive at the last minute you have the opportunity to unsettle your client, yourself, your witnesses, find you have left something behind and can do nothing about it, find you have not numbered productions and generally give the impression that you do not know what you are doing. It takes no effort to continue that impression well into the proof.

The start

There is usually a call over of cases to decide the order in which they are to be taken. When your case is taken ensure that your client is in the court and your witnesses are not. Your client should be beside you sitting on the side further away from the sheriff with the pursuer's solicitor on the sheriff's left and the defenders solicitor on the right.

Procedural matters

There may well be procedural matters to be dealt with before witnesses are called. Minor amendments, productions to be lodged, a joint minute of admissions. Do not forget to cover these in your eagerness to get on with the proof.

On the assumption that you are acting for the pursuer and no request has been made and granted for the defender to lead evidence first you now call your first witness. In family cases this will almost invariably be your own client.

General court craft

Preparation

You will come across many different attitudes to preparation for examination and cross-examination of witnesses. Criminal practitioners in particular are used to appearing in court day in day out in trials. They can have well-honed advocacy skills. In family work, by contrast, you may only have to conduct a proof as little as once a year or less. This gives you no real opportunity to gain confidence in and work on your advocacy skills. People may tell you otherwise but the bottom line is preparation pays. Even the most brilliant advocate will perform better if he or she has spent time reflecting on the questions to be asked and the line to be taken.

Officer of court

This is an element of court craft to which perhaps insufficient attention is paid. Under most circumstances you will find that your fellow professionals are honest and honourable in their treatment of you and court procedures. However, there are occasions where you may feel that another Solicitor is straying beyond appropriate boundaries. You will be likely to remember that Solicitor and treat them with caution in the future. As a Solicitor in Court your reputation is your greatest asset. Certain basic elements should be remembered.

Openness with the court

Your duty (within the necessity of respecting the court) is to present your client's case in the best way you can. You also have a duty to be truthful with the court and must not allow your client to be otherwise. To take an obvious example you must not seek to elicit from a witness a statement which you know to be false. You must not suggest in cross examination that someone is lying if you know from your own client that the witness is in fact telling the truth.

You present the facts of a case that are favourable to your client but do not give the court any information which to your knowledge is contrary to the facts.

You are not allowed to communicate confidential information about your client's case learned during the course of it even when you have ceased to act for that client or he is dead. If you are cited as a witness you should appear but formally decline to give any answer that can possibly be regarded as confidential. The court then decides whether the information is protected or not. This confidentiality does not apply if you are called by your client as a witness.

When it comes to authorities or statutes you have to refer to those that both support and undermine your contention.

You should not make a legal submission which, to your knowledge, is not sound in law.

Communication

You are a communicator. Much has been written about how little of communication comes through our words and how much comes through the quality of our voice, body language and the like. If you are really interested in being as effective as you can be in court there is no substitute for seeing yourself on a video and then deciding how far you meet the criteria for good court communication. It may be excruciating but it is better to spend an embarrassed hour becoming aware of how you present yourself than an unembarrassed lifetime presenting yourself and your cases badly.

Courtesy

It may seem strange to give this as a central element in court craft but, in spite of some evidence to the contrary, Judges are human beings too. Even a bad tempered Judge will usually respond better to the consistently courteous agent. The good sheriff will be courteous to you if you are courteous to him or her. You want to give an impression of integrity, rectitude and reasonableness on your client's behalf and the best starting point for that message is your own behaviour. That does not get round the need to be assertive. It does mean that, in general, you will get a better response from Judges, get further with witnesses, by being courteous.

Assertiveness

Being courteous does not mean being unassertive. At the end of the day the responsibility is yours to put your client's case. If you believe you have to follow a particular line to establish your case you have to be prepared to follow it in the teeth of any nonlegal obstacles that get in your way.

Brevity

You want to be accurate and sometimes that demands more words than you would like, but in general a Judge will respond best to a short, focused presentation.

Delivery and pitch

Most of us have a wide range of ways in which we present ourselves. People respond best, and judges are no different, to a clear, warm, relaxed, relatively low pitch of voice with the speed of delivery geared to the needs of the particular situation. If a sheriff or shorthand writer is taking notes you are not going to be popular if you speak at your fastest. If you are taking a witness through a fairly inconsequential and simple piece of evidence you are not going to score points for your slowest delivery. The idea is not to put on an act but to use and develop the full range of your own delivery matching the appropriate delivery to the particular situation.

Eye contact

There can be a temptation to immerse yourself in your notes failing to engage with either the witness or the sheriff. If you stand or sit with your head buried in papers do not be surprised if those around start to lose interest. You are putting a barrier between you and the judge/witness. Judges, like anyone else, get very bored looking at the back of a head in a folder. If a judge is bored he or she is unlikely to be engaged and influenced by what you say. Your papers are an essential prop to the action but they should not be the focus of the action.

Sheriffs, just like anyone else, respond better to eye contact and a sense that you are listening, watching and responding to what you hear and see. You can learn a great deal by watching the physical/facial reactions of a judge or a witness.

Objectivity

You are not a witness and therefore cannot, for instance, in your submissions give evidence yourself. You are not there to give your personal views on the world and how it should work.

Responsiveness

You are involved in a live drama. By definition things will not always happen as you expect. You need to be responsive to what happens. This does not mean that you abandon your plan of what needs to be done. It does mean that you adjust your plan where possible to fit in with reactions from the sheriff, evidence that emerges and unexpected developments while still always keeping, as far as possible, to your own strategy.

Question Forms

The way to formulate your question will dictate the type of response you get. The two basic categories we mention are:

Open questions

There are different understandings of what an open question is. In this context we are referring to questions that will tend to be prefaced with "When?", "Where?", "Who?", "What?", "How?". They allow witnesses to tell the story in their own words. They can be useful for scene setting. Depending on how they are used you can get very wide answers ("What happened next?") or narrower ones ("Who answered the door?). They tend to beused a lot in examination-in-chief.

Closed questions

These limit the information you get back. They can give you a tight control of a response avoiding a more expansive response that might introduce new information damaging to your case ("Did you go to the house?"). This form of question is particularly useful in cross-examination.

Examination-in-chief

The aim

The aim of examination in chief is to elicit from your witness the evidence he or she has that supports your client's case in a way that a judge will believe and understand. The witness may also have evidence you wish to bring out in anticipation of the other side's case. You have to consider whether to draw out evidence that may be adverse to your client's position but would be better brought out by you, through sympathetic questioning, than by the other side looking to give it its worst face.

Preparation for examination in chief

There tend to be two tiers to preparation.

The first tier

There is an identification of what has to be proved or disproved to succeed in getting what your client wants. That is in turn related to your proposition in law. If you want to establish that your client has been financially dependent to a substantial degree on her husband then you need to look for the factual triggers leading an independent mind to that conclusion. You will be able to clear the irrelevant factual clutter and concentrate on the crucial facts and the documentary and other evidence to support them.

Around the crucial facts you need to establish a coherent, believable verbal picture that makes sense to the judge. That picture is not, in itself, essential except that it gives a context and makes comprehensible what is essential.

You want a balance between allowing the witness to give his or her account in his or her own words, keeping the witness to the point, preventing the witness elaborating in a way that gives material for the other side cross-examination.

Your preparation involves giving yourself a format for checking that key evidence has been covered from each of your witnesses and, perhaps, pointers on how to elicit it. It can be done by highlighting different parts of the record or witness statement as a reminder or by a written "tick list" of the key points.

The first tier of preparation is obligatory and you will not be able to function adequately in court without having made that preparation.

The second tier

This is not necessarily regarded as essential. On occasion you may take the view that the funding provided by the legal aid board for preparation is simply not adequate cover it or that the evidence is likely to be so fluid as to make it not worthwhile. However if you do go to this next stage it can pay considerable dividends. Certainly when you first start out you should do it.

Essentially you are drawing up a format for your specific questions. In a civil action, because the record gives you notice of the facts to be proved, you can do it. The art is in ensuring that you leave sufficient flexibility in your plan to allow you to adapt it as circumstances develop. For instance it usually makes sense to take your evidence in chronological order under clearly separated, headed blocks following the order of the record. If you need to move from one block to another you can do so and return to your thread through the record. By considering your question forms before the proof you can work out which elements require closed, tight questioning, which areas require a looser open approach. You can formulate leading questions on non-controversial "scene setting" evidence and non-leading questions on controversial and crucial evidential points.

The inexperienced solicitor, without this level of preparation, will almost inevitably find themselves producing questions so untargeted that the witness does not know what is being asked or produces unwanted and even damaging evidence.

At the first tier of preparation you will have fulfilled your basic function if you manage to bring out the evidence of facts averred by you on record. At the second level the subtlety and discrimination you bring to your question forms can communicate, through your witness, a more sympathetic and compelling picture for the sheriff. You may establish some clear favourable themes to the "story".

At the end of your examination in chief remember to check your plan/record/precognition/productions as appropriate to see that the facts you want to come out have come out.

Your plan at both tiers must always have room for adjustment in the light of events and evidence in court.

The examination in chief as it happens

Whichever depth of preparation you have gone through certain basic rules almost invariably apply—

— let the sheriff put the witness on oath
— always start by leading or asking your witness his full name, age, address and job. Think about the best way to put him or her at ease
— do not be afraid to elicit "scene setting" evidence by leading questions as appropriate
— control the witness by your choice of open or closed questions
— use short questions with no preamble
— use simple precise language
— seek one fact with each question where appropriate
— follow the record as far as possible
— do not ask a question to which you do not know the answer unless the answer is certain to be of little or no significance
— make sure the sheriff and the shorthand writer can hear you
— never call a witness unless you know what he or she is likely to say
— do not betray your personal reaction to a particular response
— listen to the answer and note evidence
— with an expert witness take from him or her his or her qualifications in some detail, including the position he or she holds, years of experience, what the experience is of
— remember to get your witness to speak to productions which relate to him or her
— if you are flustered, lost or desperate for the toilet ask for a short adjournment (this is not an assault course or an endurance test but an attempt to achieve justice).

If you follow the above basic rules you can relax and let the evidence unfold to flesh out your written statement of the case.

Cross-examination

The aim

The object of cross-examination is—

— to show that the witnesses evidence is untrue/not exactly
  true/not the whole truth
— to undermine the witnesses credibility
— to elicit favourable evidence
— to put your client's evidence to the witness in so far as
  within that witness' knowledge and different from the
  witness' own evidence

Preparation for cross-examination

Because you have prepared the earlier elements of your case
properly you know the thread of the argument that runs
concurrent with the factual picture painted by your evidence
leading to what you want through a proposition in law. In cross-
examining you are focusing on the evidence that undermines or
contradicts your picture. You want to discredit that evidence.

The cross-examiner who has not got the picture clear in his/her
own mind will often end up with an aggressive, unproductive,
blunderbuss approach. The cross examiner who has a clear
picture will, with preparation, achieve some, but rarely all, of his
or her goals in attacking the witness evidence.

In preparing for the proof you will have highlighted on the
record the points that diverge from your story in the story of the
other party. You will have noted the key points of divergence. As
with examination in chief there can be two tiers to preparation.

The first tier

An analysis of what needs to be challenged remembering that if
you intend to lead evidence to contradict a witness at a later stage
you should put the question in cross examination. A failure to
cross examine may have serious consequences (see I.D.
Macphail, *Sheriff Court Practice,* p. 546 at 16.76).

Your analysis should result in a series of points to be covered
in cross examination. If the witnesses in their evidence in chief do
not mention a point negative to your client you thought you were

going to have to cross-examine on you can simply take the relevant noted point out of your list for cross examination. The other party's agent will then under normal circumstances not be allowed to introduce the matter in the re-examination. (If they try to you should object immediately and before the question is answered by the witness).

The second tier

Again this is often regarded as non-essential and yet, provided it is done in the right way, you can gain considerable benefit from it. The key is to organise your material in such a way that you have sufficient flexibility to adapt or alter your plan in the light of the evidence that actually emerges. Demarcation of particular areas of evidence to allow you to take them in a different order should you so wish is essential. Behind your line of cross-examination should be a theory of the case. This will give you the opportunity to provide the best tactical sequence for the cross-examination. The questions are always asked to establish your theory of the case and to challenge the one offered by the other side.

An experienced court practitioner may feel that they have sufficient confidence to manage without this preparation and indeed there are those who would say it is disadvantageous if it results in too rigid an approach to the cross-examination. However, the inexperienced Solicitor may have a great deal of difficulty presenting anything other than a direct confrontational contradiction of witnesses evidence without this level of preparation. That kind of approach can end up reinforcing, rather than undermining, the evidence challenged. With preparation more subtle and effective approaches can be used.

There are those who say that the best way to learn about advocacy is by watching someone with the relevant skills. There is a lot of truth in this, however, if you watch the best advocate day in day out without understanding why what he or she does works then you are unlikely to get significant benefit. A basic book such as *Advocacy Skills* by Michael Hyam is a good introduction to what works and why. Active training with role play and videos is invaluable.

The cross-examination as it happens

It is not within the scope of this book to give a detailed introduction to skills and techniques of cross examination. However, it is worth stressing that whatever happens both at the planning stage and in court you need to consider what type of questioning will assist. At the most elementary level you need to consider whether you are going to use open questions which might lead to a large amount of information emerging that you do want or close tight questions to keep the witnesses to narrow small steps and away from any destructive disclosure.

In family law cases, especially if there are ongoing family relationships to be preserved, it is almost always better to take a polite but assertive approach. With witnesses in actions that relate to the care of children and the balance of time the children spend with their parents in the future, you always need to consider what impact the questions you ask may have. There is a difficult balance to be obtained between presenting your client's case to the best of your ability and trying to ensure that the parties are not unnecessarily further alienated from each other with an inevitable negative knock-on effect on their children.

As with everything else, most of what you do comes back to common sense and plain English. A few basic points along those lines to note—

Avoid catchphrases

Try and avoid using phrases such as "I would suggest that", "I put it to you that". You do not use them in your day to day communication; there is no need for them in a court room. They add nothing to your question and irritate sheriffs.

Time

One of the greatest problems in presentation of Court cases is that rather than asking the right question, people ask any question. If you need time to collect your thoughts, to check that you have asked what you need to ask, to recover your poise, do not be afraid to take it. It is far better that there is a silence then that there should be a "witter".

Simple language

Keep your language plain and at a level the particular witness can understand.

Brief

Ask for one fact with one question. Keep your questions as short as possible.

Pace

The best cross examiners have a tremendous sense of timing. This is partly a matter of understanding what you are doing and partly instinct. If you understand the effect of moving things along quickly (the matter is straightforward and unimportant, or the witness does not have time to think and therefore may say something helpful to you etc.) then you can decide to go with that pace. If you consider what happens if the pace is slowed (you may be putting the witness on the spot, giving added significance to what is said, forcing the witness to an answer through silence) you can decide a slower pace suits. If you are nervous you may rush things and you have to be aware of that and slow yourself down. However, as you become more experienced, you should be able to become conscious of your pace and its potential effects.

Antennae out

While concentrating on exactly what you are going to say, it is easy to lose your sensitivity to the reactions from your witness and the sheriff. This is particularly so if you are too wedded to your pre-proof plan. You need to listen and look very carefully to decide what is going on for the witness and how the sheriff is reacting to what is going on. You should modify your approach to take account of perceived reaction. This does not mean deferring to an antagonistic sheriff where you believe you have to ask particular questions to establish your case but it does mean moulding your presentation as best you can to the protagonists involved, always keeping your own theory of the case and your need to prove it in mind.

Do not argue

You are there to ask questions. Do not be drawn into an argument or into answering questions from the witness.

Facts not conclusions

You are there to challenge facts. Conclusions to be drawn from those facts are for the judge and your submissions. Unless the witness is an expert you should not be seeking their opinions. This is the theoretical position but, in practice, it is true to say that different sheriffs take dramatically different views as to what are appropriate questions to ask of, for instance, a parent. The distinctions between opinion and fact are decidedly blurred. Is it an opinion to say a mother loves her child or are you stating a fact? The word "love" communicates a qualitative assessment (opinion) based presumably on factual observation. Certainly if a witness uses this kind of word you have to be prepared to look behind the qualitative statement to establish the facts it is based on—How often has the witness seen the mother with the child, what did they do together, what elements of behaviour lead the witness to the opinion the relationship was loving?

Sometimes, a witness opinion can be based on a very challengeable premise. (He cries when he comes home after contact visits therefore he "dislikes" the visits. Is it not possible that he is sad at these times because they bring home to him the reality of his parents' separation and/or his own separation from the "contact parent" he loves?) Be prepared to root out the spurious opinion masquerading as fact.

Key words

Watch out for key words and phrases used by the witness in examination in chief or in cross examination. Use them, where helpful, in your cross examination to bolster your own picture of the case or where, for instance, these have been exaggerations, to undermine the witness's credibility.

Words in general

Because we use words all the time and the whole process of a court action is dealt with through words it is sometimes possible to lose your awareness of their significance. Measure what you say to fit what you want to communicate. An overstatement from a cross examiner is just as unhelpful as an overstatement from a witness.

Listen to the answers

Remember to listen to what is said and note it appropriately. Key responses should be highlighted for possible use in your submissions.

The balance

As with every other element of your behaviour in court you are not trying to be a different person, you are trying to pitch your behaviour at the part of your own personal spectrum which best tallies with the above qualities. Over time you can modify and improve the spectrum available to you by developing your skills but the sheriff is looking for a human voice not a contortionist or a robot.

Cross-examining child witnesses

Consider carefully whether you need to cross examine a child at all. If it has to be done the need for straightforward language, simplicity, short sentences, single questions and respect (patronising adults are just as loathsome to children inside court as they usually are outside) is paramount.

Be prepared in cross examination to canvass with a child whether anyone has spoken to them about the views expressed outside the court. Probe the possibility that the person in whose favour evidence has been given might be upset if the child said something different from what they have said. Issues of loyalty are often central to a child's narration of events.

Consider repeating questions already put in examination in chief to see if the response is the same verbatim as first time round suggesting coaching.

Be prepared to ask questions on an entirely different matter to see if a child is talkative on, what you think is, a coached subject but clams up on anything else.

Cross-examining expert witnesses

An expert can be cross-examined in areas such as

— their credentials suggesting he or she is the wrong person to be giving this opinion or at least not as well qualified as your own witness
— their previous inconsistent opinions
— whether their opinion would be different if the facts set out in your pleadings were accepted
— published opinions of other authorities
— the opinion of your expert (be prepared to go into some detail on why they take a different view)
— the view that their conclusions do not follow from the data provided
— the view that the methodology used has been flawed (for instance a child psychologist basing an opinion on one short interview with a child with one of the parties present)
— the view that his or her instructions were slanted or flawed
— the view that another opinion could be equally consistent with the facts they justify their own opinion with.

The idea is to either undermine the foundations factual and/or technical on which the opinion is built or to show the opinion does not follow naturally from those foundations or to show an entirely different conclusion would be equally consistent with those foundations.

It is often helpful to have your expert in court beside you when the other side's expert is giving evidence to benefit from their input on any unexpected turn in evidence and to allow them to take in exactly what the other expert is saying. Make sure you ask the sheriff for permission for your expert to sit in. Where the client is on legal aid check whether you need sanction for the expert to sit in.

Re-examination

Re-examination can only be on new matters that have arisen in cross examination unless the sheriff allows new matters in. It is particularly important to be aware of the rules governing the examination and to be prepared to object where appropriate quickly and forcefully. Macphail, *Sheriff Court Practice* at 16.78

gives a good introduction to the essential elements to look out for. As Macphail makes clear, the limits on leading questions are the same as those for examination in chief.

Objections to evidence

Again, Sheriff Macphail's *Sheriff Court Practice* is the best introduction to this area (p. 548, paras 16.84 to 16.88). The most important point for you to note is that you should make the objections as soon as the issue arises. As stated earlier in this book one of the great bugbears of family law is the inconsistency within the courts in the application of the rules concerning fair notice. The bottom line is that your duty is to your client and if you have not been given fair notice of a line of questioning, you should not hesitate to object. Any objection you make to a question or line of evidence will be included in the record of the evidence where there is a shorthand writer.

Remember that if recording of the evidence has been dispensed with under Rule 29.18(1) you can call on the sheriff to note, in writing, the terms of objections made and the decision on those objections.

Under OCR 28.18(12) the sheriff has to record the terms of any objection and his decision on the objections in the notes to his Interlocutor disposing of the merits of the cause.

You should note that, even where an objection to a line of evidence taken by you has been sustained, you still have the right to bring other witnesses to speak to the line of evidence objected to notwithstanding the fact that the questions will be overruled. A way to avoid infuriating a sheriff by following this course is to indicate that named witnesses were going to cover the question overruled. The point should be stated before the close of the proof.

Often a sheriff will allow evidence to be heard "under reservation of all questions of competency and relevancy". This means that the evidence is heard with the question of its admissibility available to be argued at a hearing on the evidence.

Closing the proof

After your witnesses have given the evidence you need to formally close your proof. It is vital that you remember to confirm to the sheriff that included in the evidence are all the documents admitted or put to witnesses and reports of evidence taken on commission. The normal phrasing is something along the lines of "the evidence along with the productions for the pursuer/defender concludes the proof for the pursuer/defender".

Discretion

We have given you the broad rules but it is important to remember that most elements of the conduct of the proof are governed by the sheriff's discretion. Where something has gone wrong or been omitted and you consider it to be of some significance you should immediately consider whether you should ask the sheriff to exercise his or her discretion by, for instance, allowing a witness to be recalled. It is not within the scope of this book to go into all the possible scenarios for the use of a discretion. In our view you should not venture into the court for any significant hearing without having Macphail's *Sheriff Court Practice* in your possession. You will never know all the possible procedural and evidential variables likely to emerge. Macphail provides a concise starting point for an enquiry about any issue of this sort that may emerge.

Shorthand notes

Consider whether you need the notes extended and make sure that, if you do, and your client is legally aided, you seek an order for the extension from the sheriff to ensure the cost is paid by the Legal Aid Board.

Submissions

As with all other aspects of your communication you are looking for the maximum impact for what you say made with the minimum of verbiage .That means organising what you say in a coherent structured way formulated from the document you, the sheriff , the other agent have in common, the record.

Preparation

It is essential to have at least the broad outline of your submissions prepared in advance of proof. Ideally you want detail but that can create problems as almost certainly the proof will not follow the path you expect.

The best way to cope with the unexpected is to have your elements of the submission broken into separate identifiable chunks so that you can amend or drop the chunks if necessary after evidence has been heard.

If matters are the least bit complex you will make a positive start by providing the sheriff with a skeleton note of your arguments. The key is to give enough to explain the line of your argument but not so much that the line is swamped or what you have typed up as a "skeleton" does not accommodate the "flesh" of what happens in court. When a division of assets is sought a schedule showing your proposed division will always be welcome.

Before you start

If it is proposed at the end of evidence being heard that submissions be made straightaway do not be afraid to ask for a short adjournment to allow you to gather your thoughts and finalise your submissions.

Presentation of submissions

Your order of presentation should again follow on logically from the order in which things are set out in the record. A good basic approach is—

— tell the sheriff what you want (identify the craves insisted on)
— tell him the order in which you will deal with the craves
— deal with the craves in the order you have told the sheriff you will deal with them, identifying the legal basis for the request and the evidence produced to justify your client getting it
— briefly summarise your position

Do not be afraid to use headings, lists and numbers to highlight your structure.

The above does not involve running all the evidence past the sheriff again. It does mean inviting the sheriff to accept certain evidence as proved, highlighting inadequacies or inconsistencies in the other parties evidence, suggesting that certain evidence was more or less credible.

Make sure you cover everything you need to cover. For instance if you want interest indicate why it should be granted. Let the court know how a particular financial settlement can be achieved.

Finally, think about weaknesses in your position. Be prepared for questions. Your aim is to appear reasonable and persuasive.

The other agent's submissions

One of the most difficult elements of court craft is the response to any opposing submission. You are trying to listen to what they are saying while at the same time decide whether any counter submission is necessary and if so what it should be. It is easy to end up with copious notes of what the opponent said, you think, and very little idea of what you need to respond to and how. Some consistent pre-planned notation method is helpful. For instance you can have three columns on your page, a narrow one to the left, wider ones middle and right. In the left you can put a star at every point you intend to make a counter submission. In the middle you can put your note of the other side's submission. On the right you can have your own note perhaps of trigger words for your responding submission.

There is no licence for endless submissions and counter submissions. You have to gauge how much you need to say. That means watching the sheriff to weigh up his or her responses to what is said, considering whether the point has already been sufficiently covered in your principal submission and then making if necessary the most concise additional submission you can. Sheriffs by and large do not expect or like too much shuttling between agents for submissions so be prepared to be limited to your initial submission and one responding submission (indeed in certain circumstances a sheriff may choose not to afford you the opportunity of any submission beyond your initial one).

Expenses

These are normally dealt with at a later stage and are covered later in this chapter.

After the proof

Such is the exhaustion/exhilaration/relief that a proof is over the temptation is to shove the file back into the cabinet and forget the case until the judgments appears. Do not do this. A number of things still need to be done.

Witness expenses

Make sure your witnesses have the relevant forms for an expenses claim. Thank them for taking the trouble to give evidence on your client's behalf.

Your client

Your client needs to know the likely timescale for a judgment being issued. A short letter tidying up on this point and confirming when expenses will be dealt with shows you are still on the case and interested.

Your records

Remember to make sure you have made a note showing the time spent on the proof and any event in the course of the proof that may influence your submission on expenses or a possible appeal. Keep your notes on the evidence and conduct of the case somewhere safe. You may well need to refer to them again not least when you are preparing your submissions on expenses.

When the judgment arrives

Rather than sending a copy immediately to your client consider how they may react to it. Particularly where children are involved it may be better to invite the client in to discuss the judgment rather than sending it out (but remember time limits for any appeal). A client receiving bad news by post can react in ways that are unhelpful to him or her and the rest of the family. The same news received in person from a sympathetic solicitor can be assimilated and dealt with appropriately.

Appeal

The question of an Appeal has to be covered with your client. If there has not been a hearing on expenses you may well be better to wait until after that hearing before a final decision is made on appeal. If an Appeal is to be made remember the relevant time limits

Expenses

The majority of proofs are taken to *avizandum* with a hearing on expenses fixed once the judgment on the other parts of the action has been issued so you will probably need to sort out expenses at this latter stage. In family actions compared with other civil proceedings a greater emphasis tends to be put on conduct in relation to the proceedings as opposed to success (see *Little v. Little,* 1990 S.L.T. 785 at 790; *McWilliam v. McWilliam,* 1990 S.C.L.R. at 373 and *MacDonald v. MacDonald,* 1995 S.L.T. 72).

Conduct

Both parties may well have started out with the intention of achieving a fair sharing of the matrimonial property. If both parties have made a full disclosure, negotiated reasonably and moved the case forward in an appropriate way there may well be an argument that no expenses be due to or by either party where neither party has been completely successful. Where one party has failed in one of these strands, even where there is divided success, there might be an argument for expenses in relation to that particular strand.

Success

The relevance of conduct does not mean success in the proceedings is not a significant factor. Where a party has sought and obtained a particular proportion of the matrimonial property and all other factors are equal there may be an argument that, at a particular point either before or after proceedings were raised, the unsuccessful party should have recognised the validity of the claim and settled and expenses may well be awarded from that point.

What it boils down to is that the decision is one for the discretion of the judge in the case. In looking for a favourable outcome you need to draw on arguments over both conduct of and success in the proceedings.

Sanction of use of counsel/certification of expert witnesses

If you are seeking expenses remember to get the court's sanction for the use of Counsel if Counsel has been used. Have expert witnesses certified as experts by the court at the time you deal with expenses.

Modification of expenses

In legal aid cases, consider whether any motion to modify expenses to a smaller amount or nil should be made.

Uplift of fees

Where a case has been complex, consider a motion for increased fees. This can be done in both private and legal aid cases. You should make any submission based on the fees regulations or the legal aid regulations as appropriate.

Conclusion

When it is all over remember again that there is no such thing as the "perfect" proof. You are not given an hour to think about every word you will utter, every question you will ask. You do not know how the drama will unfold. Things are said and done that are not ideal. "Winning" or "losing" the proof are not the measure of whether you have done your job properly. You will win badly presented cases and lose well presented cases. The measure of your success is whether you have prepared and presented the case to the best of your ability being like the rest of us, an imperfect person working in an imperfect world.

CHAPTER 14

LEGAL AID

Introduction

Legal aid is a vital gateway to the law. It's important to remember that legal aid represents both access to justice for clients and a significant use of taxpayer's money. At the moment, a client seeking legal aid may feel rather like Alice in Wonderland when she tried to gain entry through a doorway and found herself unable to use it because either the key lay on a table too high for her to reach or she became too large to get through! People who find themselves in need of legal remedies are often not poor enough to qualify for legal aid but not rich enough to feel they can pay privately. And taxpayers may rest assured that they are obtaining full value for money! Since the rate for work carried out under civil legal aid is so low it will be viable only if done with the most aerodynamically efficient streamlining!

The trick is to ensure that the streamlining is not at the expense of good quality contact with the client. The practical management of the case must be infused with efficiency. Key points are—

— have a proper stock of forms and use them at the appropriate time
— maintain rigorous time recording
— have a system of running fee totals & alerts for the need for increases
— each time you handle the file make a mental check on how the fees stand
— keep your client informed of the rules on disclosure and clawback
— take a combined degree in semantics, logic and mathematics to be able to understand the recovery provisions!
— keep an eye on outlays & spring into action to apply for reimbursements

— for long-running files or lengthy proofs bear in mind the possibility of interim payments

Preliminaries

Make sure you are aware of the appropriate forms to use. They can be obtained from Geo. Stewart & Co Ltd, Meadowbank Works, 67 Marionville Road, Edinburgh, EH7 6AJ. Telephone: 0131 659 6010, or from the Scottish Legal Aid Board's website at http:// www.slabpro.org.uk.

An overview of the relevant forms looks like a demented Scrabble hand! The basic list is—

- the key card—it can be helpful to keep a note of the current child benefit payments as clients sometimes give a slightly inaccurate figure
- AA/APP—the basic application form
- AA/INC—the increase application form
- AA/15 (2)—"hardship" application
- Category code list
- Pro forma—form to calculate likely eligibility for civil legal aid
- CIV/SU2—notification of specially urgent work carried out under reg. 18 (1)(a)
- CIV/SU4—application for certification of urgent work to be carried out under reg. 18 (1) (b)
- CIV/APP—application for civil legal aid
- CIV/INTDOC—notice to opponent in a legal aid application
- PART G—Financial Statement
- TRANS/APP—request for transfer of legal aid (other than AA) from one solicitor to another
- SANC/APP—application for authority for employment of counsel or expert witness, or for unusual or unusually expensive work
- SLA/ROL/2—application for reimbursement where AA outlays £100 or over
- SLA/ROL/1—to be used with SLA/ROL/2 for reimbursement application where AA outlays under £100 but combined civil and AA or exclusively civil outlays £150 or over

- AMND/APP—application for amendment or extension of a grant of, or application for, legal aid
- SLA/POA/1—application for payment on account of fees in terms of reg. 11 of Civil Legal Aid (Scotland) (Fees) Regulations 1989

You should also have a copy of *The Scottish Legal Aid Handbook,* a guide to legal aid in Scotland which includes some commentary and the full text of the Legal Aid (Scotland) Act 1986 and relevant regulations. It is obtainable from the Board in both book form and from the website detailed above.

Remember that part of your advice giving is to inform a client how they stand about legal aid. If they could qualify and you are not prepared to do the work under legal aid they may still wish you to act. In that case you would be wise to confirm the position in writing. If the client does want to sign up for legal aid you need to complete the "pink form" and have the client check and sign it then and there. Also bear in mind that some clients may qualify for Civil Legal Aid although not eligible under the Advice and Assistance Scheme, and should be advised accordingly.

Advice and assistance

It is possible to send the form out for signature if requested. You must underline the importance of checking any information you may have completed for the client. When the form comes back and you sign make sure you send a letter of explanation to the Board to explain the difference in the date of signing by the client and date of commencement.

Emphasise to the client that by signing the form they—

— authorise the Board to check the information
— could be prosecuted if they've consciously provided false information
— would almost certainly have to pay the fees out of any settlement (although at a lower rate than for work carried out privately)

Considering you are likely to have to wade into this delicate territory very early in your relationship with a client it is important to deal with matters clearly but sympathetically. The client is likely to the anxious about fees anyway. You can underline that you are dealing with that aspect at the start to get it out the road and allow them to concentrate on absorbing the information they want from you about their legal position.

PART A

Be attentive about the address to be used for the client. Always ask if it is in order to write to them at their home address. In many cases that could cause serious difficulties at a delicate point in a couple's relationship. Question 15 provides the opportunity of using a different address for correspondence. Remember to take note of that for your own correspondence.

PART B

Selecting the appropriate category code does currently involve the rather grating use of "acc" for "contact" and "cus" for "residence". The Board expect related matters to be dealt with under one category code rather than a number of forms being signed to cover various strands such as divorce, children, or financial provision. While that is important from the client's point of view if he or she is liable to pay a contribution in respect of any single form signed it could become rather unwieldy if clearly distinct matters were to arise while you are acting for a client. If the advice being sought were sufficiently distinct as to be in relation to a wholly separate set of circumstances separate forms would be appropriate. The Board comments "Solicitors should, however, expect these situations to be the exception rather than the rule" (*The Scottish Legal Aid Handbook* (sixth edition, April 2001), A:11-A:12).

PART C—Financial statement

Remember that if it appears to you that your client has deprived him or herself of capital or income the resources he or she may have shed should be taken into account. (The Advice and Assistance (Scotland) Regulations 1996 Schedule 2 (4)).

Income

Since you are authorising the grant of legal aid you should ask to see evidence of income by way of a pay slip or benefit book covering the appropriate period of seven days up to and including the date of the application. If possible, have an appointments system which informs new clients to bring evidence of income and identity (but avoids them feeling alienated before they even arrive at the office!). Since it will not be workable to ensure that every client does have evidence of income available at the first meeting, remember that it is your responsibility to be satisfied that an individual qualifies. If there is any doubt, the decision to grant advice and assistance may have to wait until the information is produced. Remember that "income" means the total income from all sources which the person concerned received or became entitled to during or in respect of that period. Leave out any income tax or National Insurance contributions paid or payable. Aliment received will have to be taken into account. If the client is self employed the Board do find it acceptable to take the drawings for the relevant period as the measure of net income. The assessment for civil legal aid would be on a more detailed basis.

If your client receives jobseekers' allowance keep your fingers crossed that he or she can tell you if it is income or contributions based! People may not be familiar with that wording but be able to tell you if it is instead of income support or unemployment benefit. If any doubt remains you may need to fax the local job centre with the appropriate query and hope you receive a response.

Capital

Exclude the value of the household contents, personal clothing or car (unless unusually valuable) and the value of the client's main residence. If your client has a second home you should include the amount which could be borrowed on it. That could be done by taking into account the equity in the property and your client's income.

Exclude any asset which is the subject matter of the dispute which may include—

— any assets which are joint where your client has a realistic claim for more than a half share
— assets of your client alone which have been made the subject of a claim by his or her partner, either by formal letter or writ.
— If in doubt, check with the Board.

Remember that any payment under the Earnings Top up Scheme 1996, a back to work bonus (payable under the Jobseekers Act 1995) or any payment under the Community Care (Direct Payments) Act 1996 or under Section 12B of the Social Work (Scotland (1968) should be excluded.

Policies

For Civil Legal Aid the amount which could "readily" be borrowed on the security of any life assurance or endowment policy is to be taken into account (Civil Legal Aid (Scotland) Regulations 1996 Sched. 3, r.12). There is no specific mention of policies in the Advice & Assistance Regulations but presumably a similar approach should be taken. If the policy or policies are already being used as security in connection with the loan secured over the house then it would be safe to assume no further borrowing would be "readily" available. In many cases the policy or policies may be part of the subject of the dispute.

Deductions

Since you may be completing the form during a meeting with a very anxious client much in need of reassurance, eye contact and attention it can be only too easy to do the arithmetic of the deductions inaccurately. For that reason it is a good idea to double-check the figures with a calculator! If the form is submitted and found wanting it will be returned and you will have to trouble the client again about a matter he or she will assume had been sorted out. Remember that any changes have to be initialled by your client.

If your client has not yet separated, receives the child benefit but is unemployed (or a low income) and is being supported by the partner who has a contrary interest it is still in order to make the full deduction in respect of the children.

Contribution

Sometimes clients are able to pay the contribution immediately, which is ideal. If some or all the payment is to be deferred have a definite arrangement for payment and diary it forward to check. Legal Aid rates leave no margin for loss. Once work is completed if a contribution has been overlooked it is likely to remain unpaid.

Effective date

Remember that when the Board's authority is required because you are the second solicitor, the effective date is the date when the Board's authority is given. Also bear in mind the form must be submitted within 14 days unless it is a special reason for late submission. Carelessness or oversight would not be seen as special reason!

Reciprocal enforcement of maintenance orders

Where advice and assistance is required in connection with proceedings under Parts I or II of the Maintenance Orders (Reciprocal Enforcement) Act 1972, advice and assistance may be made available without inquiry into the applicant's resources if a certificate of exemption has been issued in relation to the applicant. The certificate in question is one from the reciprocating or convention country stating that the applicant would be financially eligible for complete or partial legal aid or exemption from cost of expenses in that country.

Extent of advice and assistance

Scottish law

The scheme covers only Scottish law. If it becomes apparent that the advice involves another jurisdiction then advice and assistance can be used to establish that and take such steps as are necessary to put the client in touch with a solicitor from the appropriate jurisdiction. It is unlikely to be possible to obtain an increase in the authorised expenditure for this which would make it rather important to be alert to issues of jurisdiction early in a first meeting.

Basic limit

There are two possible initial limits, currently £150 or £80. The higher limit only applies if you are satisfied that matters are likely to need to be resolved in court in an action for which legal aid is available and it is likely your client will qualify for legal aid on financial grounds and it is reasonable.

Increases

There is no set upper limit. The key test is reasonableness. Two aspects are utterly crucial. The first is to have some way of monitoring your expenditure as you go along. There must be a significant amount of work being carried out free of charge because of the difficulty of doing this. The second is to give ample explanation of the reason for the increase application. Clearly each subsequent increase application will merit ever fuller information about what has been done so far and the work proposed to be carried out with details of any outlays. Always remember the increases are not retrospective. If you start incurring outlays you will not be able to apply for a reimbursement whatever the scale of the outlay unless civil legal aid is granted.

Reports

If you wish to obtain a report from an expert you should obtain an estimate of the cost involved. At the same time you should warn the expert involved that the work will be carried out under legal aid which could mean a lengthy delay in payment (unless you have an exceptionally sympathetic bank manager and lead a very modest life style!). You should also explain that the Legal Aid Board will look for some breakdown in their fee note even if it is within the estimate given. Accountants and others may be bewildered at the thought of what to them is a modest outlay requiring justification, not realising that the figure involved for their limited involvement in the work may vastly exceed your fee for all the rest! Emphasise that they should not exceed the estimated cost without further authority from you. If you are looking for a report from a far flung medical or other expert witness you would have to satisfy the Board that either no such expert lurks closer to hand or that there is some particularly cogent reason to engage your expert of choice.

Urgency

In extreme urgency a telephone request for an increase can be made. Take note of the name of the person granting the increase for the file and check when the written grant comes to hand that the date coincides. If not, take that matter up with the Board immediately. If the urgency arises out with normal office hours application may be made by phone to 0771 42 43 44. Do not over use this resource!

Conveyancing

Transfers of title are a regular consequence of a negotiated settlement. The Board will consider each application on its own merits subject to the test of good and cogent reasons being provided. In general an increase in expenditure to cover the cost of a transfer is likely to be authorised if no consideration is being paid, the property will be retained for your client's occupation for the foreseeable future and your client will be able to service any secured loan. The cost of the preparation of security documents is also likely to be authorised, as is your client's share of a survey if required to establish the value of the property as a matrimonial asset. Stamp duty will not be covered under legal aid and so the costs of stamp duty on a renunciation of occupancy rights must be budgeted for elsewhere. If your client is paying money to secure the transfer there is an expectation that the conveyancing costs should also be factored in by the client. It could still be worth applying for an increase if your client can show that it stretches their borrowing capacity to the limit to obtain sufficient to cover the consideration. Remember cover only extends to work which is your client's responsibility and be careful to restrict their liability in the separation agreement.

Mediation

The costs of using a solicitor mediator or all issues mediation through the Family Mediation Service may be met under Advice and Assistance. The outlay covered will be your client's one half share. If you are making a referral to a solicitor mediator bear in mind that each session lasts about an hour and a half. It is usual for the mediation process to involve at least three sessions and the preparation of written summaries. Your increase application should cover over half the costs of six hours work at the rate recommended by the Law Society (the half share would currently total about £270). Explain to your client that it is important for you to be told if it is likely that more than three sessions will be involved to allow you to ask for further cover if appropriate.

DNA analysis

Cover for this is likely to be granted if it will settle paternity. The Board will want confirmation that there are reasonable grounds for claiming paternity. If someone is seeking to defend it should be shown that there are stateable grounds on which this could and would be challenged. There must also be a reasonable prospect that the outcome of the analysis will be accepted as determining the issue. The Board expects the cost to be shared. If the opponent would co-operate with the analysis but utterly refuses to pay and an expensive court action could be avoided by DNA profiling you could explain the situation to the Board who might accept responsibility for the overall costs so long as the outcome was determinative.

Curators ad litem *for a child*

Most such fees are met by the Pursuer. Accordingly, if in any particular case cover under the advice and assistance scheme is necessary you should provide a very full explanation.

Applications by children

If a child seeking advice is under 12 you must be of the view that the child has a general understanding to instruct a solicitor. You assess that in the course of your meeting with him or her. It will be very anxious decision to make. You will be very aware of how much responsibility a young person takes in instructing his or her own solicitor. If you do satisfy yourself about the question of their understanding it is the child who signs the form. You should also submit a letter confirming that you have satisfied yourself that the child does in fact have a general understanding of what it means to instruct a solicitor. If you are not satisfied about his or her understanding then an appropriate adult can sign part A. If the child is 12 or over there is a presumption that the child is of sufficient age and maturity to have that understanding. You may form a different view if the young person appears immature for their years. In that case an appropriate adult can become involved on their behalf. Whether the child or their parent, Guardian, carer or curator signs only the child's resources should be taken into account.

Withdrawing from acting

If you decide to stop acting you should tell the Board not only that you are no longer acting but also why. You should also tell your client that the Legal Aid Board would have to give permission before any other solicitor could become involved in acting under the advice and assistance scheme.

Submitting account

Your account must be submitted within one year of the conclusion of the work unless a special reason for the delay can be shown or the account is being submitted along with a civil legal aid account. Remember that if your client has received a settlement which means your fees are to be met under the recovery provisions the fee must be calculated on the basis of the advice and assistance rates no matter how vast a capital sum your client may have received! Neither can you charge any more than the authorised limit of expenditure. The only exception to that is, having been refused any further increase, you have explained the situation to the client and he or she has authorised you to proceed on a privately funded basis. Which brings us on to the vexed question of the potential clawback under the recovery and preservation provisions! In property recovered or preserved cases the mechanics for payment is that the solicitor must first look to his or her client's contribution for payment of the contribution, then to any expenses recovered on behalf of the client and then to any property recovered or preserved on behalf of the client. Only if there is a shortfall from these sources should an account be rendered to the Board.

Clawback

The provisions are covered under the Advice and Assistance (Scotland) Regulations 1996, reg. 16. *Excluded* from the clawback are—

— aliment or periodic allowance
— the first £2,500 in money or value of a capital award on divorce or any settlement to prevent or bring an end to such proceedings
— any main dwelling, household furniture or tools of trade

so remember that any agreed settlement for an unmarried couple will not have the benefit of the £2500 disregard.

Hardship provisions

In terms of reg. 16 (2) you can make an application on behalf of your client (using form AA/15 (2) and enclosing your account) to ask for your account to be met from the legal aid fund rather than the money or property recovered or preserved if **either** payment would cause your client grave financial hardship or distress **or** you have taken all reasonable steps to obtain payment out of the property **and** payment could only be effected with unreasonable difficulty.

Contrast with Legal Aid

Bear in mind that neither the hardship provisions nor the exemption for "any dwelling, household furniture or tools of trade" applies to Civil Legal Aid. If your client is hoping to end up with the family home a negotiated settlement is particularly desirable.

Reimbursement

Remember that if civil legal aid has been granted you can apply for reimbursement of outlays incurred under advice and assistance so long as these exceed £100 (using form SLA/ROL/2) or if the combined outlays under advice and assistance and civil legal aid amounts to £150 (using forms SLA/ROL/2 &SLA/ROL/1). Copies of the invoices must also be submitted but payment need not yet have been made.

Civil Legal Aid

There will be a number of cases in which court proceedings will be necessary and civil legal aid applied for. Your client may need protective remedies or want to be divorced. It may not have been possible to sort out arrangements for children or division of property. Proceedings may already have been started and your client may need to oppose them or make a claim.

Remember that a simplified procedure divorce application can be dealt with under the advice and assistance scheme. Eligibility under the advice and assistance scheme is a passport to exemption from the court fee so long as the appropriate form is completed.

The test for entitlement to civil legal aid is threefold—

— probable cause
— reasonableness
— financial eligibility

Cover will only be given from the date the Board are satisfied on these three points (the effective date) unless you have carried out work using the special urgency provisions, submitted the appropriate paperwork and carried out the pro forma calculation.

Probable cause

You will have to precognose your client and in most cases a witness. The precognition should show the date on which it was taken. If corroboration is not available explain that when you submit your application to the Board. (Remember that the Board may accept evidence which the court will not find sufficient. Equally, you could take steps under the urgency provisions and obtain a remedy such as interim interdict only to find the full legal aid application refused on the test of reasonableness) There may well also be documentary evidence in support of your client's case. Do not submit original documents with your application.

Divorce—merits

You must submit a precognition from your client and from at least one witness corroborating the ground of divorce. If the basis is two years non-cohabitation a letter from the spouse confirming their intention to consent must be produced. If the basis is unreasonable behaviour the Board have indicated in their "Handbook" that a "witness who can speak to statements soon after the events of the applicant alleging violence, for instance, and can speak to seeing bruising on the applicant or other evidence of violence, is acceptable. A statement of a witness which lends colour to a detailed statement of the applicant may be acceptable, even if it does not corroborate the "worst" part of the behaviour complained of. A medical report is optional, but may be essential if there is no other evidence available. To be of evidential value, it should speak to some treatment required by the applicant, for either mental or physical health, attributed to the breakdown of the marriage." In adultery cases the evidence of one enquiry agent should be sufficient. It remains to be seen whether any challenge will be made to the use of inquiry agents in terms of the right to privacy conferred by the European Convention on Human Rights. Evidence may be available from other witnesses of affectionate familiarity and opportunity. A birth certificate showing the husband registered as the father of another woman's child during the course of the marriage could be used as corroboration.

Although evidence could be available from your client's children it is best to explore if other witnesses might be available to avoid the need to involve a young person providing evidence against the parent.

Divorce—craves for financial provision

It is important from the point of view of the Board (and indeed yourself!) to make it clear in your client's precognition how any financial remedy envisaged is justified in terms of the Family Law (Scotland) Act 1985. The specific criteria laid down in the Act should be covered. If no corroboration is available to your client make that clear in the precognition.

Aliment

If the application relates to aliment for a child it would be wise to clarify why the Child Support Agency have no jurisdiction. For any application, vouched details of your client's income and expenditure should be provided with as much information as possible about the other party.

Orders relating to children

Make it clear why your client feels an order is necessary and how it will promote the child or children's welfare. Give specific details of the arrangements proposed including, if contact is the issue, what contact is proposed. If a residence order is in issue provide information about housing, school, health, finances, out of school activities and day to day care. A precognition in support will usually be necessary. Remember that it would be very unusual indeed to be granted an order simply maintaining the *status quo*.

Matrimonial interdict or exclusion order or transfer of tenancy

It is good practice, as early as possible, to measure the information you are obtaining against the statutory tests and this should be reflected in the precognitions.

Defender

If an action of divorce is raised and your client accepts the marriage is over although disputing the explanation put forward it is unlikely that any application simply to oppose the merits of the action will be granted. This may need to be carefully explained to your client. It is however quite possible that ancillary craves may be opposed or your client may wish to make a claim and in either case information should be provided in support.

Curator ad litem

Submit a copy of the pleadings, a copy of the interlocutor appointing you, copies of any statements obtained or Reports prepared in the course of your initial investigations and a note stating why you consider there is a need for separate representation.

Reasonableness

Fault based divorce

The Board formerly took the view that if the only remedy sought is divorce a client paying privately would be likely to wait and proceed on the basis of separation. Now they are asking for applications to demonstrate that "there would be a direct benefit to the applicant from the divorce action being raised immediately", including "where all ancillary contenttious matters have been settled by agreement and both parties wish to proceed with the divorce" (*The Recorder,* September 2001, where other examples are given). They will consider each application on its own merits.

If the reason divorce is the only outstanding issue is because of successful negotiations resulting in a separation agreement your client may prefer to avoid apportioning blame and instead wait out the period of separation and have the divorce expenses covered in the agreement. The position may be rather different if although there are no financial issues to resolve the marital history has been particularly troubled and involved drunken and aggressive behaviour. Your client may feel they can manage without protective remedies so long as the marriage itself is brought to an end as soon as possible. If their partner has been unreliable and dishonest your client may be reluctant to wait for the period of separation to elapse only to find their spouse remains predictably unreliable! If applying for legal aid for a fault based divorce alone in circumstances such as those outlined do make matters clear in the client and witness precognitions.

Interdict—common law

Even if a court is satisfied that interim interdict is justified the Board may decide it is not reasonable to make legal aid is available for the action. You should consider with your client whether he or she would go ahead on a privately funded basis if of "moderate but not abundant means". You must also consider whether the Board is likely to have the same view as your client! If your client did not involve the police explore the reason for that and cover it in the precognitions.

If acting for the Defender consider the likely impact of the interdict. Where the interdict would not appear to unduly restrict your client's activities legal aid is likely to be refused. To satisfy the test of reasonableness to oppose any interdict it is essential to narrate in detail whatever negative consequences your client envisages as the result of the existence of such an interdict.

Curator ad litem

You must satisfy the Board of the need for the young person to have separate representation. Focus on the risk of the young person's views being overlooked, the difference between the adult and child perspective, any particular pressure the young person is under and why separate representation is more appropriate than conveying their views in some other way.

Applications by or on behalf of children

The position is similar to applications under the advice and assistance scheme. Details of the child should be given in Part A1 of the form CIV/APP and details of the parent/guardian/carer/curator in Part A2.

Appeal

Always submit a copy of the judgment appealed against, a statement of the grounds of appeal and your comments as to the prospects of success.

Interim orders

If the subject matter of the appeal is an interim order then use form AMND/APP to apply to have the certificate endorsed to cover the appeal.

THE HAGUE CONVENTION ON INTERNATIONAL CHILD ABDUCTION AND THE EUROPEAN CONVENTION ON THE CUSTODY OF CHILDREN

The expense of taking court proceedings under the Conventions is met by the state where the proceedings are brought. Legal aid will be made available in Scotland automatically and without payment of a contribution where a person resident outwith the United Kingdom seeks to pursue a Convention application. Check the Handbook for details at **A:69–A:71.**

THE EUROPEAN JUDGEMENTS CONVENTION—See the Handbook **A:70.**

THE MAINTENENANCE ORDERS (RECIPROCAL ENFORCEMENT) ACT 1972—See the Handbook **A:71.**

Special urgency provisions

Form SU2 can be used for the steps listed on the form. If other urgency steps are envisaged you must obtain certification on form

SU4. If you have a case where that is necessary then do make sure you explain the need very clearly.

Remember that in either case it is crucial to submit the full legal aid application within 28 days of commencing the specially urgent work. The Board has no power to waive that rule. It is highly recommended to have the legal aid application completed and signed and the witness and client precognitions prepared before you proceed with the urgency step. That will normally be possible if you are acting for the Pursuer but may well not be possible if you are instructed by the Defender. If you do have to carry on with the work before the documentation has been completed make sure that you diary forward to check how matters stand well within the 28 day period. Make it clear to the client that they may have to pay the expenses themselves if the papers are not returned and the witness statements obtained by the deadline. Underline that the grant of legal aid cannot be guaranteed in any event.

Unless your client is on Income Support with no savings, you must complete the form allowing you to calculate your client's financial eligibility and notional contribution. This may well be a startlingly high figure. Nevertheless, if you have office staff to pay, family to feed or a bank manager to please you should collect that contribution from the client before you proceed. Work carried out urgently is inevitably "front loaded". There will be intense activity involving Writs, Affidavits and significant outlays including Court fees and Sheriff Officers expenses. Work to the value of the notional contribution mounts up very quickly. If the application is not granted, then there is no way of recovering the notional contribution from public funds. If it is granted, the notional contribution should be returned to the client.

The application

The client, not the solicitor, should complete the financial statement. Remember that the Board can take into account resources an applicant has deprived her or himself of and since you owe a duty to the Board as well as the client are you must steer well clear of giving any advice, or indeed endorsement of steps taken towards that end.

Make it utterly clear to your client that any change in their circumstances must be reported to the Board. So far as income is concerned, the relevant period for notifying changes is one year from the date the application is received by the Board, known as the computation period. Any changes in capital must be notified to the Board throughout the lifetime of the case.

An application for legal aid consists of the application form (CIV/APP), a statement known as the legal aid memorandum setting out briefly what steps the legal aid legal aid is to cover, the intimation form (CIV/INTDOC) and a copy of the statement/memorandum and precognitions and copies of any supporting documentation.

The statement/memorandum can be founded on during the action and so should be framed carefully and on the side of brevity!

The process

Remember that the legal aid certificate must be lodged in court and the process marked "assisted person". The certificate is only effective if lodged within one year of its issue.

Sanction

Form SANC/APP should be used to obtain the board's authority before incurring any unusually high expenditure or for work of an unusual nature, involving counsel or instructing expert witnesses. G.P.'s are not classed as experts and so sanction is not required to involve them as witnesses where that is necessary. If a hospital doctor is needed to give evidence about fact again, he or she would not be classed as an expert. If you wish to involve an expert on a matter of opinion such as a child psychologist to provide a report and potentially appear as a witness you must provide full reasons why such an expert should be involved. You must provide a detailed breakdown of the cost likely to be incurred with a statement of the basis of charge and a note of any outlays likely to be incurred. Give information about the amount and type of travel costs envisaged. Remember that when someone is in receipt of legal aid it is not open to him or her to privately fund experts the Board will not sanction.

If in any doubt about whether or not sanction is required for any step it is safer to check the position in writing with the Board.

Mediation

If your client has civil legal aid and it is decided to make a referral on a voluntary basis or by motion to a solicitor mediator or all issues mediation offered by the Family Mediation Service than the Board's authority should be requested in the same way as under the Advice and Assistance scheme. If a referral is made by the Sheriff's own decision your client's half share of the cost will be met from the Legal Aid Fund.

Retrospective sanction

The Board may grant retrospective sanction if satisfied that the employment of counsel or expert witness would have been approved and that there was special reason why prior approval was not applied for. That does not include simple oversight! Remember that retrospective sanction is not available in respect of unusually expensive work or work of an unusual nature.

Diligence

Orders for aliment or periodical allowance (including registered Agreements entered into as part of a settlement of court proceedings) can be enforced by way of execution of an arrestment or service of a charge for payment as a preliminary step before an earnings arrestment may be carried out within 12 months from the date of the decree, or date of settlement without the Board's prior approval. Apart from that provision, any step to enforce a decree (other than by a separate process such as an action of forthcoming) can be carried out under the original certificate, without any time limit but only with the prior approval of the Board. Retrospective approval can be given if the Board considers approval appropriate and that there was special reason why prior approval was not requested.

Property recovered or preserved

Apart from the following exemptions in family law cases—

— aliment, periodical allowance or CSA maintenance
— the first £2,500 in money or value paid by court order or settlement

the Board's right to be paid the expenses, which would otherwise be paid by them from any property recovered, or preserved is in priority to all other debts.

Payment of principal sums into the fund

The guidance issued by the Board in March 2001 is as follows—

> "In terms of section 17(2B) of the 1986 Act, all that has to be paid into the Fund by the solicitor for the assisted person is the net liability to the fund.

Solicitors should therefore only send to the Board

- that part of the principal sum sufficient to cover the amount of their civil account of fees and outlays (including counsel's fees) and
- a sum equal to the costs of any estimated supplementary accounts (for example, for enforcement) under deduction of the client's contribution.

The principal sum, or that part of it, which is exempted in terms of Regulation 33 of the Civil Legal Aid (Scotland) Regulations 1996 should *not* be sent to the Board.

In some cases it will be relatively straightforward for solicitors to draw up an account and have it assessed by the Board. In other cases it will not be so straightforward, with the account for the solicitor and perhaps for counsel having to be taxed. The solicitor should, therefore, retain the principal sum in an interest bearing account and remit to [the Board] either the sum which has been agreed by [the Board] or, alternatively, a sum equivalent to the best estimate that can be produced of what his account will be, including outlays and counsel's fees. The remainder of the principal sum should be retained in the interest bearing account by the solicitor until such time as a more accurate figure can be obtained and a decision taken as to whether this balance should be utilised to meet the solicitor's account of work done under advice and assistance.

As a consequence of this change in approach—

- solicitors should make sure that settlement cheques are made out in their name as opposed to the Board

- cheques in respect of expenses are unaffected and should continue to be made out to the Board

This should enable the release of principal sums more speedily in most cases and thereby avoiding the delay inherent in the present system."

Which is good news for the client but you should still warn your bank manager about the delay likely to elapse before you receive payment!

Property settlement

If your client receives or retains heritable property as a result of the action the Board will ask for the expenses to be paid but will normally allow the option of a deferred payment coupled with a Standard Security. It is very important clients realise that interest will run on any deferred payment of expenses, at judicial rate. It seems likely that deferred payment will also operate in cases involving pension sharing and again, your client must be made very aware of the situation.

Additional cases of special difficulty

The Sheriff may allow a percentage increase of no more than 50 per cent in ordinary actions or 100 per cent in summary cause to cover the responsibility in the conduct of case taking into account the following factors—

(a) the complexity of the proceedings and the number, difficulty or novelty of the questions involved;
(b) the skill, specialised knowledge and responsibility required of and the time and labour expended by the solicitor;
(c) the number and importance of the documents prepared or perused;
(d) the place and circumstances of the proceedings or in which the solicitor's work of preparation for and conduct of it has been carried out;
(e) the importance of the proceedings or the subject matter thereof to the client;
(f) the amount or value of money or property involved; and

(g) the steps taken with a view to settling the proceedings, limiting the matters in dispute or limiting the scope of any hearing; and

(h) any other fees and allowances payable to the solicitor in respect of other items in the same proceedings and otherwise charged for in the account.

(The Civil Legal Aid (Scotland) (Fees) Regulations 1989, s. 5(4))

Such a request must be made by motion, intimated to the other party or parties and to the Board.

The procedure for and timing of such a motion was considered in detail in *F. v.F.*, 2000 S.L.T. (Sh. Ct) 106 (which did not follow the reasoning in *Beveridge & Kellas v. Abercromby*, 1999 S.C.L.R. 533).

In Court of Session proceedings a fee additional to the prescribed legal aid fees may be allowed at the discretion of the Court to cover the responsibility undertaken by a solicitor in the conduct of proceedings—the additional fee is fixed by the auditor.

You should discuss matters with your client. If the case has involved a settlement any uplift in fees may affect how much he or she receives and will do so if there was no award of expenses against the opponent. The net liability will increase where a percentage uplift motion has been granted in the solicitor's favour and this will affect the balance of any free proceeds being paid back to the client. Even if the case has not been over financial issues, where there is an award of expenses against the other party an uplift could affect the amount the Legal Aid Board try to recover. The Board will usually accept payment of the amount paid out from the fund without going to taxation if the opponent agrees to pay. That will often be much less than the taxed expenses. The Board expects solicitors advising assisted clients to explain the position and take those implications into account in deciding whether or not to ask for an increase. The implications of the encroachment on a settlement may seem a weightier concern to both advising solicitor and client than more expenses payable by an unsuccessful opponent but there could be circumstances where either possibility may give pause for thought.

In fact, such increases are sparingly applied for or granted in most courts.

Modification of expenses

If your client is found liable for the opponent's expenses and your client is an Assisted Person it is possible to ask for the expenses to be modified (Legal Aid (Scotland) Act 1986, s. 18(2)—such a request must be made when or immediately after your client is found liable for expenses (or accepts liability in a joint minute) but before any interlocutor for a specific amount of expenses is pronounced. (*Gilbert's Tr. v. Gilbert*, 1988 S.L.T. 680). The motion should be intimated to the other party or parties. The Court must decide what it is reasonable for the Assisted Person to pay taking into account all the circumstances including—

—the means of the parties
—the parties' conduct in connection with the dispute.

The Court's exercise of its discretion may be open to appeal (*Cullen v. Cullen, 2000* S.L.T. 540).

As well as providing as much information as you can about those aspects you are likely to be asked to give an estimate of what the level of expenses is likely to be. Accounts do not need to have been taxed before the motion is dealt with (*McInally v. Clackmannan District*, 1993 S.C.L.R. 482).

PAYMENT OF URGENCY WORK CARRIED OUT AND LEGAL AID NOT SUBSEQENTLY GRANTED (SECRETARY OF STATE'S DETERMINATION)

If you submitted the full Legal Aid application within 28 days of the commencement of the work then even if the application is ultimately refused you may still be paid so long as the Board is satisfied that the determination criteria are met. You should be in a position to demonstrate—

1. You had reasonable grounds to believe on information available at the time the work was done that your client was financially eligible for Legal Aid and (you need to have the completed pro forma to back that up unless your client was on Income Support) **and**
2. That the work was "actually, necessarily and reasonably done" – remember you need to justify the urgency as part of the reasonable necessity)

In addition,

any likely contribution, recovery or preservation is taken into account (which means you will not be paid any amount up to the level of your client's likely contribution).

Conclusion

AA and Civil Legal Aid is the ultimate challenge to office systems. If you can derive any profit from either and do the work justice, you deserve a gold star!

CHAPTER 15

ENFORCEMENT

Introduction

Enforcement tends to cover three broad categories:

— orders relating to children
— financial orders
— property orders

Our aim is to focus on fundamentals of approaches to enforcement in family actions rather than the detail. What makes enforcement in family actions distinctive is the fact that the choices made can have particularly important implications for ongoing relationships. Before advising a client to take a particular enforcement procedure the likely effect in other directions of such a step need to be considered.

We have dealt with enforcement in two stages—

— enforcement in relation to children
— enforcement over financial orders.

We have tried to deal with them in the order we think you are most likely to come across them.

Orders relating to children

It is a sad fact that much of the frustration and anger that emerges in family actions can be traced back to failures to obey interim and final court orders on arrangements for children. There can be, on the part of some carers, an extraordinary level of stubborn anger and hatred towards another person. That would not matter so much if that other person did not also happen to be the parent of a child born to and loved by both parties. Before taking any steps towards enforcement over children a client should be encouraged to consider the impact of those steps on the children and their relationships with each parent.

The Catch 22 carer

We used to call this the Fathers Catch-22 because it is so often Fathers who are not the main carers of their children and therefore find themselves in the situation. The Catch 22 applies to anyone who is not the main carer of a child but has some form of contact with or responsibility for them.

Where an order for contact has been made the person with care is expected to encourage and instruct the child to attend for contact but is not expected to physically force them to go (*Brannigan v. Brannigan,* 1979 S.L.T. (Notes) 73; see *Cosh v. Cosh,* 1979 S.L.T. (Notes) 72 and *Blance v. Blance,* 1978 S.L.T. 74). Notwithstanding this expectation it does not take a rocket scientist to work out that such orders can be sabotaged either consciously or unconsciously.

In deciding how to get a level of contact that is in the best interests of that child the Catch 22 carer inevitably learns that the main carer nearly always has the strong hand. If the Catch 22 carer asserts that it is in the best interest of the child to have more contact with him and is prepared to go to court to obtain that contact there is a real possibility that the main carer will start to put physical and emotional barriers in the way of contact. It is important to appreciate that on most occasions this will not be a conscious choice. The main carer may well be unhappy and hurt—not the best state from which to make difficult but generous gestures. If things are handled sensitively early on it may be that the difficulty can be overcome. If not attitudes can become entrenched.

It is only honest to say that, on occasion, unhelpful behaviour can be very deliberate. A quick reference to "inappropriate sleeping arrangements" or something of that ilk can start a process that ends with a child feeling to enjoy or even go for contact will be felt as a display of disloyalty to the main carer. A potentially good relationship between a Catch 22 carer and his or her child can easily be poisoned and made unworkable.

In other words if the Catch 22 carer gets on the wrong side of the main carer by being assertive things can go wrong.

If on the other hand the Catch 22 carer decides simply to keep on the right side of the main carer, make no challenge, and take as much contact as is offered, no matter how little, then the decisive factor in decisions about the child has become not what is in that child's best interests but what the main carer wants to happen which means that things are still going wrong. Catch 22.

In the worst-case scenario the Catch 22 carer can have the full support of law through all the various enforcement procedures but still be left with no contact. Very few sheriffs can see any real point in imprisoning or fining a recalcitrant main carer. The perception is usually that this will be even more damaging for the child than the loss of contact with the other carer. If the main carer is punished, the child suffers; if the main carer is not punished and doesn't change the child suffers. A Catch 22 for the Sheriff!

Methods of enforcement over arrangements for children

Having pointed out that difficulties it is still important to note that there are powerful remedies available to enforce care arrangements.

Delivery

An order for delivery can be made to bring about contact (*Thomson v. Thomson,* 1979 S.L.T. (Sh. Ct.) 11). If that does not work then the person with care may be ordered to appear at the bar of the court to explain why contact is not taking place. If the failure amounts to a contempt of court then, in theory, it can be punished. The dilemma at the heart of the situation is that of course, as stated above, punishing a child's main carer is most unlikely to be in that child's best interests.

At its most dramatic a court may decide that the only way to bring about an appropriate relationship with both parents for a child is to reverse the residential care arrangements. Certainly the threat of such a step is often the most powerful tool available.

Contempt of court

Sheriff McPhail (*Sheriff Court Practice* (p. 33 at 2.19)) states:

> "many forms of conduct may constitute contempt of court. In civil proceedings in the Sheriff Court such conduct may include failure to obtemper an order of the court, abuse of process, breach of an undertaking, tampering with documents in the custody of the court, conduct by a witness in defiance or disregard of the court's authority, and in certain circumstances the publication of material relevant to the proceedings. Any failure to obtemper an order of the court

which is wilful or intentional, or inexcusably careless, or which involves misconduct or a flagrant disregard of the due course and administration of justice, may be dealt with under the inherent jurisdiction as a contempt of court warranting punishment."

Contempt then covers a wide range of activities. If conduct covered can also be a criminal offence the Sheriff would usually find out whether criminal proceedings were being taken. If such proceedings were being taken the Sheriff would not normally deal with it as a contempt.

If the contempt is not admitted there may need to be a hearing to establish it. In order to prove the contempt of court the evidence of one witness suffices if the contempt is in the context of civil proceedings.

Once the contempt is established the person in contempt would be ordained to appear. When it comes to punishment Sheriff MacPhail states at p. 35, 2.24:

"the courts power to punish contempt should be exercised with the greatest of care and the wisest discretion. Offenders are normally punished by admonition, fine and imprisonment or detention, or any of these."

MacPhail's view that the court should exercise restraint is mirrored by the general experience in family actions of judicial attitudes to contempt. While, in extreme cases, a court may act with severity, those in contempt are usually given every opportunity to alter their conduct.

The Sheriff can impose a maximum sentence of three months' imprisonment or a fine at level four of the standard scale or both.

Human Rights Legislation

The comments on the human rights angle over contact with children in Chapter 16 should be noted.

Financial orders

Butterworth's *Scottish Family Law Service* gives an excellent introduction to the whole subject of enforcement of financial and property orders. For more in-depth information Maher and Cusine, *The Law and Practice of Diligence in Scotland* is a good source. Our intention is to give a basic outline of the remedies available. We deal with them in the order we think you are most likely to come across them. References to the "1987 Act" are to the Debtors (Scotland) Act 1987.

The charge, poinding and warrant sale

The charge

A charge is the thing you will come across first and most frequently in situations of enforcement. It is a formal request in writing served on a debtor demanding payment by him of sums due within a specified time. It warns of specified diligences that may be used if payment of the sum due is not made.

The charge is required before proceeding to carry out a poinding and warrant sale or to carry out an earnings arrestment. (the 1987 Act, s. 90 (1)). An extract decree contains a warrant to charge. Where a summary warrant has been granted there is no requirement to serve a charge. The next stages of enforcement can be proceeded with.

The period for payment following service of the charge is 14 days within the United Kingdom and 28 days if the debtor is outside the United Kingdom or if the debtor's whereabouts are unknown (s. 90 (3)). It should be noted that the days of charge are related, not to residence or domicile in the United Kingdom, but to presence within the United Kingdom.

Where the charge has been served it is not competent to execute a poinding following that charge more than two years after the date of service, a fresh charge is required (s. 90 (5) and (6)).

Service

By an officer of court by personal service or one of its accepted equivalents (see Maher and Cusine, p. 169 at 7.06 to 7.13 for more on modes of service).

Poinding

This can follow on the charge to pay. It involves seizing corporeal moveable property belonging to the debtor which is in the debtor's hands at the time of the poinding. For a detailed discussion of what this broad statement covers, see MacPhail, *Sheriff Court Practice,* p. 980 at 29.70 to 29.85 and Maher and Cusine, *The Law and Practice of Diligence in Scotland,* p. 177 at 7.22 to 7.107.

Joint property

Property with an indivisible title between two or more people (for instance held as a member of a club as trustee) cannot be poinded because each of the joint owners cannot dispose of any share in the joint property. The qualification to this is where the joint owners are found liable in the same capacity as that in which they hold property, where a poinding can proceed on that liability.

Common property

Where each person has a right to a determinate share property can be poinded under section 41 (1) of the 1987 Act.

What cannot be poinded

Section 16 of the 1987 Act lists items that cannot be poinded. For a fuller discussion of the subsection see Maher and Cusine, *The Law and Practice of Diligence,* p. 189 at 7.44 to 7.59.

What happens

The procedure is set out in sections 20 and 21 of the 1987 Act. The officer has to exhibit—
  —extract decree (or other warrant to point)
  —certificate of execution of charge
The officer demands payment from the debtor, if the debtor is present, or any person present who appears to be authorised to Act for the debtor.

The officer values the goods (s. 20 (4)) at the price they would be likely to fetch if sold on the open market. A professional valuation can be arranged where appropriate. The officer gives the debtor a poinding schedule giving specified information including the goods poinded and their value. The debtor can redeem goods poinded by paying the officer a sum equal to the appraised value of the goods (s. 21 (4)). This can be done within 14 days after the execution of the poinding. Similarly the debtor can apply for the release of a poinded item on the basis that its continued inclusion would be unduly harsh in the circumstances (s. 23 (1)).

Report

The officer has to submit a report of the execution of the poinding to the court within 14 days after the date of execution (s. 22 (1)).

Challenges to poinding

The sheriff

The sheriff can declare a poinding invalid or as having ceased to have affect either on his own initiative or on application of the debtor (s. 24 (1)).

The sheriff can recall the poinding before warrant sale on various grounds (s. 24(3)).

Protection of spouses

A spouse can seek to have furniture and plenishings declared exempt under section 16(4) of the 1987 Act. Where orders have been granted under section 3(3) or 3(4) of the Matrimonial Homes (Family Protection) (Scotland) Act 1981, giving the right to use or possess furniture and plenishings in a matrimonial home, a poinding of such items can be challenged (see Maher and Cusine, *The Law and Practice of Diligence,* p. 205 at 7.84).

Duration

A poinding ceases to have effect one year after the date of execution of the poinding, unless an application has been made for a warrant sale before that period expires (s. 27(1)). There are qualifications to this general rule (s. 27(2) onwards).

Warrant sale

To complete the poinding the poinded goods have to be sold. This is done on the basis of a warrant from the court.

In general only the debtor's movable property in his possession at the time of the poinding can be poinded. It can only be so poinded if it is capable of being sold. Sheriff MacPhail, *Sheriff Court Practice,* p. 986 at 29.86 to 29.90 gives a good introduction to the procedure for warrant sale. (See also Maher and Cusine, *The Law and·Practice of Diligence,*p. 213 at 7.108 to 7.138).

Arrestment

What is an arrestment?

A diligence used against the moveable property of a debtor in the hands of a third party.

Who is involved?

The Arrestment procedure involves three parties—

— The creditor (known as the "**arrestor**")
— The third party (the person who is in possession of the debtor's property, (the "**arrestee**")
— The debtor (known for these purposes as the "**common debtor**")

What is the effect of arrestment?

The Arrestment does not transfer any real rights to the arresting creditor. The common debtor can authorise release of the arrested fund by mandate which failing an action of furthcoming is required.

An arrestee, who pays over the sum or hands over the property to the common debtor or some other party than the arrester, is liable to pay the arrester the value of that sum or property.

When can it be used?

An Arrestment can be made—

— on the dependence of an action
— in security of a future or contingent debt
— in execution to enforce a decree or summary warrant

What can it attach?

It attaches any obligation to account owed by the arrestee to common debtor. Maher and Cusine's *The Law and Practice of Diligence* (1st ed.), p. 115 at 5.04 states that "all debts owing by the arrestee to the common debtor and all moveable property of the common debtor held by the arrestee may be arrested in the hands of the arrestee provided that at the time of the arrestment the arrestee is under an obligation to account for the debt or moveable property to the common debtor".

The obligation obtained by the arrestor is no better than that held by the common debtor.

What is needed?

A warrant to carry out an arrestment (excepting an Arrestment earnings) is provided by—

— An extract decree for payment of money from the Sheriff Court, Court of Session, High Court of Justiciary, Court of Tiends (Debtor's (Scotland) Act 1987, s. 87 (1)).
— An extract of a document registered in the Books of Council and Session (such as a Separation Agreement) which contains an obligation to pay a sum of money under Writs Execution Scotland Act 1877, s. 3 as amended by the Debtor's (Scotland) Act 1987, s. 87.

A warrant to arrest on the dependence is provided by

— A warrant on the initial writ to cite and arrest. There has to be a crave for this.

Arrestment on the dependence

A pursuer in a court action where there is a financial claim other than for expenses can ask for a warrant to arrest on the dependence. OCR 3.5(1) states—
"A copy of—
(a) an initial writ with warrant to cite which includes a warrant to arrest on the dependence;
(b) defences which include, or a minute of amendment which includes, a counterclaim with warrant granted to arrest on the dependence endorsed on that writ,

certified as a true copy by the pursuer or defender, as the case may be, or his solicitor, shall be sufficient warrant to arrest on the dependence if it is otherwise competent to do so".

In an initial writ or summons

Where the warrant is sought in the initial writ or counterclaim the warrant will be granted automatically if the application is in order.

It is important to remember that service of the initial writ has to take place within twenty days of the execution of the Arrestment on the dependence (OCR 6.2). If this is not done the Arrestment falls. Where Arrestment takes place prior to service, the Arrestment has to be reported to the sheriff clerk forthwith (OCR 6.2 (2)). The sheriff officer will do the reporting. Check you have confirmation from the sheriff officer that the report has been made.

By motion (OCR 18.4)

In an action for aliment or financial provision on divorce you are aided by the terms of section 19 (1) to (3) of the Family Law (Scotland) Act 1985 which states—
"(1) Where a claim has been made, being—
(a)   an action for aliment, or
(b)   a claim for an order for financial provision,
the court shall have power, on cause shown, to grant warrant for inhibition or warrant for arrestment on the dependence of the action in which the claim is made and, if it thinks fit, to limit the inhibition to any particular property or to limit the arrestment to any particular property or to funds not exceeding a specified value.

(2) In subsection (1) above, "the court" means the Court of Session in relation to a warrant for inhibition and the Court of Session or the sheriff, as the case may require, in relation to a warrant for arrestment on the dependence.

This section is without prejudice to section 1 of the Law Reform (Miscellaneous Provisions) (Scotland) Act 1966 (wages, pensions, *etc.* to be exempt from arrestment on the dependence of an action)".

The court can limit the Arrestment to particular property or funds up to a specific value. The initial writ must include averments justifying the warrant.

Prescription of arrestment on dependence

Three years after the date of service of the Arrestment (Debtor's (Scotland) Act 1838, s. 22).

The prescriptive period is interrupted by an action of furthcoming or multiple poinding being raised.

Arrestment being carried out (in execution)

Basically a schedule of Arrestment is served by hand by sheriff officer on the arrestee followed up by a post copy (for the prescribed methods of service see Maher and Cusine, *The Law and Practice of Diligence,* p. 115 at 5.03). If the common debtor refuses to authorise payment of the sums arrested in the hands of the arrestee to the creditor by way of a mandate then the creditor has to bring an action of furthcoming. Once a decree is obtained in that action the arrestee is directed to pay over the funds held to the arresting creditor or, where goods are held, provides for the sale of those goods with the proceeds going to the creditor.

It is worth noting that where property is held by more than one person jointly (indivisibly by all the owners) that property cannot be arrested against the debt of one of the owners owed as an individual.

Where property is held on a common basis (divisibly in that each owner has title to a specific separate share) then it can be arrested.

For more information on what can and cannot be arrested see Maher and Cusine, *The Law and Practice of Diligence,* p. 287 at 5.05 to 5.35.

Insolvency

For information on situations where there is insolvency see Maher and Cusine, *The Law and Practice of Diligence,* at 10.36 and 10.40

Arrestments under the Debtor's (Scotland) Act 1987

The Debtor's (Scotland) Act provides three statutory diligences against earnings under section 46(1).

"The following diligences against earnings of a debtor in the hands of his employer shall replace the diligence of arrestment and action of furthcoming against such earnings—

(a) a diligence, to be known as an "earnings arrestment", to enforce the payment of any ordinary debt which is due as at the date of execution of the diligence;

(b) a diligence, to be known as a "current maintenance arrestment", to enforce the payment of current maintenance;

(c) an order, to be known as a "conjoined arrestment order", to enforce the payment of two or more debts owed to different creditors against the same earnings".

An arrestment of earnings can only be carried out by one of these methods. The diligences described can only be used to enforce a decree, the equivalent of a decree or a summary warrant. Earnings are defined under section 73 of the Act; the section gives some detail as to what is not treated as earnings.

Earnings arrestment

(The Act, s. 46(1)(a))

What is it for?

Earnings Arrestments are designed to enforce ordinary debts. Arrears of maintenance and the expenses previously incurred in executing a current maintenance Arrestment are covered. Current ongoing maintenance is not covered (see current maintenance arrestments hereinafter). The debt has to be owed at the date of service of the charge prior to the Arrestment or in the case of a summary warrant (no charge served) the debt as shown in the summary warrant.

How is it done?

The debtor has to be served with a charge (unless there is a summary warrant (the Act, s. 90 (1)). The period for payment, to be specified in the charge, is 14 days if the person on whom service is made is within the United Kingdom and 28 days if he is outside United Kingdom or his whereabouts are unknown. Where the debtor's whereabouts are unknown service is in the hands of the sheriff clerk.

Once the period for payment under the charge has expired the earnings Arrestment can be implemented against the debt or what remains of it.

The earnings Arrestment has to be implemented within two years after the charge has been served failing which a new charge is necessary (1987 Act, s. 90 (5) and (6)).

The 1987 Act sets out the procedure for implementing the earnings Arrestment. Essentially, a sheriff officer serves a schedule of Arrestment in the prescribed form on the debtor's employer (see the 1987 Act, s. 70). The schedule shows the debt, interest and expenses due, including the expenses of the schedule and charge.

What does the employer do?

On receipt of the Arrestment schedule the employer makes payments from the debtor's salary on each pay day (see the 1987 Act, s. 47). Various deductions are allowed as set out in section 49 and Schedule 2 of the 1987 Act.

The employer is expected to send money due under the Arrestment to the person specified in the schedule of Arrestment "as soon as reasonably practicable" (1987 Act section 51 (1)). These payments continue until the sum due is paid or the employer is told to stop by the creditor or the court. The creditor has to tell the employer to stop the deductions when the debt has been paid (1987 Act, s. 57 (4)).

Prescription

Claims about deductions which have, or ought to have, been made by the employer by the debtor or the creditor cannot be made more than one year after the date when the deduction or payment has, or ought to have, been made (1987 Act, s.69(4)).

Current maintenance arrestment

(The Act, s. 46 (1)(b))
Used to enforce and collect maintenance due after the date of the carrying out of the Arrestment (as opposed to before the date of the carrying out as with the earnings Arrestment). Maintenance includes aliment, periodical allowance, and sums due on a regular basis under contribution orders and similar non Scottish orders as defined in section 106 of the Act, under "maintenance order". The idea is that it is a device for getting ongoing maintenance.

What is covered?

This is an Arrestment against earnings but as stated above can only be used to obtain maintenance due in the future. It is important to note that this type of Arrestment cannot be used to obtain payment of arrears of maintenance and the expenses of the current maintenance Arrestment itself which have to be sought under the previously mentioned earnings Arrestment.

The same definition of "earnings" applies to this type of Arrestment as applies to an earnings Arrestment (section 73 (2) and (3)).

How is it done?

This type of Arrestment has to be preceded by certain key elements set out in section 54 of the Act.

Section 54 (1) (a)—Appropriate intimation

What is to be intimated depends on the type of maintenance order. For orders granted by a Scottish court for periodical allowance or aliment intimation is made by sending the debtor—
　　—a notice in form 37 (Act of Sederunt, Proceedings under the Debtors (Scotland) Act 1987 (S.I. 1988 No. 2013), rule 45)
　　—a copy of the relevant maintenance order
This has to be done by recorded delivery post to a debtor in the United Kingdom. If postal delivery fails service can be made by sheriff officer. If outside the United Kingdom it is by any competent method of service appropriate to the place where the debtor is (Act of Sederunt, rule 45 as above).

Four week gap

After the above intimation four-weeks have to pass (s. 54 (1) (b)).

One instalment unpaid

Before intimation can be made of the schedule there has to be a total of not less than one instalment of maintenance unpaid at the date of service (s. 54 (1)(c)).

Non Scottish orders

The exception to this is non Scottish orders where the order has been registered in Scotland under section 106, meeting the definition of "maintenance order" at s. 106(c) (e) (f) ,or (g) and a certificate of arrears in appropriate terms is produced at the time of registration (section 54 (2) (a) and (b). In these circumstances the Arrestment can be carried out as soon as an extract of the registered order is available.

How is it served on the employer?

As with the earnings Arrestment a current maintenance Arrestment is served by a sheriff officer serving a schedule of Arrestment on the debtor's employer in a prescribed form (Act of Sederunt, Proceedings under the Debtors (Scotland) Act 1987 (S.I. 1988 No. 2013), rule 42, Form 34).

What does the employer do?

The employer makes payments from the debtor's earnings on every pay day after service. Subject to the proviso that the employer is only bound to make the payments from the pay day occurring next after seven days from service. Within the seven day period the employer can choose whether to make the deductions section 69 (2) of the Act.

The payments continue until the creditor abandons the Arrestment, the Arrestment is recalled or varied by the court, or the order ceases to be enforceable. It is worth noting that the court can recall the Arrestment if it is satisfied that the debtor is unlikely to default from payment again (the Act, s. 55 (2)). The creditor is under a duty to inform the employer when the Arrestment no longer has effect.

How long does the order last?

It will continue until—

—the debtor is no longer employed by the employer (section 51 (2) (b))

—the Arrestment has been recalled or abandoned by the creditor (section 51 (2) (b))

—the current maintenance Arrestment itself ceases to have effect (the statute mentions the coming into effect of an order varying, superseding or recalling the maintenance order or the maintenance order ceasing to be enforceable in Scotland (s. 55 (8)) but other circumstances would have the same effect (death of an alimentary creditor, expiry of a period for which periodical allowance was granted or the like).

Review of current maintenance assessment

Forms of review are set out under section 55 of the Act a good commentary on the grounds is set out in Maher and Cusine, *The Law and Practice of Diligence,* p. 154 at 6.46 to 6.49.

Prescription

Claims over deductions which have, or ought to have, been made by the employer by the debtor or creditor cannot be made more than one year after the date when the deduction has, or ought to have been made (1987 Act, s. 69(4)).

Conjoined arrestment order

(Section 46(1))c))

This is to enforce the payment of two or more debts owed to different creditors against the same earnings. For an explanation of the procedure, see Maher and Cusine, *The Law and Practice of Diligence,* p. 155 at 6.52 to 6.75.

Where there are two or more obligations to pay maintenance, a conjoined Arrestment order is not necessary if the payee in each case is the same. For instance a wife due periodical allowance for herself and aliment for children payable to her can use a single current maintenance Arrestment to enforce payment.

The Child Support Act

The child support agency can make a deduction from earnings order to get payment of child support maintenance both future and arrears (the Child Support Act 1991, s. 31). It operates in a similar way to a current maintenance Arrestment but collects arrears as well.

If a deduction from earnings order is ineffective or inappropriate the CSA can ask the Sheriff Court for a liability order (see Child Support Act 1991, s. 33 (1)).

Arrestment in security

This is a little known and little used remedy. It is an Arrestment for a future debt due under a decree or a debt payable on the occurrence of a specified event. The matter is dealt with by way of a "precept of Arrestment" (OCR 3.5 (2)). The type of circumstances justifying this remedy are limited. It might be obtainable where, for instance, the debtor was close to bankruptcy.

Recall of arrestments

Parties can agree a recall. This does not require a judicial order.

Caution

Where the defender offers caution for the whole amount sued for or the sum covered by the Arrestment. The amount for caution depends on the particular circumstances of the case.

Nimious or oppressive

The use of the Arrestment is prejudicial or unfair to the defender. For instance where the arrested sum is disproportionate to the sum sued for or there are other funds available to meet the claim with no prospect of other creditors taking them.

Inhibition

Simply put this is a remedy to stop someone disposing of their interest in a heritable property, usually a house, to the detriment of a creditor. Because family homes are usually in joint names inhibition would be unnecessary as any sale would require signatures from both spouses for a sale or Security. It does not affect pre-existing debt and obligations such as under a Standard Security. It therefore—

—stops any voluntary disposal of the heritage

—means any subsequent voluntary Security is challengeable

—means debts contracted after the inhibition are postponed to the inhibitors claim

The above is a broad statement of the position. For a fuller explanation of these effects, see Maher and Cusine, *The Law and Practice of Diligence,* p. 251 at 9.13 to 9.17.

Inhibition can be a useful way of providing a fallback safeguard while other methods of recovery are pursued.

Inhibition on the dependence

An inhibition can be granted on the dependence of a sheriff court action (see MacPhail, *Sheriff Court Practice,* p. 354 at 11.36 to 11.42). The application for warrant to inhibit is made to the signet office of the general department of the Court of Session.

—if in Security, special circumstances have to be set out. If used under the Family Law (Scotland) Act 1985 "cause" has to be shown.

Recording in the register of inhibitions and adjudications

In general the inhibition has to be recorded to take effect. If a Notice has been lodged and the inhibition is recorded within 21 days, the inhibition takes effect from the date of the notice.

Service on the debtor

The inhibition has to be served on the debtor by a messenger at arms.

Once recorded the inhibition is taken as having been intimated to all persons.

Motion

A warrant for inhibition can be applied for by motion only where the cause is still depending and the application was not included in the original writ or summons.

Special provisions under the Family Law Act 1985 section 19(1)

This section allows the court "on cause shown" to grant warrant for inhibition on the dependence of the action where the action is for aliment or includes a claim for an order for financial provision. The court can limit the inhibition to any particular property if it thinks fit.

Inhibition in security

This is an inhibition used in relation to a future (certain) or contingent (future uncertain) debt. These might be future aliment, a deferred capital sum or circumstances such as a threat to sell property and obtain alternative property in the name of someone else (see *Wilson v. Wilson*, 1981 S.L.T. 101). There have to be special circumstances justifying it. These have to be set out in the application for inhibition.

Discharge of inhibition recall and prescription

Discharge

A formal document confirming the end of the inhibition. The discharge should be recorded in the register of inhibitions and adjudications as a purchaser would be able to reject the title if an inhibition appeared to remain undischarged on a search. (*Newcastle Building Society v. White*, 1987 S.L.T. (Sh. Ct) 81).

Recall/restriction

Can take place where the court is satisfied the inhibition has been used when not necessary as in an oppressive or unfair way.

For sheriff court actions the request for recall or restriction is made by petition to the Outer House in the Court of Session.

Prescription

Five years from the date of recording in the personal register or five years from the date of the notice (if the inhibition is recorded within 21 days). Inhibitions cannot be renewed but a creditor can reinhibit

Death

The death of the debtor extinguishes the inhibition.

Minutes for civil imprisonment

A person owed aliment under an aliment decree can seek to have the non payer imprisoned for up to six weeks under the Civil Imprisonment (Scotland) Act 1882. The failure to pay has to be wilful.

Periodical Allowance is not covered (*White v. White*, 1984 S.L.T. (Sh. Ct) 30)).

It is for the non-payer to counter the presumption that non payment is wilful (*McWilliams v. McWilliams*, 1963 S.C. 259; *Gray v. Gray*, 1993 S.C.L.R. 580).

CHAPTER 16

THE HUMAN RIGHTS ACT 1998—
IMPLICATIONS FOR FAMILY LAWYERS

Introduction

Whilst Scots Law has for many years ignored the European Convention on Human Rights, the busy family lawyer can no longer afford to do so! The 1998 Act came into force on October 2, 2000 and effectively incorporated the ECHR into United Kingdom domestic law, creating a right of action in the Scottish Courts and providing a mechanism for the amendment of any United Kingdom legislation found by the court to be incompatible with the convention.

The 1998 Act has an overriding effect on the law and affects the actions of all public authorities. A right of action lies against any public authority which is deemed to act unlawfully if it acts in a manner which is incompatible with an individual's convention rights.

No clear explanation of the term "public authority" is given in the Act, section 6 (3) of which provides a very broad definition. Public authorities include courts, tribunals and bodies whose functions are of a public nature. In general terms, any body which is wholly funded by the taxpayer or exists purely to fulfil a statutory function will be viewed as a public authority. For our purposes this includes; the Court of Session, Sheriff Courts, Children's Hearings, the Reporters Office and the Legal Aid Board.

The Act is not designed to provide a right of action between private individuals but it is applicable to private law cases. Since October 2, 2000 the courts must read and give effect to primary and subordinate legislation in a manner which is compatible with convention rights. This means for example that a Sheriff considering an application for an order under Section 11 of the Children (Scotland) Act 1995 must read and give effect to the legislative provisions with the terms of the 1998 Act uppermost in his mind. This interpretation overrides all other aids to statutory interpretation but in particular case law relating to the relevant issue. This is a challenging concept for us as family lawyers as we are used to relying on precedents to sway a Sheriff in favour of a given interpretation. The large body of case law which has developed in interpreting family law legislation is now entirely vulnerable to review.

In situations where a court cannot bend, twist or torture a legislative position in such a way as to make its application convention friendly an application can be made to the Court of Session for a Declarator of Incompatibility. This will result in the Scottish Executive issuing a Remedial Order to strike out or amend the offending legislation so as to make it convention compliant.

The Scottish Parliament cannot make legislation that is incompatible with the Convention in terms of section 29 of the Convention (Scotland) Act 1998.

The 1998 Act also stresses the need for courts to take a proactive role. This is expressed as the courts "positive obligation" to ensure respect for an individuals rights[1] a good example of this relates to the enforcement of contact orders. Most family lawyers have been faced with the problem of battling through a fraught proof to obtain their hard earned contact order, only to find that they can do little to enforce it thereafter. We have all had experiences of ineffectual applications to find particularly thrawn mothers in contempt of court when a weary Sheriff admonishes the defender who simply thumbs her nose at the court and continues to ignore the order. To date, very few Sheriffs take a bolder line and as was seen in the case *Gibney v. Gibney* [2] when they do so, risk being overturned on appeal

This issue was considered by the European Court in the case of *Hokkanen v. Finland* [3.] This case underlines the obligation put on domestic courts to take all reasonable steps possible, short of physical coercion of a child (and subject to consideration of the child's views where of sufficient age and maturity to express them), to enforce contact orders and to deal with the recalcitrant parents. The courts must provide access to and a mechanism for enforcement of a real and effective remedy in such cases. This is likely to be an area of rapidly growing caselaw over the next few years.

Proceedings for judicial review against decisions of public authorities such as local authorities, the Reporter to the Children's Hearing and the Legal Aid Board are also likely to be more common.

Practitioners should bear in mind that the pursuer in such proceedings must be the "victim"[4] of the convention rights violation and that proceedings must ordinarily be brought within one year of the Act in question[5]. Courts can grant whatever orders appear just and equitable including interdict, an award of damages, or an order *ad factum praestandum*. Courts are directed to Strasbourg case law when quantifying damages and are given a discretion to allow proceedings outwith a year of the violation if this is considered to be equitable in all the circumstances.

In determining applications, courts must have regard to the "proportionality" test which requires a reasonable balance between the rights of the individual complaining of the violation and the rights of the community as a whole. A "margin of appreciation" is also afforded to each member state to allow the courts to take account of the prevailing social and moral climate at the time of the application. The level of the margin of appreciation afforded will depend on the nature of the right violated. For example: the basic right not to be tortured in terms of Article 3 would be subject to a very narrow margin of appreciation as it is considered that there is a consensus on such policy issues between contracting states. In a more complex social policy area such as privacy or the rights of transsexuals a wider margin of appreciation will be afforded.

A good example of application of the proportionality test is the case of *Dudgeon v. U.K.*[6] where the European Court considered that the effect on the individual of the criminalisation of homosexual acts between consenting adults over twenty one was disproportionate to the Government's aim of protecting the health and morals of others.

At the heart of the convention is the concept that it is a living instrument which adapts to meet changes in social moral and political context[7]. This means that precedents may be of little practical application even where the facts are entirely in point as attitudes and the prevailing moral climate may have moved on in the intervening period.

Article 8

> 1. *Everyone has the right to respect for his private and family life, his home and his correspondence.*
> 2. *There should be no interference by a public authority with the exercise of this right except such as is in accordance with the law, and if necessary in a democratic society in the interests of national security, public safety or the economic well being of the country, for the prevention of the disorder of crime, for the protection of health or morals, or for the protection of the rights and freedom of others.*

For family lawyers, this is perhaps the most relevant article of the convention. The body of case law on Article 8 is worthy of an entire book in itself. We hope to provide you with an overview which will help with its practical application to your everyday practice.

Article 8 is a qualified right and requires a structured approach to its practical application. We should ask ourselves the following questions:

1. Did the alleged violation interfere with the client's right to respect for his family life ?
2. Was the violation of the individuals' right lawful in accordance with Scottish Law?
3. If so, did the interference with the individual's right pursue a legitimate aim within the terms of paragraph 2 of Article 8 ?
4. Was the interference necessary ?
5. Was the interference with the individual's right to family life proportionate to the aim sought to be achieved and within the margin of appreciation afforded ?

What is meant by "family life"?

The key principle to take on board is that the approach is a reality based test. The is alien to family lawyers in Scotland where legal and biological relationships take centre stage in establishing parental rights. "Family life" is essentially a question of fact rather than a question of genetics. In the case of *G. v. Netherlands* [8] the genetic link between a sperm donor and a child was held to be insufficient to create "family life" between the two. When invoking the provisions of Article 8 practitioners should stress to the court the facts of the case. The huge advantage of this reality based approach is that each case is determined on its own facts and merits. This should encourage practitioners to consider convention points in as wide a range of cases as possible and not to be deterred by a lack of precedent.

How does this reality based approach fit into the various family relationships?

Parents and minor children

The European Court have found family life to be established between a mother and child and between a father married to the child's mother and his child. Family life continues after divorce [9]

A more difficult issue is whether family life exists between unmarried fathers and their children. This group will have to establish that as a matter of fact a family relationship existed between them and their child.

In *Keegan v. Ireland* [10] the applicant had lived with his fiancée and the couple planned to have a baby. The fiancée got pregnant and the couple separated during her pregnancy. Mr Keegan's fiancée decided to give the child up for adoption. Mr Keegan was not notified of the adoption proceedings and complained that this violated his Article 8 rights. The European Court looked at a number of factors but in particular the length of the parties' relationship which lasted over two years during which time they had co-habitated and the fact that the applicant and his partner had planned the pregnancy together. The court decided that from the moment of the child's birth there existed between Mr Keegan and his daughter a bond amounting to "family life".

This rules bears an interesting similarity to the Scottish Executive's proposals in the Consultation Paper *Improving Scottish Family Law* which suggests giving legal recognition to the relationship between children and a father named on the birth certificate as an appropriate way forward. This approach looks at the factual reality of the relationship between the parents at the time of the child's birth.

The case of *Boughanemi v. France*[11] also underlined the fact that family life may be established even when a father and child have never lived together in the one household.

In *Marckx v Belguim*[12] the court considered Article 8 in the context of Article 14 which prohibits discrimination on grounds such as sex, race, colour, language, religion, political or other opinion, national or social origin, association with a national minority, property birth or other status. The court held that while a state could encourage traditional family values, it may not discriminate against illegitimate families unless such discrimination pursues a legitimate aim.

It is the qualification in paragraph 2 of Article 8 which has to be founded upon to justify treating unmarried fathers differently to those married to the child's mother. States may found on a margin of appreciation afforded to them and the United Kingdom courts have thus far justified their approach as being a means to identify "unmeritorious" fathers[13]. This is a social policy area likely to be subject to ongoing change.

Other family relationships recognised under Article 8

The European court has recognised the concept of family life between siblings[14], grandparents[15] and an uncle and nephew[16]. The dicta in these cases focus on the fact that real family life existed and still existed at the time of the application, looking at the factual reality of the family's home life and whether a level of dependency existed.

Gays, lesbians and transsexuals

Recent case law helps us identify the right to these groups as ripe for challenge under Article 8. The Portuguese case of *da Silva Mouta*[16a] (December 21, 1999) held that it was inappropriate to discriminate against a parent of one sexual orientation over another in a residence dispute. Family life was also found to exist between a transsexual parent and his child in *X., Y. and Z. v. U.K.*[17] to enable him to be registered on the child's birth certificate as the child's father.

The recent English case of *Fitzpatrick v. Sterling Housing Association Ltd*[18] found that a homosexual partner was entitled to succeed to his deceased cohabitant's tenancy. The House of Lords construed the reference in the relevant legislation to "family" as encompassing same sex relationships but again looked at the factual reality of the situation including the degree of mutual interdependence, the sharing of life as a family unit and the level of commitment and support enjoyed by the couple to distinguish this from a transient superficial relationship or mere cohabitation between two friends as a matter of convenience.

Cases for gays and transsexual partners who seek parental rights orders or adoption orders may emerge under this heading

In summary: practitioners should look at the day to day facts of the situation in their client's life in order to decide whether despite the biological and legal relationships "family life" within the meaning of Article 8 can be averred. Having got over this hurdle and identified that a public authority such as a court in applying the legal provisions to the client is interfering with that right we then go back over the questions posed early in this chapter and must ask ourselves is the interference with the client's right lawful or can the legal provision be applied in a more convention friendly way?

If the violation is lawful, is it necessary to pursue a legitimate aim falling within the terms of paragraph 2 of Article 8 ? This last question is often where the practitioner must carefully consider the convention case law and the balance between the rights of the individual and the interests of the community as a whole[19].

The scope for these issues arising in family law cases is vast and within the confines of this chapter we can only give you an initial flavour. The important factor to take on board is the flexibility of approach and the absence of absolutes in the court's approach. A good example of this is found in comparing two fairly recent cases on adoption: The first, *Soderback v. Sweden*[20] deals with step-parent adoption. The child's birth mother and partner applied for an adoption order. The child's birth father who had been estranged from the child's mother for some time objected to the adoption. The adoption was granted by the Swedish courts. The European Court took the view that any violation of the father's right to family to family life was justified by the legitimate aim of consolidating and formalising the child's family ties. The adverse effect on the father's relationship with the child (who he had not seen since birth) was viewed to be disproportionate (of lesser importance) in looking at the child's overall best interests.

The second case *Johansen v. Norway*[21] concerned an application for deprivation of a mother's parental rights when her child was placed with foster carers. The mother objected to the severance of her parental rights with a view to adoption which she complained interfered with her right to family life under Article 8. The European Court considered that the severance of links between a mother and child constituted a breach of the mother's right to family life and that in that case it was not justified by a sufficiently legitimate aim. The court distinguished *Soderback* on the basis that in this case the mother had previous care of her child and had developed family life with her.

Article 6: the right to a fair trial

In the determination of his civil rights and obligations, everyone is entitled to a fair and public hearing within a reasonable time by an independent and impartial tribunal established by law. Judgement shall be pronounced publicly but the press and public may be excluded from all or part of the trial in the interests of morals, public order or national security, when the interests of juveniles or the protection of private life of parties so require, or to the extent strictly necessary in the opinion of the court where publicity would prejudice the interests of justice.

Article 6 applies to both private and public law family cases coming before the courts or children's hearings. The key principle underpinning this article is fairness. A margin of appreciation is afforded to the domestic courts of each contracting state but subject to the issue of whether the end result produced a fair hearing overall.

Article 6 guarantees:

(a) the right of access to a court
(b) the right to a fair hearing
(c) the right to a hearing within a reasonable time
(d) the right to have the matter heard before an independent and impartial tribunal
(e) the right to a public hearing and judgement

The right of access to a court is not absolute. Restrictions such as time bar may be applied if they pursue a legitimate aim. In some cases overriding considerations such as the welfare of a child may take precedence over procedural niceties, *e.g.* in an emergency situation. However, the limitations cannot go so far as to impair the essence of the right of access to the courts.

The right of access to the court often involves a right to legal aid to enable the applicant to raise proceedings. The Legal Aid Board is a public authority whose decisions may be subject to judicial review in certain circumstances.

In *Airey v. Ireland*[22], the applicant who suffered physical and mental cruelty at the hands of her husband failed to obtain a judicial separation from him due to the absence of legal aid funding to enable her to do so. She claimed a violation of Article 6 in that her right to access to the court was effectively denied. The European Court held: "Article 6 paragraph 1 may sometimes compel the state to provide for the assistance of a lawyer if such assistance proves to be indispensable for an effective access to court either because legal representation is rendered compulsory as is done by the domestic law of certain contracting states for various types of litigation or by reason of the complexity of the procedure or of the case".

The key issue is therefore whether legal representation is compulsory or whether by reason of the complexity of the case it is necessary to ensure equality of arms between the parties. The state must provide a real and practical effective remedy for an applicant not merely one which is theoretical or illusory.

Article 6 does not prevent the Legal Aid Board from imposing a means test for funding. Most challenges will be in relation to the application of the merits test—obvious examples being the absence of funding for defence of interdict cases or divorce cases on the merits. The recent case of *S. v. Miller and Lord Advocate*[22a] which came before the Inner House on March 30, 2001 considered the issue of availability of legal aid funding for children's hearings. The Appeal Court held that contrary to the Legal Aid Board's policy to date of refusing legal aid for all children's hearings, that it was desirable in order to ensure a fair hearing in certain cases that legal aid was made available. The arguments in this case were based on the Airey case and provide a good example of a practical application of the 1998 Act to the Legal Aid practice of a family lawyer. The application of this decision may well be extended to the provision of legal aid for CSA tribunals in due course.

The right to a fair hearing when looked at against the background of Article 8 may well affect the admissability of evidence in certain cases. In many adultery divorce cases evidence such as letters, diaries, and credit card statements are obtained by covert means or alternatively evidence may be in the form of an enquiry agents' report. It is questionable whether the right of one party to have all the evidence throwing light on disputed facts to allow justice to be done will prevail over the party's right to a respect for his private life, home and correspondence.

The issue of confidentiality of certain pieces of evidence in family cases is also relevant. In *McMichael v. U.K.*[23] breaches of Article 6 and 8 were found where parents were not given sight of documents placed before a children's hearing which put them at a disadvantage and did not give then equality of arms. The *S.* case, extended this to the requirement to provide documentation to a child in such proceedings following an Article 6 point being made.

The issue of confidentiality of children's views which are at present often submitted to the court in sealed envelopes is also pertinent. This is likely to involve a delicate balancing of the parents' Article 6 rights and the child's Article 8 rights in order to decide if keeping the views of the child confidential achieves a sufficiently legitimate aim to risk prejudicing the parents' rights to a fair hearing with access to all pieces of evidence before the court[24].

Litigants have a right to an oral hearing before an independent and impartial tribunal. This provision may well impact on the approach on the court to making determinative orders at Child Welfare hearings and indeed the recent caselaw on procedural difficulties in relation to non-harassment orders is a good example of the type of issues which arise.

The delays often encountered in taking cases involving questions of parental rights and responsibilities to a full conclusion has often been remarked upon by the appeal courts. Article 6 may assist us in obtaining a speedy determination of cases, expediting procedure, obtaining earlier proof dates or invoking the early disposal procedure for Inner House Appeals. The circumstances of the case and the importance of making a correct determination with all available evidence before the court and the importance of the issues at stake must be balanced against this[25].

The scope for points under Article 6 is very wide and this article should always be borne in mind in relation to issues of fairness or procedural irregularity alongside the substantive law points raised under the Act such as the areas we have explored under Article 8.

If this Chapter has left you feeling less intimidated by the 1998 Act and inspired you to think latterly as to the issues raised in some of your cases then we have achieved our aim.

Notes

1. *X. & Y. v. Netherlands* (1988) 8 E.H.R.R. 235.

2. 1999 Fam. Law 30.

3. (1994) 19 E.H.R.R. 139.

4. s. 7(1) (b) of the 1998 Act, *A. & B. v. U.K.* (1998) E.H.L.R.R. 82.

5. s. 7(5) (a) of the 1998 Act.

6. (1981) 4 E.H.R.R. 149.

7. *Tyrer v. U.K.*, 2 E.H.R.R. 1.

8. (1993) 6. E.H.R.R. C.D. 38.

9. *Berrehab v. Netherlands* (1988) 11 E.H.R.R. 327.

10. (1994) 18 E.H.R.R. 342.

11. (1996) E.H.R.R. 228.

12. (1979) 2 E.H.R.R. 330.

13. *McMichael v. U.K.* (1995) 20 E.H.R.R. 205.

14. *Moustaquim v. Belguim* (1991) 13 E.H.R.R. 802.

15. *Marckx v. Belgium* (1979) 2 E.H.R.R. 179.

16. *Boyle v. U.K.* (1994) 19 E.H.R.R. 179.

16a. 2001 Fam. L.R. 2.

17. (1997) 24 E.H.R.R. 143.

18. (1999) 4A 11 E.R. 705.

19. *Soering v. E.H.,* 11 E.H.R.R. 344.

20. (1998) E.H.R.L.R. 343.

21. (1996) 23 E.H.R.R. 33.

22. 1979 2 E.H.R.R. 305

22a. 2001 S.L.T. 531.

23. (1995) 20 E.H.R.R. 205.

24. *Dosoo v. Dosoo,* 1999 S.L.T. (Sh. Ct) 86; *McGrath v. McGrath,* 1999 S.L.T.(Sh. Ct) 90.

25. *Hokkanen v. Finland* (1994) 19 E.H.R.R. 139.

APPENDIX OF STYLES

Because practice varies from one jurisdiction to the next and interpretation of the law is never still, these styles should not be seen as definitive , but we hope they are a helpful starting point. Please note our comments at the end of Chapter 7 about how to use the style writs.

1. File Label
2. Interview Sheets—couple
3. Interview Sheets—young person
4. Questionnaire about matrimonial property
5. Draft Schedule of Matrimonial Property
6. Statement of Income & Expenditure
7. Business information - information checklist
8. Useful addresses for client.
9. Pension Sharing Clauses—written agreement and writs, annex & letter
10. Separation Agreement
11. Separation Agreement Checklist
12. Contract in connection with sale of matrimonial home
13. Pre-marriage Contract
14. Parent & Child Contract
15. Letter to Pursuer client in connection with options hearing
16. Letter to client re non-harassment order
17. Letter to police re non harassment order
18. Motion to sist for legal aid
19. Minute of Amendment changing action to 2 year separation with consent
20. Motion in relation to above
21. Joint Motion re Joint Minute in divorce
22. Joint Minute—divorce
23. Court Attendance Sheet
24. Court Attendance Record
25. Initial Writ—divorce
26. Initial Writ—Exclusion Order
27. Initial Writ—Paternity Residence & Contact /Interdict
28. Minute to Sist —child as party
29. Notice to Admit
30. Specification

APPENDIX—STYLES

Style 1

Example of File Label

NAME & ADDRESS	CLIENT REFERENCE
	DATE OF BIRTH
	PRIVATE / LEGAL AID

| SUBJECT MATTER | SLAB REF:
AA:
CIV: |

| DATE | OPENED | CLOSED | TO BE DESTROYED |

| CONTACT DETAILS
TEL:
HOME:
WORK:
MOBILE:
E-MAIL: | ADDITIONAL INFORMATION: |

Style 2

Interview Sheets— Couple

MARRIED / UNMARRIED COUPLE		
Date of first interview:	date of amendments:	
FULL NAME OF CLIENT:		
Current Address:	ADDRESS FOR CORRESPONDENCE	
TO BE DISCLOSED: YES/NO		
Is that the Family Home - YES/NO		
Rented / Owned Client / Partner / Joint		
Telephone number: Home	Work:	Mobile:
E-mail Address		
Age	D.O.B.	
Occupation:		
Place of Work:		
If unemployed, previous Employment:		
Means of identification produced:-		
FULL name of relevant partner:		
Current address:		
Is that the Family Home - YES/NO	Rented / Owned	Client / Partner / Joint
Age	D.O.B.	
Occupation		
Place of Work		
Date and Place of Marriage		
OR date relationship started		
Date of Separation		
Names and D.0.B.'S of Client's Children: (1)		
(2)		
(3)		
(4)		
Any not from this relationship?	Any other relevant children?	
Children with client/partner:	Contact	
If unmarried, is father shown on birth certificate?		
Schools Attended:		
Child Minder:		
M&B Certificates: Produced / to be ordered?	Where registered?	
Habitually resident in Scotland?		
Previous decree of divorce/parental orders		
Date and Court		

FINANCIAL INFORMATION

INCOME DETAILS	CLIENT	RELEVANT PARTNER
Income Support		
Which Office?		
Working Family Tax Credit		
Renewal Date		
Child Benefit		
Pay from Employment		
Is O/T usual		
Job Seekers Allowance		
Contribution Based	YES/NO	YES/NO
Incapacity Benefit		
Other Benefit (Specify)		
Investments/other		
Aliment received		

EXPENDITURE	CLIENT	RELEVANT PARTNER
Housing costs		
Rent/loan repayments		
Endowment policies		
Building contents		
Gas/electricity		
Telephone		
Car costs		
Food		
Council tax		
Aliment paid		
CONTRIBUTION?	AMOUNT	DATE TO BE PAID
Benefit book/pay slip examined?	Place of birth:	
N.I. number:	**Mother's original surname:**	
Is client living with new partner?	YES/NO	
If YES, do they have an income?	YES/NO	
If YES, give details of income and capital:		

CAPITAL DETAILS
Relevant date values unless marked otherwise as current (c)

MATRIMONIAL/SHARED HOME	CLIENT	PARTNER	JOINT
Value of house			
Amount of loan			
Name and Address of lenders			
Reference number			
Net value of house			
Endowment loan			
YES/NO			
Policy details			
OTHER ASSETS			
Time share/holiday home			
Household contents			
OtherInsurance policies			
Bank Accounts			
Savings			
Investments			
Pensions			
Business Interests			
Vehicles			
Others			
Any inheritance or gifts or previous assets			
Other resources			
LIABILITIES			
Bank loans			
Car loans			
Credit cards			

SEPARATION AGREEMENT FRAMEWORK

List Proposals   Amendments

CHILDREN
Based With

Contact With

DIVISION OF ASSETS	**CLIENT**	**PARTNER**
Matrimonial Home		
Time share/Holiday home		
Household contents (see overleaf if very detailed)		
Insurance Polices		
Bank Accounts		
Savings		
Investments		
Pensions		
Business Interests		
Vehicles		
Other		
Capital Sum		

APPORTIONMENT OF LIABILITIES	**CLIENT**	**PARTNER**
Bank Loans		
Other Loans		

FINANCIAL SUPPORT:

PA:	AMOUNT:	DURATION:
ALIMENT		
SUCCESSION CLAUSE:	YES/NO	
PROGRESS SHEET		

Summarising Letter to be sent?	YES/NO	
Couple Counselling discussed	To be Attempted	YES/NO/PERHAPS
Mediation:	To be Attempted	YES/NO/PERHAPS

If Yes - CALM/FMS

SUMMARY

Style 3

Interview Sheet—Young Person

YOUNG PERSON	
Date of first interview:	Date of amendments:
FULL NAME OF CLIENT:	
Current Address:	ADDRESS FOR DATABASE & CORRESPONDENCE (IF DIFFERENT FROM CURRENT ADDRESS):
Telephone number:	
Age:	D.O.B.:
Current Place of Education:	
Occupation:	Place of Work:
Means of identification produced:-	
Who does client live with: Mother/Father/Other:-	
Full name of Mother:	
Address:	
Occupation:	
New Partner: YES/NO	
Full name of Father:	
Address:	
Occupation:	
New Partner: YES/NO	
Siblings:	
1)	
DOB:	Lives with:
2)	
DOB:	Lives with:
3)	
DOB:	Lives with:
Step Siblings	
1)	
DOB:	Lives with:
2)	
DOB:	Lives with:
3)	
DOB:	Lives with:
How much contact with other parent:-	

INFORMATION ABOUT STUDIES
Course (including place of education if not yet started:
Start Date:
Finish Date:
Any placements or special costs - Detail:

FINANCIAL INFORMATION	
Income from work:	
Any other Income:	
Any Capital:	
Place of Birth:	
NI no:	Mother's maiden name:
Contribution Amount:	Date to be paid:

PROJECTED INCOME & EXPENDITURE

Income	
Grant	
Other:	

Accommodation	
Holidays	
Books	
Food	
Clothes	
Travel	
Other:	

INCOME DETAILS	**FATHER**	**MOTHER**
Income Support		
Which Office?		
Family Credit		
Renewal Date		
Child Benefit		
Single Parent Supplement		
Pay from Employment		
Is O/T usual		
Job Seekers Allowance		
Contribution based	YES/NO	YES/NO
Incapacity Benieft		
Other Benefit (specify):		
Investments/other		
New Partner's Income		

EXPENDITURE	**FATHER**	**MOTHER**
Housings costs		
Rent/Loan repayments		

ACTION TO BE TAKEN

Style 4

Questionnaire About Matrimonial Property

<u>**For**</u>

Name_____

Address_____

_____

It is important that all the values are shown for the date you and your partner separated. If you have not yet separated then please use the most recent value for each asset and give the date of the information.

Date of Separation		Today's Date:	

If any assets were wholly or mainly acquired as a gift or inheritance to either of you please show this as that affects how far they might be considered matrimonial property.

1. Matrimonial Home **Address:**	
Is it owned/rented?	Owned/rented
Who is the owner/tenant?	You/your partner/joint
Have you had this valued if owned?	YES/NO
If, YES has this been by an Estate Agent?	YES/NO
Or by a Surveyor?	YES/NO
What was the date of the Survey?	
What is the value they indicated?	£
If not, what do you think the house might fetch if it was sold now?	£

If you have obtain a survey of the property could you please let us have a copy.

2. Please give the name, address and loan reference number for the Bank or Building Society who advanced you the money to pay for the house.	
How much of the loan is outstanding?	£

If there is more than one loan secured over the house, please give details of any other lenders involved and the outstanding balance.

If you have a recent statement showing how much is outstanding could you let us have a copy.

3. Holiday Home/Timeshare/Other Property

Please give details of any holiday home/timeshare/other property you owned and the value of this. Please show if the value is an estimate or it has been suggested by a professional and if so, the identity of the professional involved.

Who is the owner?	You / Your Partner / Joint
Who has the documents of ownership?	

4. Bank Accounts

Please give details of credit balance in any Bank accounts you or your partner held. Please indicate if the accounts are yours, your partner's or joint.

Name	Address	Account No	Balance (at date of separation)	Balance (now)

If you have copies of statements confirming these figures please let us have them.

5. Savings Accounts

Please give details of credit balances in any Savings Accounts you or your partner held. Please indicate if the accounts are yours, your partner's or joint.

Name	Address	Account No	Balance (at date Of separation)	Balance (now)

If you have copies of statements confirming these figures please let us have them.

6. Shares & Investment

Please give details of any shareholdings or other investments held by you your partner or jointly and their value giving a note of whose name they are in. Please indicate if this value is an estimate and if not, the identity of whoever has given you the information.

Company	Shareholdings & Investments	Value

7. Household Contents

Please indicate the value of the household contents. Let us know if this is an estimate or, if it has been valued professionally, the identity of the valuer. The value to use is the resale, not the replacement value.

Have any of the contents already been shared out?

8. Vehicles

Do you own a car?	YES/NO	Does your partner own a car?	YES/NO

If YES, please detail the model and registration	You	Your Partner
What was the value of the vehicle?	£	
Is this an estimate?	YES/NO	
If NO, was the value provided by a professional person?	YES/NO	
If so, could you supply a copy of the valuation.	YES/NO	

9. Pension Fund

Have you been in an occupational pension scheme?	YES/NO

If YES, could you please attach or now request & forward to us a cash equivalent transfer value for this if possible, from the period you have worked during the marriage up until the separation. (You can ask the pension fund for this although they may not provide it calculated for the exact period. An appointment may be necessary).

Have you had a private pension policy	YES/NO

If YES, please give details of the Company involved and attach or request and provide a fund value from the Company which they should give you on request.

Was your partner in an occupational pension scheme?	YES/NO

If YES, for what period of time and from what employer during the time you were married and lived together?

Was your partner in a private pension policy	YES/NO

If YES, please give details if you can.	
Are there any state scheme pensions rights for you? Or your partner?	YES/NO

10. Endowment Policies

Please give details of the name, address and policy number of each policy and their surrender value. If you would like us to obtain the surrender value please let us know and we will send you a mandate to sign to allow us to do this.

If you have obtained a surrender value could you please let us have a copy of this.

10. Endowment Policies cont.

Company	Policy no	Surrender Value	In name of Wife/ Husband or Joint
If any of the Policies were taken out before the marriage, could you please show the date the policy was started.			
Who has the original policy documents?			

11. Business Assets

Do you have any interests in a business that started after the marriage?	YES/NO
If YES, please give details and attach accounts for the last 3 years if possible.	

Does your partner have any business interests which started during the marriage.	YES/NO
If YES, please give details.	

12. Other Assets

Please give details of any other assets either of you owned or have any significant value.

LIABILITIES

Please try to provide copy Statements for any liabilities

Do **you** have any Bank loans?	YES/NO

If YES, please give details		
Bank & Address	Account number	Balance

Does your **partner** have any Bank loans?	YES/NO

If YES, please give details		
Bank & Address	Account number	Balance

Do you have any Bank loans **jointly**?	YES/NO

If YES, please give details		
Bank & Address	Account number	Balance

Do you have a car loan?	YES/NO	Did your partner?	YES/NO
If YES, please give details of lenders and amounts outstanding.			
You	Lender:	Amount: £	

Your Partner	Lender:	Amount: £

Do **you** have any credit card debts?	YES/NO

If YES, please give details

Bank & Address	Reference number	Balance

Does your **partner** have any credit card debts?	YES NO

If YES, please give details

Bank & Address	Reference number	Balance

Please give details of any other loans owed by you or your partner at the date of separation.

Have any of the assets gone up substantially in value since you separated.	YES/NO

If YES, please give details.

Have any of the liabilities been reduced more by one or other of you since the separation	YES/NO

If YES, please give details.

Have any of the assets been wholly or mainly acquired as a gift or inheritance or from pre-marriage resources by either of you?	YES/NO

If YES, please give details

Did either of you own any of the assets before the marriage?	YES/NO

If YES, please give details

Style 5

DRAFT WITHOUT PREJUDICE SCHEDULE OF MATRIMONIAL
PROPERTY

as at (date of draft)

For

NAMES & ADDRESSES

DATE OF MARRIAGE—
RELEVANT DATE—

If figures are estimated they are preceded by 'E'

Assets in name of	Husband	Wife	Joint
Matrimonial Home (Address)			
Value Balance of secured loan			
Net Value			
Holidayhome/timeshare/ Other property (Address) Value			
Bank Accounts Give details of balance			
Savings Accounts Give details of balance			
Shares & Investments Give details			
c/f			

Assets in name of	Husband	Wife	Joint
b/f			

Household Contents

Vehicles
Value

Interest in Pension Fund
Give details

Insurance Policies
Give details

Business Assets
Give details

Other Assets
Give Details

| TOTAL | | | |

| **Liabilities in name of** | **Husband** | **Wife** | **Joint** |

Bank Loans

Car Loans

Credit Card Loans

Other:-

TOTAL			

Total matrimonial Assets   £
Total matrimonial Liabilities   £
                                        -------.-----
Net Matrimonial Property   £
                                        ====.===

Style 6

STATEMENT OF INCOME AND EXPENDITURE PER CALENDAR MONTH FOR *(please put in name and address of client)*

(Please give full details of your average monthly income and expenditure)

Income

Net Pay from employment	£
Income from Benefit	£
Child Benefit	£
Other Income *(please give details of source of income)*	
	£
TOTAL	£

Expenditure
(Please show your expenditure for your current address)

* Rent OR * Mortgage Repayments	£
House Maintenance	£
Council Tax	£
Electricity	£
Gas	£
Telephone	£

Insurances – Endowment
          - Buildings
          - Contents
	£
	£
	£

Food	£
Clothes	£

TV Licence	
	£
Petrol	
	£
Car Tax	
	£

Car Maintenance	
	£
Playgroup	
	£
School Fees	
	£
Holidays	
	£
Other normal expenses:- (Please specify)	
	£
TOTAL	£

Notes

1. Do you share any of those expenses?	YES/NO
If YES, could you indicate what contribution is made by someone else	£

2. Is your income or outlays going to change much in the near future?	YES/NO
If YES, please give details.	

**

3. Are you making a contribution to the costs of the former matrimonial home?	YES/NO
If YES, please indicate what outlays.	

```

```

**
NOTE 3 SHOULD ONLY INCLUDED IF CLIENT IS NOT LIVING IN MATRIMONIAL HOME**

Style 7

Business Valuation—Information Checklist

❑ Company Memorandum & Articles of Association and details of share structure

❑ Shareholders Agreement

❑ Partnership Agreement

❑ Previous disposals of shares in the company or interest in partnership

❑ Copy detailed financial accounts for the last three years

❑ Last Annual Return submitted to Companies House

❑ Copies of the Management accounts at relevant dates

❑ Minutes of Directors Board Meetings

❑ Any budgets or financial forecasts

❑ Accounts for company pension scheme

❑ Copy income tax returns

❑ Background information on the business including major customers, business history, etc.

❑ Confirmation that accounts have been agreed by the Inland Revenue

❑ Analysis of the Directors Loan Account or partners capital account for the last three years

❑ Analysis of the directors remuneration shown in the accounts, allocated between the directors and details salaries, bonuses and pension contributions paid by the company

❑ The specific working roles of each director or partner in the business

❑ Further information on the roles of the other key staff within the business, the work carried out and the salary paid to each.

❑ If necessary request access to business records

❑ Personal bank statements

Kindly provided by Alan Robb of Robertson Craig & Co., 3 Clairmont Gardens, Glasgow.

Style 8

Some Useful Addresses for Clients

<u>**Counselling**</u>

COSCA
(formerly Confederation of Scottish Counselling Agencies)
18 Viewfield Street
Stirling
FK8 1UA
Tel 01786 475140
E-mail: cosco@compuserve.com
Website: www.cosca.org.uk
A National organisation which can provide a list of accredited independent
counsellors.

British Association for Counselling
1 Regent Place
Rugby
Warwickshire
CV21 2PJ
Tel 01788 550899
e:mail: bac@bac.co.uk
The U.K. representative body which can provide lists of organisations and
individuals in Scotland.

Couple Counselling Scotland
40 North Castle Street
Edinburgh
EH2 3BN
Tel 0131 225 5006
Fax 0131 220 0639
Source of information about local services

Counselling Unit
University of Strathclyde
76 Southbrae Drive
Jordanhill
Glasgow
G13 IPP
Tel 0141 950 3359
Fax 0141 950 3329
Free counselling service to individuals by participants on the Diploma course in
counselling which is run by the unit.

Tom Allan Centre
23 Elmbank Street
Glasgow
G2 4PD
Tel 0141 221 1535

Wellspring
13 Smith's Place, Edinburgh
EH6 8NT
Tel 0131 553 6660

The Association of Person-Centred Therapy
40 Kelvingrove Street
Glasgow
Tel 0141 332 6888

ParentLine Scotland
Tel 0808 800 2222—Confidential telephone support for parents who want to talk over worries, problems and concerns—available Monday, Wednesday and Friday 10 a.m. to 1 p.m., Tuesday and Thursday 6 p.m. to 9 p.m. and Saturday and Sunday 2 p.m. to 5 p.m.

Other Organisations

C.A.L.M. (Comprehensive Accredited Lawyer Mediators)
Secretary—Stephen Brand, c/o Messrs Thorntons, Solicitors
40 Castle Street
Dundee
Tel 01382 229111
Mediation for child and financial issues

Family Mediation Scotland
127 Rose Street South Lane
Edinburgh
EH2 4BB
Tel 0131 220 1610

Scottish Women's Aid
12 Torphichen Street
Edinburgh
EH3 8JQ
0131 221 0401
Can provide details of local Women's Aid Groups who will be able to provide support and help for women and children who have been subject to domestic violence.

One Parent Families Scotland
13 Gayfield Square

Edinburgh
EH1 3NX
Tel 0131 556 3899/4563
E-mail opfs@gn.apc.org
web www.gn.apc.org.opfs
Offers information and support.

Stepfamily Scotland
5 Coates Place, Edinburgh
EH3 7AA
Tel 0131 225 8005
Helpline 0131 225 5800

Child Support Agency
P.O. Box 55, Brierly Hill, West Midlands
DY5 1YL
National Enquiry Line 01345 133 133
Information and leaflets available.

British Agencies for Adoption & Fostering
40 Shandwick Place
Edinburgh
EH2 4RT
Tel 0131 225 9285
Fax 0131 226 3778
e-mail scotland@baaf.org.uk
web www.baaf.org.uk
Legal Consultant: Alexandra Plumtree

Style 9

Clauses, pleadings, annex and letter

Pension Sharing

Bear in mind the steps outlined in Chapter 4.   Let the "pension arrangement"
have a look at the proposed wording of all relevant documents.   Read the notes
which follow the clauses.

Separation Agreement

Remember the actual sharing is only implemented on divorce and only if the
relevant paperwork is intimated on time.
Add within the body of the Separation Agreement the following clauses—

<u>PENSION SHARING</u>

(a)   The **Husband/Wife** has shareable pension rights with **(details of
        pension arrangement).** The parties intend this Agreement to make
        provision for the **Wife/Husband to receive a** share of the
        Husband/Wife's pension rights as part of financial settlement on
        divorce. The **Husband/Wife** has intimated to the pension arrangement
        his/her intention to share **his/her** pension interests with the
        Wife/Husband.

(b)   The **Wife/Husband** is to receive ***either amount [plus interest at
        amount per cent per year from DATE until transfer]** of the
        Husband's/Wife's relevant benefits OR *amount* per cent of the
        cash equivalent of the Husband's/Wife's relevant benefits at the
        date of transfer*** as provided for in the annex to this Agreement.

(c)   In the event that the **Husband/Wife** dies before the pension sharing is
        implemented, it is agreed that a capital sum of ***Amount*** with interest
        at ***Amount*** per cent each year from the date of the later signature on
        this document will be payable to the **Wife/Husband** by the
        Husband's/Wife's executors in place of pension sharing, payable
        within six months of the estate of the **Husband's/Wife's** death.

(d)   In the event that the **Husband/Wife** dies before the pension sharing is
        implemented, it is agreed that a capital sum of ***Amount*** with interest
        at ***Amount*** per cent each year from the date of the later signature on
        this document will be paid to the **Husband's/Wife's** estate not later
        than *date*.

(e) In the event that the **Husband's/Wife's** relevant pension benefits are transferred from (**details of pension arrangements**) before the transfer of the pension share is implemented then it is agreed that the **Wife/Husband** shall receive a capital sum of *Amount* within one month of the date of decree of divorce with interest *Amount* per cent each year from the date of the second signature on this document on any balance unpaid, until payment.

(f) (i) **Either—**

In the event that the pension in respect of which pension sharing is provided for is in payment to **the Husband/the Wife** prior to the implementation of the pension sharing provision, the parties shall be entitled to negotiate an alternative provision. In the event that agreement cannot be reached, the parties will be entitled to seek or propose an alternative in divorce proceedings at the instance of either. The remaining terms of this agreement shall stand and the parties shall be bound by them.

OR

(ii) In the event that the pension in respect of which pension sharing is provided for is in payment to **the Husband/the Wife** prior to the implementation of the pension sharing provision [and (**Details of pension arrangement**) indicate in writing that they will no longer be able to implement the pension sharing provision,] then **the Wife/the Husband** shall be entitled to a capital sum of * Amount* with interest at *Amount* per cent a year from the date of the later signature on this document from the **Husband/the Wife**, payable within four months of the date of decree of divorce.

Notes

1. Add details of the value and date of valuation of the pension benefits to the pre-amble setting out the matrimonial property.

2. Remember that the Agreement must be registered in the Books of Council and Session and that there must be a separable annex in correct terms.

3. If state scheme rights are involved it is necessary to receive confirmation from the Secretary of State that shareable state scheme rights are held in name of the transferor prior to the Agreement being concluded. The last sentence of (a) would not be necessary.

4. Bear in mind the doubt over a provision for interest and consider, where a specific amount is provided for, adding a separate clause: "Interest at *Amount* per cent per year will accumulate in respect of *Amount of pension share* from DATE until implementation of the pension sharing provision. The accumulated interest will be paid by the Husband/Wife to the Wife/Husband within one month of implementation of the pension sharing provision".

5.   If a provision for payment in the event of death is included, give very careful thought to the practicalities. Pension sharing may be used because there are few other resources. Where is the money to come from?

6.   Since pension sharing is directed to a specific "pension arrangement" the provision will be defeated if there is a transfer to another "arrangement" before implementation. This might be voluntary or involuntary. The consequence of either needs to be provided for.

7.   The number of contingent provisions which have to be made for pension sharing in a Separation Agreement does reinforce how important it is to try to have the divorce following as soon as possible to avoid events which might frustrate the original intention.   A particularly difficult situation to provide for is the possibility that the transferor might retire after the arrangements are made, but before the pension sharing is implemented.   In some circumstances, that could possibly diminish the fund so much that pension sharing would be thwarted.   It might have an unforeseen impact on the transferor's income
Two possible ways of dealing with this are suggested.   It is daunting to contemplate re-negotiation, especially when other assets have already been distributed.   On the other hand, providing for a specific capital sum may be fine on paper but, depending on the resources, difficult or impossible to implement.   It might be accepted that payment of a capital sum instead of pension sharing should only happen if the pension sharing order cannot be implemented because of the impact of the early retirement.   If so, the provision within the square brackets in (f)(ii) could be left in.
Practice alone will make the risk assessment easier and infinite care and extensive advice is going to be necessary initially before choices are made.   It would seem good practice for the transferee's solicitors to always check with the pension fund how matters stand before divorce is initiated and to obtain a mandate from the transferor at the time of the Separation Agreement to allow them to do that.

For pension sharing to be craved in the divorce writ add the following—
Craves

A.   To make a pension sharing order in terms of Sections 8(1)(baa) and 8A of the Family Law (Scotland) Act 1985 providing that the Defender's shareable pension rights in the **give details** scheme administered by **give details including address** be subject to pension sharing for the benefit of the Pursuer and that EITHER amount per cent of the cash equivalent of the Defender's relevant benefits at the date of transfer be transferred to the Pursuer OR £amount [with interest accrued at *amount* per cent a year from *date* until the date of transfer be transferred to the Pursuer;] and that the charges for implementing pension sharing order shall be apportioned equally between the Pursuer and Defender.

B.   To grant warrant for intimation of this Initial Writ by way of notification that a pension sharing order may be made in respect of the Defender's pension rights to *give details name and addresses of managers of pension fund*.

C.   To ordain said *give details of pension fund* to provide to the Court (firstly) a valuation of the pension rights or benefits accrued under the Defender's pension arrangement with them, [as at the relevant date, Date] within three months and (secondly) The relevant information in terms of the Pensions on Divorce etc (Provision of Information) Regulations 2000 (S.I. 2000 No. 1048) 2(3)(b–f) and 4(2) within one month.

Pension Sharing Writ

Article of Condescendence

The Defender is a member of give details of Pension Scheme administered by Name and Address. This is an occupational pension scheme within the meaning of the Pensions Act 1993. The Defender's pension rights thereunder are shareable in terms of the Welfare Reform and Pensions Act 1999. The value of the Defender's pension rights as at relevant date for the purpose of calculating the net value of the matrimonial property was give information if known or "was believed to be in excess of estimate figure". The Defender joined the scheme following the parties' marriage. The said value was accordingly referable to the period of the marriage. No order under section 12A(2) or (3) of the Family Law (Scotland) 1985 has been granted nor is any qualifying agreement between the parties in effect relating to the Defender's shareable rights in the Scheme.

IF INFORMATION NOT AVAILABLE ADD
The Defender has refused or delayed to provide details of his pension interests. It is accordingly necessary for the pension arrangement to provide the relevant information.

Plea-in-Law

The necessary order for financial provision sought by the Pursuer being justified in terms of Section 9(1)(a) add in any other relevant sections of the Family Law (Scotland) Act 1985 and reasonable having regard to the parties resources, decree therefor should be granted as craved.

Notes

Remember that the wording will be different for state scheme rights.

Letter by Scheme Member giving notification

Name & address of pension trustees

Date

Dear Sirs,

Scheme Reference Details
Section 23 of the 1999 Welfare & Pensions Act
Statutory Instrument 2000 No. 1048, regs 2(2), 3(b)–(f) and 4(2)

We act on behalf of **name and address of client** in connection with financial provision following **his/her** separation. Our client has pension interests through yourselves. A Pension Sharing Order or provision may be made. We look forward to receiving the relevant information in terms of the above Act and regulation 3(b–f) and 4(2) within 21 days.

IF VALUATION NOT YET OBTAINED ADD—
Could you also provide a valuation in terms of Regulation 2(2) within three months? The parties married on **Date**. The relevant date is **Date**.

We enclose a mandate signed by our client.

Yours faithfully

Remember to enclose mandate from client

Annex in Relation to Pension Sharing Provision in Agreement

BETWEEN

Full name and address of Husband and Wife

(a)   Information in relation to **name of Husband/Wife** as transferor—

   (i)   All names by which **he/she** has been known:

   (ii)   Date of Birth:

   (iii)   Address:

   (iv)   National Insurance Number:

   (v)   The name and address of the pension arrangement to which the pension sharing provision relates:

   (vi)   The transferor's membership number or policy number in that pension arrangement:

(b)   Information in relation to the **name of Wife/Husband** who is the transferee—

   (i)   All names by which the transferee has been known

   (ii)   Date of Birth:

   (iii)   Address:

   (iv)   National Insurance Number:

   (v)   If the transferee is a member of the pension arrangement from which a pension credit is derived the membership number of the transferee in that pension arrangement—

EITHER

(c)   The amount to be transferred to the transferee (name) is— **£Amount** [Together with interest from [date] at [specify] % a year to the date of transfer.*]

OR

(c)   The specified percentage of the cash equivalent of the relevant benefits on the valuation day to be transferred to the transferee (name) is **Amount %.**

(d)   The transferee has given **his/her** consent, in accordance with paragraph 1(3)(c), 3(3)(c) or 4(2)(c) of Schedule 5 to the 1999 Welfare Reform and Pensions Act to the payment of a pension credit to the person responsible for a qualifying arrangement as follows—

        (i)   The full name of that qualifying arrangement

        (ii)   Its address

        (iii)   If known, the transferee's membership number or policy number in that arrangement

        (iv)   The name or title, business address, business telephone and, where available, the business facsimile number and electronic mail address of a person who may be contacted in respect of the discharge of liability for the pension credit.

(e)   The transferor and transferee have arranged that the apportionment of charges levied by the person responsible for the pension arrangement will be as follows—***GIVE DETAILS***

(f)   The transferor confirms **he/she** has intimated to the pension arrangement his/her intention with respect to pension sharing on [DATE]. The pension arrangement has acknowledged receipt of the intimation

               ————Transferor
               ————Transferee
               ————Pension arrangement

* Bear in mind the possible doubt over the provision for interest*
Remember that (d) is only appropriate if the pension credit is being taken as an external credit.

Annex in Relation to Sharing of State Scheme Rights in Relation to Pension Sharing Provision in Agreement

BETWEEN

Full name and address of Husband and Wife

(a)　　Information in relation to **name of the Husband/the Wife** as transferor—

　　　　(i)　　　Full name

　　　　(ii)　　Date of Birth:

　　　　(iii)　Address:

　　　　(iv)　National Insurance Number:

　　　　(v)　　**EITHER**

　　　　　　　　The amount to be transferred is— **£Amount** [together with interest from [DATE] at [Specify] % a year to the date of transfer.*]

　　　　OR

　　　　　　　　The percentage of the cash equivalent on the transfer day of the transferor's relevant state scheme rights immediately before that date to be transferred is **Amount %**.

(b)　　In relation to the name **Wife/Husband** who is the transferee—

　　　　(i)　　　Name by which the transferee is or will be known

　　　　(ii)　　Date of Birth:

　　　　(iii)　Address:

　　　　(iv)　National Insurance Number:

(c)　　The transferor **name** and transferee **name** have received confirmation from the Secretary of State that shareable state scheme rights are held in the name of the transferor and that on the grant of decree of divorce a pension sharing agreement will be implemented.

　　　　　　　————Transferor
　　　　　　　————Transferee

* Bear in mind the possible doubt over the provision for interest*
Make sure you have seen confirmation from the Secretary of State.

Style 10

SEPARATION AGREEMENT
and Schedule

between

(Referred to in this document as "the Wife")

and

(Referred to in this document as "the Husband")

The Wife and the Husband were married at ------(PLACE)----- on **(DATE, MONTH, YEAR)** and have ***(No.) child/children, (CHILD'S NAME)** born **(DATE, MONTH YEAR)** and **(CHILD'S NAME)** born **(DATE, MONTH YEAR)** and **(CHILD'S NAME)** born **(DATE, MONTH, YEAR)** OR no dependent children*. The Wife and the Husband *separated on **Date** /stopped living together as husband and wife on **Date***.

Having taken independent legal advice the parties wish to set out the following agreement in writing —

PREAMBLE

(A)   *Refer to Schedule*

The matrimonial property at the relevant date [and the parties' current income and expenditure] is detailed in the Schedule attached and signed as relating to this document. Having taken independent legal advice the parties wish to set down the following agreement in writing:-

(B)   *Narrate Assets/Liabilities*
It is accepted by both parties that the matrimonial assets and liabilities

at the relevant date comprised—

[The Husband has a net monthly income of £   and the Wife has net monthly income of £   together with Child Benefit.]

(C)   *No Assets/Liabilities*
         The parties had no significant capital assets or liabilities at the relevant
         date. [The Husband has a net monthly income in the region of £
         and the Wife has a net monthly income in the region of £   together
         with Child Benefit of £   .]

1.   CHILDCARE ARRANGEMENTS
(A)   *Children Based with One Parent*
         The **child/children**   *(give details)* shall live with **the Wife/the
         Husband. He/She/They** shall have the following contact with the
         Husband/the Wife–
         (a) alternate weekends from 6.00 p.m. on Friday until 6.00pm on the
         immediately succeeding Sunday (b) the first two weeks of the school
         summer holidays (c) one week during the Christmas holiday period
         (including Christmas Day and New Year's Day in alternate years) (c)
         one week during the school Easter holidays. These arrangements may
         be altered if both parents agree.

(B)   *Shared Care*
         The parents will continue to share the care of their **child/children
         (GIVE DETAILS)**. The **child/children** shall live with the Wife
         *from (give details) to   * each week and with the Husband for the
         remainder of the week. The holidays shall be divided as follows—
         (GIVE DETAILS)

(C)   *General Legal Position*
         Each Parent shall consult with and take account of the views expressed
         by the other and where appropriate their **child/children** in any major
         decision affecting or concerning the welfare, health, education or
         wellbeing of the **child/children**. *Either parent has the authority to
         take the **child/children** out of the United Kingdom without the written
         consent of the other parent but only for a reasonable holiday period not
         exceeding **2/3** weeks. OR Neither parent has the authority to take the
         child/children out the United Kingdom without the prior written
         consent of the other parent.*

2.   HOUSEHOLD CONTENTS
(A)   Transfer to One
         The Husband/the Wife agrees to transfer any interest **he/she** has in
         the furniture and other moveable items in the matrimonial home at
         (ADDRESS) ("the home") to **the Wife/the Husband** [other than
         list which **he/she** will collect from the matrimonial home within
         four weeks of the later signature on this document.]

(B)   Sharing/Unspecific
         The furniture and other moveable items in the matrimonial home at
         (ADDRESS) have been divided by mutual agreement.

(C)   Specific Division

The parties have agreed to divide the furniture and other moveable contents in the matrimonial home at **(ADDRESS)** in terms of the attached Schedule of Division of Contents. The **Husband/the Wife** will collect **his/her** share within four weeks of the date of the later signature on this document.

3.   **MATRIMONIAL HOME**

(A)   *TENANCY TRANSFER/RENUNCIATION*

The **Husband/the Wife** agrees to the transfer of the tenancy of the matrimonial home at **(ADDRESS)** ("the home") to **the Wife/the Husband,** and agrees to move out of the property two weeks after the date of the later signature on this document. **He/She** will sign a Form of Renunciation of occupancy rights in home (in terms of the Matrimonial Homes (Family Protection) (Scotland) Act 1981 as amended) and deliver the Renunciation to **the Wife/the Husband** within two weeks of the later signature on this document.

(B)   *OCCUPANCY   RIGHTS/TRANSFER/POSSIBLE   SALE/JOINTLY OWNED*

3.1   **The Husband/the Wife** agrees that the **Wife/the Husband** shall have sole occupancy rights in the [jointly owned] matrimonial home at **(ADDRESS)** ("the home") until the **younger/youngest** of the **child/children** attains the age of **sixteen/eighteen** years. **He/she** shall not during that time take any steps to force the sale of the home.

3.2   At any time until the said child **(NAME OF YOUNGEST CHILD)** attains the age of **sixteen/eighteen** years **the Wife/the Husband** may offer in writing to pay over to **the Husband/the Wife** ******a one half **(or other proportion)** share of the net value of the home at that future date under deduction of the amount of secured loan then outstanding having had the value of the home established by an independent valuer OR the sum of £**Amount**   [with interest at **Amount** % a year from the date of the later signature on this document until payment].   ****** The **Husband/the Wife** agrees to co-operate with **the Wife/the Husband** to deliver whatever validly signed Deed or Deeds are necessary to convey a good marketable title [so far as affecting **his/her** interests] and to vest the whole right title and interest in the home in the name of the **Wife/the Husband** and to revoke any special destination and (if it is still appropriate to so do) to sign and deliver an Affidavit renouncing **his/her** occupancy rights in the home and a letter of obligation in appropriate terms in exchange for the appropriate consideration. **The Wife/the Husband** shall exhibit and then record in the Land Register a Deed of Variation or Discharge of any standard security in agreed terms validly executed by the creditors discharging **the Husband/the Wife** of all liability and obligations in respect of said secured loan. Prior to settlement the **Husband's/Wife's** solicitors shall show to the **Wife's/Husband's** solicitors a clear Form 10/P16 or 12 report as appropriate in the property and personal registers in relation to the home. **The Husband's/the Wife's** solicitors shall provide a letter of obligation in the Law Society of Scotland recommended style at settlement.

3.3   At the end of the period of occupation (unless previously transferred to **the Wife/the Husband,**) the home will be sold and **the net free proceeds, after settlement of the outstanding balance of the secured loan, other debts and expenses of sale, shall be divided equally between the Husband and the Wife OR in the following proportion **[State proportion]** OR the **Husband/the Wife** will receive the **sum of £**   plus interest on that figure at the rate of   % per annum from the date of the later signature on this document until payment and the **Wife/the Husband** the balance of the net free proceeds.** Both parties agree they will not exercise any diligence on the free proceeds of sale.

(C)   *PROVISION FOR RUNNING COSTS DURING PERIOD OF SOLE OCCUPATION*

3.4   During the said period of occupation the responsibility for sums due under the secured loan [and related endowment premiums] shall be met *solely by the **Wife/the Husband** OR equally between the Husband and the Wife and if either pay a greater share of said payments during this period he or she shall be entitled to recover from the other such excess over and above one half of the total payments during the same period.* The **Wife/the Husband** undertakes to maintain the home in its present condition. The costs of any structural repairs not covered by insurance will be met *equally between the parties OR solely by the **Wife/the Husband.*** Neither party will increase the borrowing in relation to the home during said period. The **Wife/the Husband** shall be solely responsible for other outgoings such as Council Tax, fuel and telephone bills, decorating and the costs arising from wear and tear.

(D)   *SALE WHERE ONE PARTY SOLE OWNER OR JOINT OWNERS AND HALF SHARE EACH*

3.1   Both the Wife and Husband agree that the matrimonial home at **(ADDRESS) ("the home")** will be put on the market within 2 weeks of the date of the later signature on this document. ** **The Husband/the Wife** agrees to pay over to **the Wife/the Husband** one half of the free proceeds of the sale of the home (after repayment of the secured loan and all reasonable estate agents and legal expenses). In exchange **the Wife/the Husband** agrees to sign an Affidavit consenting to the sale of the home in terms of the Matrimonial Homes (Family Protection) (Scotland) Act 1981 as amended and any other documentation necessary to effect the sale. OR The free proceeds of sale (after repayment of the secured loan and all reasonable estate agents and legal expenses) will be divided equally between the parties. **

3.2 *By signing this document both Parties authorise and instruct **(DETAIL SOLICITORS ACTING IN SALE)** or any other firm of solicitors instructed in the sale of the home to distribute the free proceeds in accordance with the terms of this paragraph. Both parties agree they will not exercise any diligence on the free proceeds of sale. The property will be put on the market at a price of **AMOUNT**. Both parties undertake to co-operate fully to facilitate a sale of the property. No reasonable offer for the property will be refused. If the property remains unsold at the end of three months the parties will review the price asked to encourage a sale.

(E) *SALE—JOINT OWNERS—UNEQUAL DIVISION*

3.1 Both the Wife and the Husband agree that the matrimonial home at **(ADDRESS)** (**"the home"**) will be put on the market within two weeks of the date of the later signature on this document. **The Husband/the Wife** shall receive **POUNDS STERLING (£   )** from the free proceeds of the sale (after deduction of all reasonable and necessary Estate Agent and Legal expenses) the balance being payable to **the Wife/the Husband** [(unless the free proceeds are less than **(INSERT AMOUNT)** POUNDS STERLING **(£   )** in which case the free proceeds shall be divided equally between the Husband and Wife).]

3.2 By signing this both Parties authorise and instruct **(DETAIL SOLICITORS ACTING IN SALE)** or any other firm of solicitors instructed in the sale of the home to distribute the free proceeds in accordance with the terms of this paragraph.   Both parties agree they will not exercise any diligence on the free proceeds of sale. The property will be put on the market at a price of ***AMOUNT***. Both parties undertake to co-operate fully to facilitate a sale of the property. No reasonable offer for the property will be refused. If the property remains unsold at the end of three months the parties will review the price asked to encourage a sale.

(F) *NARRATION OF OUTLAYS WHEN HOUSE BEING SOLD*

Both parties agree that until the date of entry following the sale of the matrimonial home the monthly payments of the secured loan will be met by **the Husband/the Wife**, Council Tax and other utilities by **the Wife/the Husband**. [In the event of a material change of circumstances the responsibility for those payments may be reviewed at the written request of either party and failing agreement ***be determined by Court/OR by an arbiter mutually appointed, or, failing agreement, by an arbiter who is a Family Law specialist**

selected and appointed by the President or Vice President for the time being of the Law Society of Scotland and conducted in accordance with the Arbitration Rules of the Law Society of Scotland current at the date of appointment of the arbiter whose decision will be final and binding on the parties.]

(G) *ONE PARTY RECEIVING MATRIMONIAL HOME FOR NO SPECIFIC CONSIDERATION*

3.1 **The Husband/the Wife** agrees to convey to **the Wife/the Husband** [**his/her** one half *pro indiviso* share in] the home at   **(ADDRESS) ("THE HOME")** and to give **him/her** sole occupation. He/She shall co-operate with **the Wife/the Husband** to deliver whatever validly signed Deed or Deeds as are necessary to convey a good, marketable title [so far as affecting **his/her** interests], and to vest the whole right, title and interest in the home in name of **the Wife/the Husband** [alone, and to revoke any special destination] together with a validly executed and notarised Renunciation of any or all rights available to **him/her** under the Matrimonial Homes (Family Protection) (Scotland) Act 1981 (As Amended) in respect of the home. All this shall be completed as soon as reasonably practicable, but no later than eight weeks from the date of the later signature on this document.

3.2 In exchange for delivery of said Deed or Deeds of conveyance and Renunciation **the Wife/the Husband** shall free and relieve **the Husband/the Wife** of all obligations in respect of any Standard Security presently secured over the home. **She/He** shall exhibit and then record in the Land Register a Deed of Variation or Discharge of any Standard Security in agreed terms validly executed by the Creditors discharging **the Husband/the Wife** of all liability and obligations in respect of said secured loan.

3.3 Prior to settlement the **Husband's/Wife's** solicitor shall show to the **Wife's/Husband's** solicitors a clear Search form 10/P16 or 12 Report as appropriate in the property and personal registers in relation to the home. At settlement, **the Husband's/the Wife's** solicitors shall provide a letter of obligation in the Law Society of Scotland recommended style.

(H) *ONE PARTY PURCHASING THE OTHER'S SHARE*

3.1 **The Wife/the Husband** agrees to convey to **the Husband/the Wife** [**her/his** one half *pro indiviso* share in] the home at **(ADDRESS) ("the home")** and to give **him/her** sole occupation in exchange for receiving ****£Amount** OR one half of the net value of the home, after deduction of the amount then outstanding in terms of the loan secured over the property. The net value of the home will be established by an independent valuer chosen by the parties or, failing agreement, appointed by the Dean of the Faculty of Solicitors for the area in which the property is situated. OR in exchange for receiving the capital sum payable in terms of this Agreement** **The Wife/the Husband** will also be discharged from any liability under any loan presently secured over the home. **The Wife/the Husband** shall co-operate with **the Wife/the Husband** to deliver such validly executed Deed or Deeds as are necessary to convey a good, marketable title [so far as affecting **his/her** interests], and to vest the whole right, title and interest in the home in name of **the Wife/the Husband** [alone, and to revoke any special destination] ** together with a validly executed and notarised Renunciation of any or all rights competent to under the Matrimonial Homes (Family Protection) (Scotland) Act 1981 (As Amended).

3.2   In exchange for delivery of those Deeds **the Husband/Wife** shall pay over the consideration due in terms of this paragraph and shall exhibit and thereafter record in the Land Register a Deed of Variation or Discharge of the Standard Security in agreed terms validly executed by the Creditors discharging **the Wife/the Husband** of all liability and obligations in respect of the said secured loan. The Parties agree that the conveyancing to effect the transfer will be concluded and the money paid over within eight weeks of the date of the later signature on this document. If the titles and conveyancing drafts have been made available by the **Wife's/Husband's** solicitors within four weeks of the date this document receives the second signature and the full consideration is not paid over within eight weeks of the date of the later signature on this document interest on any sum outstanding will be payable by **the Husband/the Wife** to **the Wife/Husband** at 8% per annum until settlement is made in full unless the **Wife's/Husband's** solicitors have failed to return the conveyancing drafts by then. In that case interest will run at 8% per annum from one week after the date of the return of the conveyancing drafts.

3.3   Prior to settlement **the Wife's/the Husband's** Solicitors shall show to the **Husband's/Wife's** Solicitors a search Form 10/P16 or Form 12 Report (as appropriate) in the property and personal registers in relation to the home. At settlement, **the Wife's/the Husband's** Solicitors shall provide a letter of obligation in the Law Society of Scotland recommended style.

(I)   *NARRATION OF OUTLAYS WHEN TRANSFER AT THIS STAGE*
        The Wife/the Husband will be solely responsible for payment of the secured loan and outlays in respect of the home, including Council Tax and utilities from the date of the later signature on this document.

4.   ENDOWMENT POLICY/POLICIES
(A)   *SURRENDER AND EQUAL DIVISION*
        The life **assurance policies/policy number/s with (DETAILS)** [will be re-assigned to the parties and on re-assignation] will be surrendered, the proceeds to be divided equally between the Parties.

The surrender of the **Policy/ies** will be requested within two weeks of ** the date of the later signature on this document OR the date of entry following on the sale of the matrimonial home.**

(B) *ASSIGNATION TO ONE PARTY*

The life **assurance policies/policy number/s with (DETAILS)** will be assigned by **the Husband/the Wife** to **the Wife/the Husband** and [relevant policy documents and] **assignation/s** will be delivered **together with the Disposition as already referred to OR within six weeks of the date of the later signature on this document **. After the date of the later signature on this document **the Husband/the Wife** will have no liability for premiums on said policies payable after that date.

(C) *WARRANTIES*

The policy/policies are warranted to be free from any restriction or assignation and to be assignable and the premiums up to date. If there are any arrears outstanding at the date of the later signature on this document they will be the responsibility of **the Husband/Wife.**

(D) *SALE OF POLICY*

(After the date of entry following the sale of the former matrimonial home), An open market value shall be obtained for the policy number **(DETAILS)** with **(NAME OF INSURANCE COMPANY).** [**The Husband/the Wife** shall have the option, within four weeks of the value's being obtained, of paying one half of the open market value or surrender value, whichever is higher to **the Wife/the Husband.** In exchange **the Wife/the Husband** will deliver to **the Husband/ the Wife** within one week an Assignation of **her/his** whole right, title and interest, to the policy and its benefits. Following delivery of said Assignation **the Husband/the Wife** will stop being liable for payment of the premiums on said policy. If **the Husband/the Wife** does not take up said option] T/the said policy will be disposed of at the best sum obtainable and the proceeds divided equally between the Husband and the Wife.

(E) *MAINTAINING JOINT POLICY*

The policy number **(DETAILS)** with **(NAME OF INSURANCE COMPANY)** [presently used in connection with the loan secured over the matrimonial home] will be maintained in joint names of the parties. **The parties will each pay one half of the relative premiums OR the Husband/the Wife** will be solely responsible for payment of the relative premiums.** On maturity the proceeds of the policy [after repayment of the loan secured over the matrimonial home] will be spilt equally between the parties or his or her executors. Neither party will sign any deed or issue any instructions which would affect the other party's right as beneficiary to the Policy either on death or on maturity.

4.   TRANSFER OF SHARES

The **Husband/the Wife** will transfer to the **Wife/the Husband** his/her interest in **DETAIL SHARES**. He/she *will sign the relevant* transfer documents and deliver them to **the Wife/the Husband** within 4 weeks of the later signature on this document **The Husband/the Wife** will have no right to benefit from the shares in any way after this document is signed by both parties.

6.   CANCELLATION OF CURRENT INSTRUCTIONS IN HOUSE TITLE OR POLICY DOCUMENT/S
Evacuation of Destination
The parties agree that any survivorship destination contained in the title to the home [or in any joint Endowment Policy] will not operate and the subjects described in the title to the home [or policy] will pass to the respective executors of the parties in the event of either or both parties dying prior to the home [or Policy] being **sold or transferred** as provided for in this Agreement. Both parties, as testified by their signatures to this Agreement, specifically revoke such survivorship destination with the consent and concurrence of the other party.

7.   CAPITAL SUM
(A)   IMMEDIATE PAYMENT
The **Husband/the Wife** shall pay to **the Wife/the Husband (AMOUNT)** a capital sum of **(Amount)** within eight weeks of the date of the later signature on this document with interest at the rate of 8% a year on any balance unpaid by that time until payment.

(B)   TIED INTO HOUSE TRANSFER
The **Husband/the Wife** shall pay to **the Wife/the Husband** a capital sum of **(Amount)**. Payment shall be made when the transfer of ownership of the matrimonial home is effected on the terms narrated in relation to that provision with interest at the rate of 8% as year on any balance unpaid at the due date until payment.

(C)   INSTALMENTS (NO INTEREST)
The **Husband/the Wife** shall pay to the **Wife/the Husband** a capital sum of **(AMOUNT IN WORDS)** POUNDS STERLING **(£Amount)**. The capital sum shall be payable by instalments of **£Amount** per month. The first instalment will be due and payable one month after the date of the later signature on this document. No interest shall be payable except if two or more consecutive instalment payments are outstanding. In that event the whole balance of the capital sum still

remaining to be paid shall become immediately due and payable, with interest at the rate of 8% a year on the whole sum or the balance outstanding from time to time until paid.

(D)   *DEFERRED CAPITAL*

The **Husband/the Wife** agrees that the **Wife/the Husband** shall be paid a capital sum of **£**   [with simple interest at the rate of   **% a year** from the date of the later signature on this document on the balance outstanding until payment] on **Date,** the retirement or death of the **Husband/the Wife** whichever occurs first. In the event of non-payment on the due date, interest on any balance outstanding shall run at 8% a year until payment.

"EARMARKING"

In the event of divorce proceedings by either party before payment of the capital sum the **Wife/Husband** will be entitled to ask the Court to order payment of a capital sum equal to the capital sum and interest outstanding to the date of the order, together with interest on the capital sum from the date of the order at 8% a year and to make an order in terms of Section 12A of the Family Law (Scotland) Act 1985. requiring the trustees or managers of the pension scheme [provide name and contact address of scheme and any identifying reference number] to pay to the **Wife/the Husband** the whole or such part of the sum due in terms of this clause as can be met from the lump sum which remains payable at the time of divorce in terms of the said scheme on the retirement or death of the **Husband/the Wife.**] Upon the making of such an order **the Husband/theWife** will no longer be bound to make payment in terms of the capital sum and interest in terms of this Agreement.

8.   FINANCIAL SUPPORT

(A)   *SPOUSAL ALIMENT/PERIODICAL ALLOWANCE*

The **Husband/the Wife** shall pay to **the Wife/the Husband** the sum of **£**   per **week/month** by way of spousal aliment or periodical allowance payable   ****until her/his** death or remarriage OR for a period of **(number)** years from the last date this Document is signed OR until their child **(GIVE DETAILS)** attains the age of **(GIVE DETAILS).****

(B)   *ALIMENT*

The **Husband/the Wife** shall pay to the **Wife/the Husband** the sum of **£**   per **week/month** as aliment for [each of] the said **child/children,** for so long as the **child/children is/are** under the age of eighteen, **remain/s** in the care of the **Wife/the Husband** and the **Husband/the Wife remain/s** liable to aliment the said **child/ren** in terms of the Family Law (Scotland) Act 1985   or the Child Support

Act 1991 or any subsequent statutory provision amending or replacing same. If an assessment of child maintenance is carried out by the Child Support Agency then **the Child Support Agency Assessment will supersede this Agreement OR if the Child Support Agency Assessment for the said **child/children** of the marriage is at a rate higher than provided for in this paragraph, the sum due to the Wife as spousal aliment or periodical allowance as provided for above shall be reduced by an amount equal to the difference between the maintenance assessment and the sum due in terms of this clause and the Husband's liability shall be reduced accordingly in respect of aliment or periodical allowance for the Wife**.

(C) *TIMING OF PAYMENTS*

The [child & spousal] aliment [*or periodical allowance*] shall be payable **weekly/calendar monthly** in advance beginning * as at the date of the later signature on this document OR whenever the Husband and Wife separate* with interest at 8% a year on any arrears from the date the arrears fall due until paid.

(D) *SCHOOL FEES*
The **Husband/the Wife** undertakes to pay to **(GIVE DETAILS OF SCHOOL)** when requested by them all fees due to them in respect of the attendance of the said **child/children** at the school including costs of any mandatory extra curricular activities directly relating to the said **child's/children's** education. The **Husband/the Wife** also undertakes to pay for all elective extra curricular activities (providing that the parties agree beforehand that such activities should be undertaken). In the event that the **child/children is/are** removed from that school the **Husband/the Wife** undertakes to make payment of all fees and other outlays as provided for above for such other school as may be chosen by the **Husband/the Wife** in consultation with the **Wife/the Husband (and the <u>child/children</u> if appropriate) for the said child/children.**

(E) VARIATION
INDEX LINKING
The [spousal aliment or periodical allowance for **the Wife/the Husband** and] aliment for the children [other than school fees] payable by **the Husband to the Wife** shall be varied on the First of **Month** of each year in accordance with the percentage increase or decrease of the Retail Price Index published during the preceding month of **Month** in each year.

(F) *MATERIAL CHANGE OF CIRCUMSTANCES*

The child [or spousal] aliment or [periodical allowance] [including liability for school fees and outlays] shall be open to variation on the application of either Wife or Husband in light of a material change in either Wife or Husband's financial circumstances. In the absence of their agreeing the terms of any such variation, application may be made to a Court, Agency or Tribunal of competent jurisdiction for variation or assessment.

(G)   *PROVISION FOR ANNUAL REVIEW & MATERIAL CHANGE—ARBITRATION*

The **aliment [for the **Wife/the Husband** and periodical allowance and aliment] for the **child/children** [including liability for school fees and outlays] shall be subject to an annual review which shall take into account inflation for the preceding twelve months, and the respective financial positions of the Parties involved. The first review shall take place on the first anniversary of the date of the later signature on this document and so forth annually after that until liability for aliment ends as stipulated previously in this Agreement. The revised payment will be effective from the relative anniversary provided that the Party seeking review intimates their intention in writing to the other Party at least four weeks before the relative anniversary. Otherwise the revised payment will be effective from four weeks after the date of giving such notice.

The of [child and spousal] aliment [or periodical allowance] [or liability to pay school fees and outlays] shall also be subject to review in the event of a material change of financial circumstances of either Party. The revised payment in that case will be effective from eight weeks after the party seeking the review intimates their intention of this in writing to the other party. Within four weeks of intimation of the request for review the parties undertake to provide vouched details of income and expenditure. In the event of the Wife and Husband failing to come to a mutually agreed sum at any review whether annual or in relation to a material change of circumstances within twelve weeks of intimation that review is sought then the matter will be referred to Arbitration by an Arbiter who is a Family Law Specialist selected by the parties or, failing agreement on the identity of the Arbiter within two further weeks, selected and appointed by the President or Vice-President for the time being of the Law Society of Scotland and conducted in accordance with the Arbitration Rules of the Law Society of Scotland current at the date of appointment of the Arbiter whose decision will be final and binding on the Parties.

(H)   *CREDIT TRANSFER*

Payment of said **sum/s** of [child and spousal] aliment [and periodical allowance] shall be made by credit transfer into a Bank account to be nominated by the **Wife/the Husband** or such other account as from time to time may be designated for this purpose by the **Wife/the Husband.**

(I)   *POSSIBLE UNEMPLOYMENT OF HUSBAND/WIFE*
If the **Husband/the Wife** becomes unemployed no [child or spousal] aliment [or periodical allowance] shall be payable to the **Wife/the Husband during** such unemployment from the date the **Husband/the Wife** intimates a copy of a letter confirming such unemployment from the appropriate government department to the **Wife/the Husband** until the date the **Husband/the Wife** starts work again. The **Husband/the Wife** undertakes to recommence payment immediately on resumption of employment.

9.   MOTOR VEHICLES
Both Husband and Wife agree that ownership of the vehicle **(GIVE DETAILS)** will be *transferred **to/retained** by the **Husband/the Wife.** The **Husband/the Wife** will solely make repayment of the related loan agreement **(GIVE DETAILS)** despite the fact that it is in joint names. If the **Wife/the Husband** fails to make the repayments then the vehicle will be sold if it will realise enough to repay the outstanding loan and any free proceeds will be divided equally between the Wife and Husband.]

10.   *SPECIFICATION   OF   PROPERTY   PRESERVED   AND APPORTIONMENT OF LIABILITIES*
In addition to the provisions narrated above the Wife will retain the following assets which belong to her—   She will take sole responsibility for the following liabilities—   The husband will retain the following assets which belong to him—   He will take sole responsibility for the following liabilities—
OR
All other assets in name of the Husband will be retained by him as his own absolute property. All other assets in name of the Wife will be retained by her as her own absolute property. Each party will be responsible for any debts incurred by him or her in his or her sole name no matter when such debts were incurred.

11.   *SUCCESSION*
Both Parties renounce for all time coming his or her legal right to inherit by way of prior rights or on intestacy from the other arising from the fact of their marriage. Both parties accept that the terms of this document shall be binding on their executors.[with the exception of liability for payment of aliment OR periodical allowance.]

12.   *DISCLOSURE*

Each Party warrants that he or she has made full disclosure of his or her significant financial resources.

14.   **EXPENSES**

Each Party shall meet his or her own legal costs in respect of the negotiation, preparation and registration of this Agreement [To avoid doubt, each Party shall bear his or her own expenses incurred in relation to the transfer of title to the matrimonial home. The **Wife/the Husband** as transferee will bear all normal conveyancing search and registration outlays with the exception of the Stamp Duty on the Renunciation of Occupancy Rights which will be the responsibility of the **Husband/the Wife** as transferor. In the event that a defect in title is disclosed, the parties will also share any additional costs necessary to achieve a good marketable title.] **The Wife's/the Husband's** solicitor will send the Agreement to be registered and order two extracts, one for each party. The parties will share equally the costs of registration.

OR

The **Husband/the Wife** shall pay the **Wife's/the Husband's** legal expenses in relation to concluding this Agreement as agreed or as may be taxed by the Auditor of the appropriate Sheriff Court.

15.   **ACKNOWLEDGEMENT OF FAIRNESS & REASONABLENESS**

The Parties acknowledge that in reaching the terms of this Agreement they have had the opportunity of the benefit of separate legal advice and that having regard to the whole circumstances prevailing at the date of separation and as at the date of this document, the terms of settlement are fair and reasonable. This Agreement shall not prevent either Husband or Wife commencing divorce proceedings and shall remain in force so far as still applicable after any such divorce. [Both Parties acknowledge that they are aware of the implications of the Child Support Act 1991.]

16.   **IMPLEMENTATION CLAUSE**

Both parties undertake to sign all documents necessary to give effect to the provisions of this Agreement.

17.   **RECONCILIATION**

In the event that the parties effect a reconciliation before divorce and cohabit continuously for a period of twenty six weeks or more then any terms of this Agreement which remain operative will be considered null and void. In the event of any subsequent separation and divorce the childcare and financial and property arrangements will be considered of new.

And both Parties consent to registration of this document for preservation and execution: IN WITNESS WHEREOF—

NON MUTUALITY CLAUSE

(It may also be appropriate to add a clause stating that neither party would be entitled to withhold performance of an obligation in terms of the agreement because of non performance of an obligation owed by the other party in terms of the agreement. If including such a clause take care to specifically exclude linked, mutual obligations from the provision.)

17.   *RECONCILIATION*

In the event that the parties effect a reconciliation before divorce and cohabit continuously for a period of twenty six weeks or more then any terms of this Agreement which remain operative will be considered null and void.   In the event of any subsequent separation and divorce the childcare and financial and property arrangements will be considered of new.

And both Parties consent to registration of this document for preservation and execution: IN WITNESS WHEREOF—

SCHEDULE OF MATRIMONIAL PROPERTY

In relation to separation agreement

between

Please put in client's name and address and their partner's name and address

Assets in name of	Husband	Wife	Joint
Matrimonial Home (Address)			
Figure at Valuation Secured loan			
		--------.----	
Net Value			
Holidayhome/timeshare (Address) Figure at Valuation			
Bank Accounts Give details of balance			
Investments Give details of balance			
Shares			

Give details

c/f			

Assets in name of   **Husband**   **Wife**   **Joint**

b/f			

Household Contents

Vehicles
Details of Valuation

Interest in Pension Fund
Give details

Insurance Policies
Give details

Business Assets
Give details

Other Assets
Give Details

	TOTAL	

Liabilities in name of	**Husband**	**Wife**	**Joint**
Bank Loans			
Car Loans			
Credit Card Loans			
Other—			
TOTAL			

Total matrimonial Assets   £
Total matrimonial Liabilities   £
--------.-----
Net Matrimonial Property   £
====.===

NOTES—

Style 11

DRAFT SEPARATION AGREEMENT CHECKLIST

NAME OF CLIENT:

1.   Check full names of parties as shown on marriage certificate or interview sheet are used - including former names and maiden names and check date of marriage. If either party divorced check previous names.

2.   Check addresses are correct with up to date file details.

3.   Check that if client is receiving Advice and Assistance that she/he remembers about the clawback.

4.   Check that Agreement covers all assets and liabilities and all provisions discussed with client. Check in particular that position regarding pensions, insurance policies, any vehicles and debt have been covered.

5.   Check that full names of children given in document and that dates of birth are correct. Check correct wording used if children born before marriage and if there are children accepted into the marriage. If no children of marriage check that first paragraph shows this. Check that if child born to couple while wife still married to earlier husband this is explained.

6.   Check that the Schedule of Matrimonial Property is completed if appropriate.

7.   Check if it is appropriate to renounce succession in the estate of the other party.

8.   Suggest to client that a Will should be prepared.

9.   If title to be transferred or policies are affected are these now available and have the details been checked against the information in the Agreement.

CHECKLIST

Use the checklist to go through the draft separation agreement before it is sent out to the client. It will make you cross refer against the other information you have on file. It will remind you of points to cover in your discussion with the client.

Style 12

AGREEMENT OVER PROCEEDS OF HOUSE SALE

CONTRACT

between

[name-and-address-of-first-party]

and

[name-and-address-of-second-party]

The parties were married on [date] at [place]. They separated on [date]. They wish to make arrangements for the sale of the matrimonial home at [address]. They wish to make arrangements for the division of any free proceeds following on the sale. The parties have taken independent legal advice. They have agreed as follows—

1.   The matrimonial home at [address] will be marketed and sold as soon as reasonably practicable by [name-of-solicitor] or any other firm or firms the parties may choose to instruct to carry out said marketing and sale. The parties will consult with each other in respect of all steps required to be taken to effect the sale, neither party withholding their acceptance of any reasonable offer for the purchase of the said property.

2.   On the sale from the sale price the following shall be deducted—

    (a)   the sum required to redeem the secured loan with [name-of-bank/building-society];

    (b)   all reasonable and necessary fees directly relating to the sale including the estate agent's fees, all advertising costs, solicitor's fees and all properly incurred and vouched outlays.

3.   On the sale after payment of the deductions referred to above, the net free proceeds of sale shall be divided between the parties as follows—

[insert-details]

Neither party will exercise any diligence on the sum paid over to the other party under this provision

or

On the sale after payment of the deductions referred to above the net free proceeds of sale will be placed in name of [name-of-account-holder] in trust for the parties and shall be retained there until a final written agreement is reached by the parties on the destination of said balance or a division of matrimonial property is ordered on divorce. In the event of no agreement being reached prior to divorce and no order being made in relation to said balance on divorce it will be divided equally between the parties.

In the event of the death of either of the parties prior to any such agreement or divorce the proceeds shall be divided as follows—

[insert-details]

4. By their subscription of this contract, both parties authorise and instruct [name-of-solicitor] or any other firm of solicitors instructed in the sale of the property to act in accordance with the terms of this contract.

5. If either party buys a property following their separation and prior to divorce the other party will provide any formal renunciation of occupancy rights or other necessary documentation or Affidavits required to discharge or confirm the non-existence of rights under the Matrimonial Homes (Family Protection) (Scotland) Act 1981 as amended.

6. In the event of any dispute or difference between the parties as to—

    (a) interpretation of or the operation or construction of any provision of this contract (including whether an offer for the purchase of the said property is reasonable in terms of clause 1).

    (b) the rights, duties or liabilities of either party to this contract.

    The dispute shall be submitted to the decision of an arbiter mutually chosen, whom failing an arbiter to be appointed by the Sheriff of [insert-jurisdiction] whose decision shall be final and binding on the parties.

7.   Both parties undertake to sign all deeds or other documents necessary to give effect to all or any of the provisions of this contract. In the event of either party refusing or delaying to sign any such deed or other document the parties by their signature to the contract hereby authorise and empower any arbiter appointed to sign any such deeds or documents on their behalf.

8.   Each party will be responsible for their own legal costs and outlays in respect of the negotiation, preparation, execution, registration and implementation of this contract other than as already provided for under clause 2. The cost of the registration of this contract and of obtaining two extracts of it shall be borne equally by the parties and an extract of the contract shall be provided to each party as soon as possible after the last date of execution of the contract.

9.   This contract is made in the understanding that it is without prejudice to the parties rights to any capital sum, other property transfer order or other order of whatsoever nature whether under common law or statute, either on divorce or death including any claims in terms of the Divorce (Scotland) Act 1976 or any re-enactment thereof or in terms of the Family Law (Scotland) Act 1985 or any re-enactment of it.

10.   The parties consent to registration of this document for preservation and execution: IN WITNESS WHEREOF

Style 13

Pre-Marriage Contract

DRAFT PRE-MARRIAGE CONTRACT
and Schedule

between

NAME AND ADDRESS OF FIRST PARTY
(Referred to in this document as "Miss   ")
and

NAME AND ADDRESS OF SECOND PARTY
(Referred to in this document as "Mr   ")

The parties are about to marry. They wish to record an agreement in relation to the ownership and potential division of property in the event of a subsequent divorce. The parties have had independent legal advice. They have agreed as follows—

1.   Miss **Name** is the owner of the assets detailed in the schedule signed as relating to this document and acquired those assets prior to her meeting Mr. **Name**. Both parties agree that those assets are not matrimonial property as defined by the Family Law (Scotland) Act 1985 (the 1985 Act). Mr **Name** does not own any financial assets.

2.   Both Parties agree that if any of the assets on the schedule referred to are sold and the proceeds used to purchase another asset or assets in Miss **Name's** name then the source of funds for the subsequently acquired asset or assets will be fully recognised. The subsequently acquired asset or assets will be retained by Miss **Name** and not taken into account in the division of matrimonial property. This condition will apply to any future sales and purchases deriving from the same source of funds.

3.   If any of the assets detailed on the schedule signed as relating to this document are sold and the proceeds reinvested in an acquisition, whether heritable or moveable, in joint names of the parties then the proportion of the funds deriving from Miss **Name's** assets will be taken into account and that proportion of the purchase price of the post marriage acquisition at the will be credited to Miss **Name** and not taken in to account in the division of property. Such proportion shall be treated in similar manner in relation to any subsequent sale and purchase transaction deriving from the same source of funds.

4.   Both parties accept that, having had the benefit of legal advice this agreement is fair and reasonable taking into account the parties financial and personal circumstances and relevant legislation.

5.   Each party will be responsible for their own legal costs and outlays in respect of the negotiation, preparation, execution and registration of this contract .

Both parties consent to the registration of this document for preservation and execution

Notes

The lack of enthusiasm being displayed in decision to give weight to source of funds arguments may increase pressure to draw up pre marriage contracts. This is a very basic example of the possibilities. It is very important to emphasise to parties that while such a document may be persuasive should financial provision on divorce prove necessary, it is not possible to enter into any agreement which can be guaranteed to be free from potential challenge. This might, however, avoid some factual disputes at least. It could become very difficult to track the funds unless clear paperwork was retained.

Style 14

Parent and Child Contract

CONTRACT

between

(referred to in this document as "the **Mother/Father**")

and

hereinafter referred to in this document as "the **Son/Daughter**")

The parties are **Father/Mother** and **Son/Daughter**. The **Son/Daughter** was born on **Date**. The **Father/Mother** is in employment. **He/She** has a net monthly income of **Amount**. The **Son/Daughter** remains in relevant full time education namely [details of course]. [Under a decree granted by **State Court** Sheriff Court on **Date** the **Father/Mother** was ordained to pay to **Name** the sum of **Amount** per week as aliment for the **Son/Daughter** until **he/she** reached the age of eighteen.] The **Son/Daughter** was eighteen on **Date**.

1.   The **Father/Mother** shall pay to the **Son/Daughter** the sum of **Amount** STERLING (**£Amount**) per week by way of aliment. The aliment shall be payable for so long as the **Father/Mother** remains liable to aliment the **Son/Daughter** in terms of the Family Law (Scotland) Act 1985 or any subsequent statutory provision amending or replacing that Act.

2.   The aliment shall be payable weekly in advance beginning as at the last date of signing of this agreement with interest at eight per cent on any arrears from the date the arrears fall due until paid.

3.   The **Son/Daughter** undertakes to advise the **Father/Mother** immediately when **he/she** ceases to be in full time education.

4.　　　　　The aliment shall be open to variation on the application of either **Father/Mother** or **Son/Daughter** in light of a material change in either **Father/Mother** or **Son's/Daughter's** financial circumstances and in the absence of their agreeing any such variation application may be made to a Court of competent jurisdiction for variation by either party.

5.　　　　　Payment of the aliment shall be made by credit transfer into a Bank account to be nominated by the **Son/Daughter** or such other account as from time to time may be designated for this purpose by the **Son/Daughter**.

6.　　　　　Each party shall meet their own legal costs in respect of the negotiation, preparation and registration of this contract. The parties acknowledge that prior to reaching the terms of this contract they have been advised to take separate legal advice.

And both parties consent to registration of this document for preservation and execution: IN WITNESS WHEREOF

Style 15

LETTER TO PURSUER CLIENT INFORMING THEM ABOUT OPTIONS HEARING

NAME & ADDRESS

DATE

Our Ref:

Dear

I thought I would let you know that I have now been informed by the Court that ***DEFENDER*** has to lodge his written opposition by ***DATE***. From that date and until ***DATE*** is allowed for each side to make adjustments in response to what is being said by the other. Both parties and Solicitors on their behalf must attend ***Detail Court*** Sheriff Court ***CHECK WHICH COURT*** on DATE at ***TIME*** am for what is called the Options Hearing. At that point the Sheriff has to decide whether a date should simply be fixed for the parties and their witnesses to attend at a Proof and give evidence or if there should be legal argument instead. In a few cases the Court might continue the period allowed for adjustment of the written pleadings.

I will be in touch with you long before then as we will have to discuss the Defences and our response to these but it is important that you take note to be able to attend Court on the ***DATE***.

In addition there is another very important date for your diary. A Child Welfare Hearing has been fixed to take place on (DATE) at 11.00a.m. You will have to be present at **DETAIL** Sheriff Court at that time. The purpose of the Child Welfare Hearing is to give the Sheriff an opportunity of hearing what each side wants in relation to the child/ren and make any interim orders necessary in relation to the child./ren.

Yours sincerely
OFFICE REMINDER TO SECRETARY
CHECK FILE AND RETURN THE WRIT AND INVENTORY TO COURT IF THEY ARE STILL IN OFFICE

Style 16

LETTER TO CLIENT ENCLOSING COPY PAPERS RELATING TO NON-HARASSMENT ORDER

Name & Address of Client

> Date

> Our Ref:

Dear **Name of Client**

I enclose the non-harassment order granted by the Court together with the papers which confirm the order has been formally intimated to **Name of Defender**.

I have also told the Police of the existence of this order. I hope you do not have any further problems but if there are any difficulties do just let me know.

Yours sincerely
ENCL/

Style 17

LETTER TO POLICE INTIMATING NON-HARASSMENT ORDER

Chief Constable/Officer in charge

Date
Our Ref:

Dear Sirs

Case No

Pursuer v. Defender

We enclose a copy of a Decree in which a non-harassment order was granted. We also enclose a copy of a Certificate of Intimation confirming that this has been intimated to the Defender. While we appreciate the procedure is rather different from an order with a power of arrest, we felt it appropriate that you should have notice of this paperwork in view of the potential consequences of a breach.

Yours faithfully

Style 18

MOTION TO SIST FOR LEGAL AID

SHERIFFDOM OF (insert Sheriffdom)

Court Ref No.

MOTION FOR PURSUER

in the cause

--PURSUER

against

------------------------------------DEFENDER

Date

The Pursuer respectfully moves the Court—

1. To sist the cause to allow his/her Legal Aid application to be processed.

2. To discharge any hearings which have already been fixed in the cause.

List the documents or parts of process lodged with the Motion:-

Copy acknowledgement from The Scottish Legal Aid Board of Legal Aid application.

IN RESPECT WHEREOF

Solicitor

AGENT FOR PURSUER

Style 19

MINUTE OF AMENDMENT FOR PURSUER AMENDING RECORD BY CHANGING ACTION TO 2 YEAR SEPARATION WITH CONSENT

SHERIFFDOM OF

MINUTE OF AMENDMENT FOR PURSUER

in the cause

---------------------------PURSUER

against

------------------------- DEFENDER

(NAME OF SOLICITOR) for the Pursuer craved leave of the Court to amend the Record by—

1. Deleting the first crave and substituting therefor—

   "1.   To divorce the Defender from the Pursuer on the ground that the marriage has broken down irretrievably as established by the parties' non-cohabitation for a continuous period of 2 or more years and the Defender's consent to the granting of decree of divorce."

2. Deleting the remaining craves.

3. Deleting articles ***Insert Numbers*** and substituting the following—

   "3.   After their marriage, the parties lived together until (DATE) when they separated.   Since then they have not lived together nor had marital relations.   The marriage has broken down irretrievably.   There is no prospect of a reconciliation.   The Pursuer seeks decree of divorce. The Defender is prepared to consent to the granting of decree of divorce."

4. Deleting article ***Number of article/s covering child related issues*** and substituting—

   "4.   (child's name) has remained with the Pursuer throughout the period of separation. She has regular contact with the Defender. The Pursuer has ample adequate accommodation for (child's name). She is well cared for. She enjoys a good relationship with both parents."

5. Deleting articles ***Number of article/s covering financial issues*** and substituting therefor—

   "5.   The parties have reached agreement on financial provision on divorce.

6. Deleting Pleas-In-Law ***detail pleas-in-law covering now redundant issues*** inclusive.

IN RESPECT WHEREOF
Solicitor

Agent for Pursuer

SHERIFFDOM OF
MOTION

Style 20

MOTION ALLOWING MINUTE OF AMENDMENT & JOINT
MINUTE WHERE ACTION CHANGED TO 2 YEAR
SEPARATION

MOTION FOR PURSUER

in the cause

-- PURSUER

against

--DEFENDER

The Pursuer moves the Court to—

1.   Allow the Minute of Amendment to be received.

2.   Allow the Record to be amended in terms of the Minute of
      Amendment, and

3.   Thereafter to grant warrant to intimate to the Defender a copy
      of the Pursuer's Record as amended, together with a Notice in
      Form F19 and a Notice of Consent in Form F20.

Part of Process lodged with Motion—

Minute of Amendment for Pursuer.

IN RESPECT WHEREOF

Solicitor

Agent for Pursuer

Style 21

JOINT   MOTION—DIVORCE/CHILDREN/   CAPITAL ETC.

JOINT MOTION

in the cause

-----------------------------------PURSUER

against

--------------------------------DEFENDER

for the Pursuer and   for the Defender
respectfully move the Court to—

1.   Recall the sist granted on ***Date***
      (Check that this is necessary, not necessary if case not sisted).

2.   Allow the Joint Minute No   of Process to be received.

3.   Allow the action to proceed by way of Affidavit evidence.

IN RESPECT WHEREOF   IN RESPECT WHEREOF

Solicitor   Solicitor

<u>AGENT FOR PURSUER</u>   <u>AGENT FOR DEFENDER</u>

Style 22

SHERIFFDOM OF

JOINT MINUTE

DIVORCE/ARRANGEMENTS FOR CHILDREN/CAPITAL SUM/TRANSFER OF POLICY/PERIODICAL ALLOWANCE/EXPENSES.

JOINT MINUTE

in the cause

-------------------------------PURSUER

against

-------------------------------DEFENDER

for the Pursuer and   for the Defender concurred in stating to the Court that in the event of decree of divorce being granted, the parties have agreed as follows—

1. Subject to the approval of the Court—

    (a)   The children of the marriage ***child/ren's name/s & DOB*** shall reside with the ***Pursuer/Defender***.

    (b)   The ***Defender/Pursuer*** shall be entitled to have contact with the children of the marriage*child/ren's name/s and date of birth as follows—

        Set out precise arrangements

2. (a)   The Defender will pay to the Pursuer a capital sum of (AMOUNT) within one month of decree of divorce being granted, with interest at 8 per

cent a year from the date the same falls due until payment.

(b)   The Defender will transfer to the Pursuer within one month of decree of divorce being granted in **(NAME OF COMPANY)** Life Policy No. **(INSERT NUMBER)** on the parties joint lives **X00000000.**

(c)   The Pursuer will transfer to the Defender within one month of decree of divorce being granted her interest in **(NAME OF COMPANY)** Policy No. **(INSERT NUMBER)**.

(d)   The Defender shall be liable to pay the Pursuer periodical allowance until **(Date).** Payment at the rate of (£   ) per week/month will commence from the date of decree with interest at 8 per cent a year from the date the same falls due until payment.

3.   Craves **{INSERT NUMBERS}** for the Pursuer and **{INSERT NUMBERS}** for the Defender will be dismissed.

4.   (a)   The Defender shall be liable to the Pursuer in the sum of **£*AMOUNT*** sterling being the agreed expenses of the action.

OR

(b)   There shall be no expenses found due to or by either Party.

The parties craved and hereby crave the Court to interpone authority hereto and grant decree in terms hereof..

IN RESPECT WHEREOF   IN RESPECT WHEREOF

Solicitor   Solicitor

AGENT FOR PURSUER   AGENT FOR DEFENDER

Style 23

COURT ATTENDANCE SHEET

Name of client:_____ Date:_____

Meeting with client before Hearing: YES/NO   Time Engaged:_____

Meeting with witnesses: YES/NO Time Engaged:_____

Meeting with client after Hearing: YES/NO Time Engaged:_____

Waiting Time:_____   Hearing Time:_____

Which Court:_____   Travelling Time:_____

OUTCOME OF HEARING

_____

_____

_____

_____

_____

Continued Hearing: YES/NO   Date:_____
Instructed for Court Diary: YES/NO

Style 24

Court Attendance Record

CLIENT_____

TYPE OF
ACTION_____

PARTIES_____

'A'
NOS_____

COURT DATE	REASON FOR CALLING	OUTCOME	TIME SPENT

STYLE WRITS

Style 25

Initial Writ—Divorce

DIVORCE (BEHAVIOUR/2 YEAR SEPARATION WITH CONSENT/FIVE YEAR SEPARATION/DESERTION/ADULTERY)

ALIMENT & PERIODICAL ALLOWANCE/DELIVERY/SALE OF JOINTLY OWNED PROPERTY/TRANSFER OF POLICY
SHERIFFDOM OF [INSERT SHERIFFDOM]

INITIAL WRIT

in the cause

Full name and address of Pursuer
..................................……........PURSUER

Against

Full name and address of Defender
..................................…………....DEFENDER

CRAVES

The Pursuer respectfully craves the Court—

DIVORCE

1.   To divorce the Defender from the Pursuer on the ground that the marriage has broken down irretrievably as established by the Defender's behaviour/Parties' non-cohabitation for a continuous period of two or more years and the Defender's consent to the granting of decree of divorce/Parties' non-cohabitation for a continuous period

of five years or more/Defender's desertion of the Pursuer for a continuous period of two years or more/Defender's adultery.

2. To grant warrant to intimate this Initial Writ to (NAME AND ADDRESS OF PARAMOUR), as a person with whom the Defender is alleged to have committed adultery in terms of Rule 33.7(1)(b).

CAPITAL SUM

3. *[In the event of the Pursuer's crave for an order for the transfer of the Defender's whole, right, title and interest to and in the property known as (ADDRESS) in terms of crave being refused]* To make an order for payment by the Defender to the Pursuer of a capital sum of (AMOUNT) POUNDS STERLING with interest on it at the rate of eight per cent per year from the date of citation or such other date as the court thinks fit until payment in terms of The Family Law (Scotland) Act 1985 Section 8(1)(a) (and to grant warrant to arrest on the dependence).

TRANSFER OF TITLE/ORDER OVER OCCUPANCY

4. (a) To make an order for the transfer by the Defender to the Pursuer of the Defender's whole right, title and interest to and in the property known as (ADDRESS) and the furniture and plenishings therein in terms of the Family Law (Scotland) Act 1985, section 8(1)(aa).

    (b) To ordain the Defender to sign and deliver to the Pursuer a valid Disposition of his whole right, title and interest to and in (ADDRESS), within one month of the said order or within such other period as the Court may direct which failing, to make an order dispensing with the signature of the Disposition by the Defender and directing the Sheriff Clerk to sign the Disposition or any other documentation necessary to effect the transfer in terms of the Family Law (Scotland) Act, 1985, section 14(2)(k).

    (c) Which failing to make an order granting the Pursuer the sole right to occupy the matrimonial home at (ADDRESS), excluding the Defender from it and from the use of the furniture and plenishings therein in terms of the Family Law (Scotland) Act 1985, section 14(2)(d) until (NAME OF YOUNGEST CHILD) attains the age of sixteen years or to such other date as the Court may appoint.

INTIMATION UNDER RULE 33.7(i) WHERE TRANSFER OF PROPERTY IS SOUGHT

5.   To grant warrant to intimate this action to (NAME AND ADDRESS OF HERITABLE CREDITOR) as a creditor of the Parties in a loan secured over the home in terms of Rule 33.7(i).

ORDER FOR SALE

6.   To grant an order for sale of the parties' property at (ADDRESS) and for that purpose.

    (a)   To appoint (SURVEYOR'S ADDRESS) to inspect the property with a view to reporting on an appropriate market price for the property.

    (b)   To appoint (SOLICITOR'S ADDRESS) to sell the property by private bargain, in such manner and on such conditions as the court shall direct.

    (c)   To order the Pursuer/Defender to execute and deliver to the purchaser or purchasers of the property such Dispositions and other deeds as shall be necessary to transfer the Defender's right to, title and interest in the property.

    (d)   In the event that the Defender refuses or delays to sign the required deeds to dispense with such signature and delivery and to direct the Sheriff Clerk to sign said deeds.

    (e)   To make such order regarding the price of the property when sold, after deduction of any debts or burdens affecting it and all other expenses attending the sale as to the Court seems proper (or to find and declare that the price of the property, when sold after deduction of any debts and burdens affecting it and all other expenses attending the sale be divided equally between the Parties) (subject to deduction from the Defender's/Pursuer's share thereof and payment to the Pursuer/Defender of any capital sum ordered by the Court under crave) all in terms of the Family Law (Scotland) Act 1985, Sections 14(2)(a) and (k).

TRANSFER OF POLICY

7.   To make an order for the transfer by the Defender to the Pursuer of the Defender's whole right, title and interest to and in (NAME OF INSURANCE COMPANY) policy number (NUMBER) and to order the Defender to sign and deliver to the Pursuer a valid Assignation of his whole right, title and interest in and to the Policies within one month of the order or within such other period as the Court may direct.

TRANSFER OF CONTENTS

8.   To make an order for the transfer by the Defender to the Pursuer of the Defender's whole right, title and interest in and to the furniture and plenishings within the matrimonial home at (ADDRESS) in terms of The Family Law (Scotland) Act 1985, section 8(1)(aa).

ALIMENT / PERIODICAL ALLOWANCE

9.   To grant decree against the Defender for payment to the Pursuer of the sum of (AMOUNT) per week as interim aliment payable weekly and in advance with interest at the rate of eight per cent per year on each weekly payment from the due date until paid.

10.(a) To grant decree against the Defender for payment to the Pursuer of a periodical allowance of (AMOUNT) per week payable weekly in advance until (the death or remarriage of the Pursuer/for 3 years from the date of decree to follow this action or to such other date as the Court may appoint) with interest at the rate of eight per cent per year on each weekly payment from the due date until paid in terms of the Family Law (Scotland) Act 1985 Section 8(1)(b).

OR

10.(b) To grant decree against the Defender for payment to the Pursuer of a periodical allowance of (AMOUNT) per week payable weekly in advance until (NAME), reaches the age of sixteen or to such other date as the Court may set with interest at the rate of eight per cent per year on each weekly payment from the due date until paid in terms of the Family Law (Scotland) Act 1985 Section 8(1)(b).

GENERAL ENABLING CRAVE

11.   To make such other order as is expedient to give effect to the principles set out in section 9 or to any order made under section 8(2) both sections of the Family Law (Scotland) Act, 1985 in terms of Section 14(2)(k) of the said Act.

EXPENSES

12.   To find the Defender liable for the expenses of this action.

ARTICLES OF CONDESCENDENCE

Background

1.   The Parties are as designed in the instance. They were married at (PLACE OF MARRIAGE) on (DATE). They have (NUMBER) child/ren, under the age of 16 (GIVE FULL NAME AND DOB OF EACH CHILD). (After each name insert—hereinafter referred to as FIRST NAME).

The relative extracts of entries from the Register(s) of marriage and birth is/are produced.

Jurisdiction

2.   The parties are habitually resident in Scotland. The Pursuer has been resident within the Sheriffdom of (SHERIFFDOM) for a period exceeding forty days immediately before the raising of this action. The Pursuer knows of no proceedings continuing or concluded in Scotland or elsewhere which relate to the marriage or are capable of affecting its validity or subsistence *[or which are in respect of the children of the marriage]*.

(N.B. Brussels II. Where appropriate consider applicability of jurisdiction based on Art 2(1).)

GROUNDS OF DIVORCE

Behaviour

3.(a)   The marriage has broken down irretrievably as established by the Defender's behaviour. **(narrate specific details of behaviour set out as separate articles of condescendence if appropriate).** The Defender's said behaviour adversely affected the Pursuer. **(narrate effects set out as separate articles of condescendence if appropriate).** The parties separated on (DATE). They have not lived together nor had marital relations since that date. The Pursuer cannot reasonably be expected to cohabit with the Defender. There is no prospect of a reconciliation. The Pursuer now seeks decree of divorce.

2 Years with consent

3.(b)   After their marriage, the parties lived together until about (DATE). They separated on that date. They have not lived together or had marital relations since that date. The marriage has broken down irretrievably. There is no prospect of a reconciliation. The Pursuer seeks a divorce. The Defender is prepared to consent to the granting of decree of divorce.

5 year Non-cohabitation

3.(c)   After their marriage, the parties lived together until about (DATE). They separated on that date. Since then they have not lived together nor had marital relations. The marriage has broken down irretrievably. There is no prospect of a reconciliation. The Pursuer seeks a divorce.

Desertion

3.(d)   The Pursuer was willing to live with the Defender. From (DATE) the Defender would not live with the Pursuer. The parties have not lived together nor had marital relations since that date. The Pursuer has not refused a genuine and reasonable offer by the Defender to adhere. The marriage has broken down irretrievably. There is no prospect of a reconciliation. The Pursuer seeks a divorce.

Adultery

3.(e)   After their marriage, the Parties lived together until about (DATE). They separated on that date. Since then they have not lived together nor had marital relations. The Defender has formed an adulterous relationship with (NAME AND ADDRESS OF PARAMOUR) designed in the (NUMBER) crave and hereinafter referred to as (PUT IN NAME). **[narrate facts justifying conclusion of adultery]** Since at least (DATE) the Defender and (NAME) have lived together at (ADDRESS) They have committed adultery there. They associate together in public. They attend social events together. The marriage has broken down irretrievably. There is no prospect of a reconciliation. The Pursuer now seeks a divorce.

CAPITAL SUM

4.   The matrimonial property at the relevant date comprised the following—

  (a)   matrimonial home at (**address**) worth about £(**AMOUNT**) subject to a secured loan of £(AMOUNT) with (**name**)

  (b)   a (**give details**) policy number   (**give details**) with a surrender value of £(AMOUNT);

  (c)   pension interests of the Pursuer with (**name**) with a cash equivalent transfer value of £(AMOUNT)

  (d)   Pension interests of the Defender with (**name**) with a cash equivalent transfer value of £(AMOUNT).

The matrimonial debt comprised—

  (a)   (**give details**) account number, overdraft of (AMOUNT)

  (b)   Car loan with (**give details**) of (AMOUNT)

The Pursuer seeks a fair share of the net value of the matrimonial property **(insert details of both parties' current resources)**. The orders sought are reasonable having regard to the resources of the parties.

SPECIAL CIRCUMSTANCES

5.   **(Narrate facts relevant to proposition in law under the 1985 Act special circumstances including economic advantage/disadvantage, burden of care of children, dependence to a substantial degree, severe financial hardship, terms of any agreement, source of funds, destruction, dissipation or alienation of assets, nature of property, liability for expenses of valuation or transfer, source of funds (set out as separate article of condescendence if appropriate)** The said circumstances justify a departure from an equal division of the matrimonial property **(if not already in insert details of current resources and aver that the orders sought represent a fair sharing of the net value of the matrimonial property and are reasonable having regard to the resources of the parties).**

TRANSFER/ORDER OVER OCCUPANCY

6.   The Pursuer seeks an order for the transfer to her of the Defender's share of the matrimonial home, of the furniture and plenishings in it and of the related Endowment Policy/Policies as capital payment. The order sought represents a fair a sharing of the matrimonial property. In the event of such a transfer order being made the Pursuer would relieve the Defender of all liability and obligation to the Heritable Creditors **(give details)** in respect of the matrimonial home. The Heritable Creditors **(give details)** will consent to a transfer order. *[Failing transfer of the Defender's interests in home to her the Pursuer seeks an order finding her entitled to the sole right of occupation of said home until **(name of child)** attains the age of sixteen to provide a stable background for him/her]. [In this event] she also seeks the sum of (AMOUNT) by way of a capital sum].*

ALIMENT/PERIODICAL ALLOWANCE

7.   The Pursuer is employed as **(give details)**/ *is unemployed.* The Defender is employed as **(give details)** *is unemployed.* His income is £(AMOUNT) net per month. His expenditure is approximately (AMOUNT). He is called upon to provide full details of his income and expenditure. The Pursuer has an income of about **(give details)** and expenditure of about (give details) **(ensure averment is supported by lodging statement of income and expenditure,**

insert facts covering earning capacity and other circumstances as appropriate). The support sought by the Pursuer is reasonable in the circumstances. The Pursuer seeks a periodical allowance (**insert facts confirming dependence to a substantial degree/economic burden of care of children/severe financial hardship)**. An order for the payment of a capital sum or for transfer of property would be inappropriate and/or insufficient to meet the Pursuer's entitlement on divorce (**insert facts confirming inappropriate/insufficient,** *e.g.* **lack of capital available)**.

NO FINANCIAL SETTLEMENT—UNEMPLOYED

8. The Pursuer and Defender are both unemployed. The Pursuer is in receipt of State Benefits. Neither the Pursuer nor Defender had any substantial capital or other assets at the relevant date. In the circumstances the Pursuer does not make any financial claim.

FINANCIAL MATTERS AGREED

9. The parties have agreed the financial aspects of the separation. A copy of the Separation Agreement entered into between them is produced. In the circumstances the Pursuer does not make any financial claim.

PLEAS-IN-LAW

DIVORCE

1. The marriage of the Parties having broken down irretrievably, decree of divorce should be granted as first craved.

CAPITAL SUM/FINANCIAL PROVISION

2. The orders for financial provision sought by the Pursuer being justified and reasonable having regard to the resources of the parties in terms of the Family Law (Scotland) Act 1985 Section 9(1) (INSERT APPROPRIATE SUB-SECTIONS) (INSERT OTHER RELEVANT SECTIONS) decree for them should be granted as craved.

TRANSFER OF TITLE

3. The transfer of Property Orders sought of the Defender's interests in the home, the furniture and plenishings therein and the related Endowment Policy/ies *[which failing an order regulating the occupancy of the home and the use of the furniture and plenishings therein]* being justified and reasonable having regard to the resources of the parties, decree for them should be granted as craved in terms of the Family Law (Scotland) Act 1985, sections 8(1)(aa), 9(1) (INSERT RELEVANT SUB-SECTIONS) (INSERT OTHER RELEVANT SECTIONS).

SALE

4. The order for sale of the matrimonial home being justified by the principles set out in the Family Law (Scotland) Act 1985 Section 9(1) (INSERT RELEVANT SUB-SECTIONS) (INSERT OTHER RELEVANT SECTIONS) and reasonable having regard to the resources of the Parties, decree should be granted as craved.

TRANSFER OF CONTENTS

5. The Pursuer being entitled in the circumstances to an order for the transfer to her of the Defender's interest in the furniture and plenishings in the matrimonial home, decree for it should be granted as craved.

SPOUSAL ALIMENT

6. The sum sued form as aliment being reasonable in the circumstances, decree for it should be granted as craved in terms of The Family Law (Scotland) Act 1985 Sections 3, 4 and 6(1)(b).

PERIODICAL ALLOWANCE

7. An order for periodical allowance being justified in terms of Section 9(1) (INSERT SUB-SECTIONS) of the Family Law (Scotland) Act 1985 and the payment of a capital sum being insufficient financial provision for the Pursuer, the Pursuer is entitled to an order for periodical allowance and decree for it should be granted as craved.

IN RESPECT WHEREOF

Solicitor
(Address)
AGENT FOR PURSUER

Style 26

Initial Writ—EXCLUSION ORDER/INTERDICT/NON-HARASSMENT ORDER

SHERIFFDOM OF (insert sheriffdom)

INITIAL WRIT

in the cause

Full name and address of Pursuer
....PURSUER

Against

Full name and address of Defender
....DEFENDER

<u>CRAVES</u>

The Pursuer respectfully craves the Court—

INTERDICT/ POWER OF ARREST

1.   To interdict the Defender from molesting the Pursuer by
      (a)   abusing her verbally
      (b)   threatening her
      (c)   using violence towards her
      (d)   putting her into a state of fear and alarm or distress
all within the jurisdiction of the Sheriffdom of (SHERIFFDOM) and to grant interim interdict and to attach a power of arrest to the said interdict and interim interdict in terms of the Matrimonial Homes (Family Protection) (Scotland) Act 1981, section 15;

EXCLUSION ORDER AND ANCILLARY CRAVES

2.   (a)   To grant an exclusion order suspending the Defender's right to occupy the matrimonial home at (ADDRESS) and to grant the order

in the interim in terms of the Matrimonial Homes (Family Protection) (Scotland) Act 1981, section 4.

(b)   To grant warrant for the summary ejection of the Defender from the matrimonial home at (ADDRESS) by officers of the Court in terms of the Matrimonial Homes (Family Protection) (Scotland) Act 1981, section 4(4)(a).

(c)   To interdict the Defender from entering the matrimonial home at (ADDRESS) without the express permission of the Pursuer and to grant the order in the interim and to attach a power of arrest to the interdict in terms of the Matrimonial Homes (Family Protection) (Scotland) Act 1981, section 4(4)(b), section 4(6) and section 15.

(d)   To interdict the Defender from removing any furniture or plenishings from the matrimonial home at (ADDRESS) except with the written consent of the Pursuer or by a further order of the Court and to grant the order in the interim in terms of the Matrimonial Homes (Family Protection) (Scotland) Act 1981, section 4(4)(c) and section 4(6).

NON-HARASSMENT ORDER

3.   To grant a non-harassment order requiring the Defender to refrain from molesting the Pursuer [insert period] by abusing her verbally, by telephoning her, by threatening her or by using violence towards her, within the jurisdiction of the Sheriffdom of (SHERIFFDOM) and from calling at or entering the house occupied by the Pursuer at (ADDRESS) or any future house she may move to or occupy within the said jurisdiction.

INTIMATION FOR CERTAIN ORDERS UNDER MAT. HOMES (F.P.) (S.) Act 1981 (OCR 33.7(1)(k))

4.   To grant warrant to intimate this Initial Writ to (NAME & ADDRESS OF COUNCIL) as landlords of the matrimonial home at (ADDRESS) in terms of Rule 33.7 (k).

EXPENSES

5.   To find the Defender liable for the expenses of this action.

ARTICLES OF CONDESCENDENCE

BACKGROUND

1.   The Parties are as designed in the instance. They were married at (PLACE OF MARRIAGE) on (DATE). They have (NUMBER) child/ren, (GIVE FULL NAME AND DOB OF EACH CHILD). (After each name insert—"hereinafter referred to as FIRST NAME").

The relative extracts of entries from the Register(s) of marriage and birth is/are produced (not essential where no crave for divorce, section 11 order).

JURISDICTION

2.   The Defender resides at (INSERT ADDRESS). He has been resident there for at least three months immediately preceding the raising of this action. He is domiciled there. In any event, the Pursuer seeks interdict against the Defender prohibiting him from certain behaviour as detailed in (INSERT CRAVE) within the Sheriffdom of Lothian and Borders. This court has jurisdiction. The Pursuer knows of no proceedings continuing or concluded in Scotland or elsewhere involving the present course of action and the parties to this action. To the knowledge of the Pursuer no agreement exists prorogating jurisdiction over the subject matter of the present cause to another court.

INTERDICT/POWER OF ARREST

3.   **(give details of behaviour and effects of it justifying order sought. Set out as separate articles of condescendence if appropriate).** The Pursuer is apprehensive that the Defender may again behave abusively and violently towards her. She seeks the protection of an interdict, interim interdict and power of arrest as craved.

EXCLUSION ORDER

4.   **(If not already narrated under interdict give details of behaviour or anticipated behaviour and effects or anticipated effects on health of pursuer and/or child justifying order sought. Set out as separate articles of condescendence if appropriate). Insert facts relevant to arguments under Section 3(3), 4(2) and 4(3) of the Matrimonial Homes (Family Protection) (Scotland) Act 1981 (narrate details of behaviour in relation to furniture and furnishings justifying interdict)** The matrimonial home at (ADDRESS) belongs to (DETAILS OF OWNERSHIP/TENANCY) The Defender's conduct is likely to injure the physical and/or mental health of the Pursuer. The making of the orders sought is necessary for the protection of the Pursuer and/or child of the family. The orders sought are justified and reasonable in the circumstances.

NON-HARASSMENT ORDER

5.   **(give details of behaviour including at least two incidents and effects of it justifying order sought. Set out as separate articles of condescendence if appropriate).** The Pursuer is frightened and distressed by the Defender's said conduct. She has good reason to believe that the behaviour may be repeated. The Defender's said

conduct amounts to a course of conduct. The Defender by the said conduct intends to harass the Pursuer. The Pursuer has requested the Defender to stay away from her and not to call at her said house.

PLEAS-IN-LAW
INTERDICT

1. The Defender having molested the Pursuer in the manner condescended on, there is reasonable cause to believe he will continue to do so and Interdict should be granted as craved.

2. In the circumstances and having regard to the balance of convenience, interim interdict should be granted as craved .

3. There being no circumstances to indicate that a power of arrest is unnecessary, such a power should be attached to the aforesaid interdict and interim interdict in terms of the Matrimonial Homes (Family Protection) (Scotland) Act 1981, section 15

EXCLUSION ORDER

4. An exclusion order being necessary for the protection of the Pursuer and/or said children from reasonably apprehended conduct of the Defender which would be injurious to her/their health, an exclusion order suspending the Defender's occupancy rights, and orders ancillary thereto should be granted as craved and should be granted in the interim in terms of the Matrimonial Homes (Family Protection) (Scotland) Act 1981.

CONTENTS

5. The Defender having damaged the furniture and plenishings in the matrimonial home and having shown an intention to persist in said behaviour, the Pursuer is entitled to interdict as craved in terms of the Matrimonial Homes (Family Protection) (Scotland) Act 1981, section 4(5)(a).

NON HARASSMENT ORDER

6. The Defender has pursued a course of conduct amounting to harassment of the Pursuer. He intended to harass her. If he did not intend to do so it would appear to a reasonable person that his conduct amounted to harassment of the Pursuer. The Pursuer is entitled to a non harassment order as craved in terms of the Protection from Harassment Act 1997, section 8(5)(b)(ii).

IN RESPECT WHEREOF

Solicitor
(Address)
AGENT FOR PURSUER

Style 27

Initial Writ—PATERNITY, RESIDENCE & CONTACT /INTERDICT AGAINST THE REMOVAL OF A CHILD

SHERIFFDOM OF (insert sheriffdom)

INITIAL WRIT

in the cause

Full name and address of Pursuer
PURSUER

Against

Full name and address of Defender
DEFENDER

CRAVES

The Pursuer respectfully craves the Court—

PATERNITY

1.   To find and declare that the Pursuer is the father of **(name and date of birth of child)** a child born to the Defender on **(date of birth)**

RESIDENCE

1.   To make a Residence Order directing that **(NAME AND DATE OF BIRTH OF CHILD)** the child of the marriage between the parties shall live with the Pursuer and to make the order in the interim.

2.   To make a residence order directing that (NAME AND DATE OF BIRTH OF CHILD) **child** of the marriage shall live (a) for the whole of one week with the Defender (b) the whole of the next week with the Pursuer on an alternating basis with each week to begin at (o'clock)

on (day of week) and to make the order in the interim.

CONTACT

3.   [*Failing the granting of a Residence order*] To make a Contact Order providing that [(NAME OF THE CHILD)] **child** of the marriage shall have contact with the Pursuer each weekend [TIMES] on a residential basis and holiday contact each year as follows—
and to make the order in the interim.

OTHER PARENTAL RIGHTS AND RESPONSIBILITIES

4.   To deprive the Defender of the following parental responsibilities in relation to (NAME AND DATE OF BIRTH) namely the responsibility (to safeguard and promote the **child's** health, development and welfare) [to provide direction and guidance to the **child**] [to maintain personal and direct contact with the **child** on a regular basis] [to act as the **child's** legal representative].

5.   To deprive the Defender of the following parental rights in relation to (NAME AND DATE OF BIRTH) namely the right [to have the **child** living with him or otherwise to regulate the **child's** residence] [to control, direct or guide the **child's** upbringing] [to maintain personal relations and direct contact with the **child** on a regular basis] [to act as the **child's** legal representative.]

INTIMATION ON CHILD/DISPENSING WITH INTIMATION

6.   To grant warrant to (intimate this action) [to dispense with / postpone intimation of this action] on (NAME AND DATE OF BIRTH) (ADDRESS) in terms of Rule 33.7(1)(h) or [GIVE REASONS TO DISPENSE AS APPROPRIATE] in terms of Rule 33.15.

DELIVERY

7.   To order the Defender to deliver to the Pursuer (NAME OF CHILD) presently in (his/her) care and control and failing (him/her) doing so within the period the Court requires to grant Warrant to Officers of Court to search for the **child** by if necessary breaking open locked places in the course of the search and to uplift the **child** and take possession of (him) and deliver (him) to the Pursuer (and to order interim delivery).

INTERDICT

8.   To Interdict the Defender from interfering in any way with the Pursuer's care and control of (FULL NAME OF CHILD) and to grant interim interdict (and to attach a Power of Arrest to the interdict in accordance with the Matrimonial Homes (Family Protection) (Scotland) Act 1981 Section 15(1))

9.   To Interdict the Defender from taking (FULL NAME OF CHILD) child of the marriage out of the Sheriffdom except with the written consent of the Pursuer or by further order of the Court and to grant interim interdict (and to attach a Power of Arrest to the interdict in accordance with the Matrimonial Homes (Family Protection)

(Scotland) Act Section 15(1)). (N.B. note the powers of the court under section 35 of the Family Law Act 1986 to grant interdict or interim interdict prohibiting the removal of a child from the U.K. or any part of the U.K. or out of the pursuer's control and to remove passports under section 36).

EXPENSES

11. To find the Defender liable for the expenses of this action.

ARTICLES OF CONDESCENDENCE

BACKGROUND

1. The Parties are as designed in the instance. They were married at (PLACE OF MARRIAGE) on (DATE). They have (NUMBER) child/ren, (GIVE FULL NAME AND DOB OF EACH CHILD). (After each name insert- hereinafter referred to as "FIRST NAME"). The relevant certificates of marriage and birth are produced herewith.

JURISDICTION

2. The **child** has lived in Scotland since (PERIOD). The **child** is habitually resident at the address in the instance which is in the Sheriffdom of (SHERIFFDOM). This court has jurisdiction. The Pursuer is unaware of any proceedings in Scotland or elsewhere continuing or concluded which relate to the said **child.**

PATERNITY

3. The Pursuer and Defender were involved in a relationship from to (**narrate facts confirming paternity**).

RESIDENCE

4. Throughout the marriage the Pursuer took the main responsibility for (NAME OF CHILD) **(Insert details of care arrangements. From birth or other appropriate date to date of action in chronological order. Consider housing, health, school, relationships, day to day care arrangements, financial arrangements, views of child, other relevant factors. Set out in separate articles of condescendence if appropriate).** The Parties have been unable to agree on arrangements for **(name of child). (Insert reasons why it is better that an order be made than no order be made).**It is better that an order be made than that no order be made. It is in the best interests of (NAME OF CHILD) to reside with the Pursuer.
   OR
   CONTACT (Unmarried Father)

5. As the natural father of (NAME OF CHILD) the Pursuer has a positive contribution to make to his upbringing. It is beneficial for

(NAME OF CHILD) to know both natural parents and their extended families as he grows up **(Insert facts backing request. Consider development of sense of identity/self-esteem/emotional, practical, financial, help/support in care. Insert facts confirming negative effects in the absence of regular contact, consider adverse effect on relationship with father/resentment from child to mother for preventing contact) (Insert reasons why it is better that an order be made than no order be made)**It is better that an order be made than no order be made. It is in the best interests of (NAME OF CHILD) to have the contact craved with the Pursuer.

OR

REMOVAL OF PARENTAL RIGHTS AND RESPONSIBILITIES

6.   The Defender has failed to fulfil his parental responsibilities and responsibilities in the best interests of (NAME OF CHILD). In particular **(give facts) (insert reasons why it is better that an order be made than no order be made)**It is better that an order be made than that no order be made. It is in the best interests of (NAME OF CHILD) that the Defender's parental rights and responsibilities in relation to him are removed.

7.   **DELIVERY**

The Pursuer seeks delivery of (name of child) **(narrate facts justifying delivery)**. In all the circumstances an order for delivery should be granted as craved.

8.   **INTERDICT**

The Defender has threatened to remove (NAME OF CHILD) from the care of the Pursuer **(narrate facts justifying order sought). (Insert reasons why it is better that an order be made than no order be made).** It is better that an order be made than that no order be made. It is in the best interests of (NAME OF CHILD) that an interdict be granted as craved.

NO ORDER

9.   The parties co-operate over the care of (NAME OF CHILD) He lives with the Pursuer/Defender and he has contact with the Defender/Pursuer. **(details of amount and nature of contact)**He is well cared for. There is no need for any order to be made in relation to (NAME OF CHILD).

PLEAS-IN-LAW

PATERNITY

1.   The pursuer being the father of the said child, is entitled to decree as craved.

RESIDENCE ORDER

2.   It is in the best interests of the said **child** to reside with the Pursuer and therefore the order for residence should be granted as craved in terms of the Children (Scotland) Act 1995 Section 11(2)(c).

CONTACT ORDER

3.   It is in the best interests of the said **child** to have contact with the Pursuer and therefore the order for contact should be granted as craved in terms of the Children (Scotland) Act 1995 Section 11(2)(d).

REMOVAL OF PARENTAL RESPONSIBILITIES

4.   It is in the best interests of the said **child** that the Defender's parental responsibilities be removed and therefore the order depriving the Defender of his parental responsibilities should be granted as craved in terms of the Children (Scotland) Act 1995 Section 11(2)(a).

REMOVAL OF PARENTAL RIGHTS

5.   It is in the best interests of the said **child** that the Defender's parental responsibilities be removed and therefore the order depriving the Defender of his parental rights should be granted as craved in terms of the Children (Scotland) Act 1995, Section 11(2)(a).

DELIVERY

6.   It is in the best interests of the said child to be delivered to the Pursuer and therefore the order for delivery should be granted as craved.

INTERDICT TO PREVENT REMOVAL OF CHILDREN

7.   The Defender is liable in the circumstances condescended on to attempt to remove the said **child** from the care and control of the Pursuer. Interdict and interim interdict should be granted as craved.

IN RESPECT WHEREOF

Solicitor
(Address)
AGENT FOR PURSUER

Style 28

Minute in Terms of OCR 14

<u>SHERIFFDOM OF (insert sheriffdom)</u>

MINUTE IN TERMS OF OCR 14

for

[name of child], child of the parties to the
action, residing at [address]

in the cause

Full name and address of Pursuer
....PURSUER

against

Full name and address of Defender
....................................DEFENDER

The Minuter craves the court:

1.   To sist the Minuter as a party to the action.

2.   To make an order for the Minuter to lodge Defences.

3.   [insert-order-sought]

4. To grant warrant for service of this Minute on the Pursuer and Defender.

STATEMENT OF FACTS

1. The Minuter (hereinafter referred to as [insert-first-name]) is the child of the parties to the action. [he/she] is [age] and was born on [date-of-birth]. [he/she] lives with [his/her] mother. The Defender lives at [address]. The Pursuer lives at [address].

2. **(narrate facts and background justifying entry into process**.

3. **(narrate facts justifying order sought set out as separate numbered statements of fact if appropriate**.

PLEA IN LAW

1. The Minuter having an interest in the proceedings in terms of Section 11(3) of the Children (Scotland) Act 1995 and it being appropriate in the stated circumstances the orders sought should be granted as craved.

IN RESPECT WHEREOF

Solicitor
(Address)
Agent for Minuter

Style 29

Notice to Admit under OCR 29.14

SHERIFFDOM OF (insert sheriffdom)

**NOTICE TO ADMIT FOR [PURSUER/DEFENDER]
UNDER OCR 29.14**

in the cause

Full name and address of Pursuer

.................................……..……….PURSUER

against

Full name and address of Defender

...................................……….DEFENDER

[NAME-OF-SOLICITOR] for the [Pursuer/Defender] calls on the [Pursuer/Defender] to admit for the purposes of this cause only that:-

1. The parties separated on [date-of-separation].

2. Number [number] of Process is a Medical Report on the [Pursuer/Defender] prepared by [name-of-doctor] and accurately records the opinion of [name-of-doctor].

3. On [date-of-separation] the parties had matrimonial property including—

    (a) [name-of-insurance-company] Policy No. [number] worth £[amount] and worth £[amount-(insert-more-recent-date-if-appropriate].

    (b) Motor Car Registration No. [number] worth £[amount].

(c)   The [Pursuer/Defender's] [name-of-company] Pension Policy No. [number] worth £[amount] with a cash equivalent transfer value of £[amount].

4.   On [date-of-separation] the parties had matrimonial debts including—

(a)   Overdraft on [name-of-bank] Account No. [number] of £[amount].

(b)   An unpaid loan with [name-of-lender] Account No. [number] of £[amount].

5.   Number [number] of Process is a report prepared by [name-of-company], Chartered Surveyors, and is a true and accurate statement of their opinion as to the value of the matrimonial home at [address].

6.   The copy documents number [number] to number [number] in Inventory of Productions for the [Pursuer/Defender] No. [number] of Process are accurate and properly authenticated copies of original documents.

7.   Document Nos. [number] to [number] in the Inventory of Productions for the [Pursuer/Defender] No. [number] of Process are accepted as original and properly authenticated documents.

So that, in the event that the [Pursuer/Defender] does not intimate a notice of non admission of said facts and documents, the [Pursuer/Defender] may be deemed to have admitted them, in terms of O.C.R. 29.14.

IN RESPECT WHEREOF

Agent for [Pursuer/Defender]

Style 30—Specification of Documents

<u>SHERIFFDOM OF [Sheriffdom]</u>

SPECIFICATION OF DOCUMENTS FOR
THE RECOVERY OF WHICH A
COMMISSION AND DILIGENCE IS
SOUGHT BY THE PURSUER

in the cause

Full name and address of Pursuer
....PURSUER

against

Full name and address of Defender
.....................................DEFENDER

1.   <u>Wages</u>

All contracts of employment, wage records, statements, pay slips, forms
P60, PAYE records, tax returns and assessments (save in so far as in the
hands of the Inland Revenue) and other documentation in the hands of (a)
the Defender and (b) [employer's-name-and-address] in order that
excerpts may be taken therefrom at the sight of the commissioner of all
entries therein showing or tending to show the Defender's income for
[his/her] employment with from [dates-required] to the date of any
interlocutor granting this motion.

2.   <u>Banks/Building Societies</u>

All bank and building society statements, passbooks, cheque books, counterfoils and other documentation in so far as in the hands of the Defender or anyone else on [his/her] behalf showing or tending to show the balances of any accounts maintained by the Defender therein as at [date-of-separation] and to the date of any interlocutor granting this motion.

3. All lists of investments, stock, share and debenture certificates and dividend counterfoils, bonds, deposit receipts, insurance and assurance policies, IOU's, unit trusts, personal equity plans, pension plans and other documents relating to the period [appropriate-starting-point] to the date of any interlocutor granting this motion so that excerpts may be taken from them at the sight of the commissioner of all entries showing or tending to show the extent and value of the moveable property in which the defender had an interest at [date-of-separation] and has an interest at the date of any interlocutor following on this motion.

4. Buildings

All title deeds, back letters, dispositions, estate accounts, valuations, tenancy agreements and other documentation for the period [appropriate-starting-date] to the date of this motion showing or tending to show the extent and value of all heritable property in which the defender had an interest as at [date-of-separation] and has an interest at the date of any interlocutor following on this Motion.

5. Building Society Repayments

All building society statements and other correspondence of whatsoever nature showing or tending to show the amount repaid to [name-of-bank/building-society] since the date of purchase of [address-of-property] from [appropriate-date] to the date of any interlocutor following on this motion.

6. Medical Records—Hospital

All medical records relating to the defender, including case notes, reports, letters, cards, charts, illustrations, x rays, photographs and other documents in the hands of [name-of-hospital] in order that excerpts may be taken therefrom at the sight of the commissioner of all entries therein showing or tending to show the cause, nature and extent of injuries sustained by the defender on [date].

7.   Medical Records—G.P.

All medical records relating to the defender, including case notes, reports, letters, cards, charts, illustrations, x rays, photographs and other documents in the hands of [name-of-doctor-and-address-of-surgery] in order that excerpts may be taken therefrom at the sight of the commissioner of all entries therein showing or tending to show the cause, nature and extent of injuries sustained by the defender on [date].

Note — remember intimation to Lord Advocate for submission to the court where recovery of NHS hospital records is sought (not required for G.P. practice or health centre records).

8.   Pension

All booklets, statements, memoranda, schedules, correspondence and other documents of whatsoever nature showing or tending to show the terms, nature and value of the defender's occupational pension from (insert details) on (insert date of separation).

9.   Failing principals, drafts, copies or duplicates of the above or any of them.

IN RESPECT WHEREOF

Solicitor,

Agent for Pursuer

INDEX